# The Machine at Work

# The Machine at Work
## Technology, Work and Organization

**Keith Grint and Steve Woolgar**

Polity Press

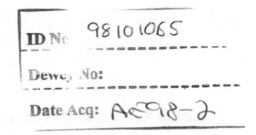

Copyright © Keith Grint and Steve Woolgar 1997

The right of Keith Grint and Steve Woolgar to be identified as author of this work has been asserted in accordance with the Copyright, Designs and Patents Act 1988.

First published in 1997 by Polity Press in association with Blackwell Publishers Ltd.

2 4 6 8 10 9 7 5 3 1

*Editorial office:*
Polity Press
65 Bridge Street
Cambridge CB2 1UR, UK

*Marketing and production:*
Blackwell Publishers Ltd
108 Cowley Road
Oxford OX4 1JF, UK

*Published in the USA by*
Blackwell Publishers Inc.
Commerce Place
350 Main Street
Malden, MA 02148, USA

**Library of Congress Cataloging-in-Publication Data**

Grint, Keith.
   The machine at work : technology, work, and organization / Keith Grint and Steve Woolgar.
     p.    cm.
   Includes bibliographical references and index.
   ISBN 0-7456-0924-4 (hardcover).—ISBN 0-7456-0925-2 (pbk. : alk. paper)
     1. Employees—Effect of technological innovations on. 2. Human -machine systems.   3. Work—Forecasting.   I. Woolgar, Steve.
II. Title
HD6331.G75   1997
331.25—dc21
                                  96-37740
                                       CIP

Typeset in 10 on 11½ pt Times
by Wearset, Boldon, Tyne and Wear
Printed in Great Britain by TJ International Ltd, Cornwall

This book is printed on acid-free paper.

# Contents

# Acknowledgements

Parts of the argument in this book evolved as the result of our teaching the course 'Work, Organization and Technology' at Brunel University. Our thanks to students on that course, and to colleagues in CRICT (Centre for Research into Innovation, Culture and Technology), especially Donna Baston, Chris Carne, Geoff Cooper, Clare Fisher, Rosalind Gill, Christine Hine, Leslie Libetta, Janet Low, Janet Rachel and Stuart Shapiro. Further afield many others have provided encouragement and assistance, including: Olga Amsterdamska, Richard Badham, John Burnett, Mark Elam, Hans Glimmel, David Held, Magnus Johansson, Nick Jardine, Oskar Juhlin, Steve K, Mihaela Kelemen, Marianne de Laet, John Law, Val Martin, Ulf Mellstrom, Russell Mills, Janet Moth, Adrian Randall, Howard Rosenbrock, Leigh Star, Lynn Winkworth, Ray Thomas and Frank Webster. Finally, we would like to thank Jacqueline and Sandra, Katy and Alex, Madeleine and Beki, and Kris and Francesca for everything else.

An earlier version of part of chapter 3 appeared as S. Woolgar, 'Configuring the User: The Case of Usability Trials' in Law, J. (ed.): *A Sociology of Monsters: Essays on Power, Technology and Domination*. Sociological Review Monograph 38 (London: Routledge, 1991), 58–100. A version of chapter 4 was published as K. Grint and S. Woolgar, 'On Some Failures of Nerve in Constructivist and Feminist Analyses of Technology' in Woolgar, S. (ed.): *Feminist and Constructivist Perspectives on New Technology*, a special issue of *Science Technology and Human Values*, 20, 3 (1995), 286–310; and also in K. Grint and R. Gill (eds.), *The Gender–Technology Relation* (London: Taylor and Francis, 1995), 48–75.

We would also like to acknowledge the support of the ESRC's Programme on Information and Communication Technologies (PICT) and EASST (European Association of Studies of Science and Technology).

# Introduction: *Deus ex Machina*

> If there were no God, said the eighteenth century Deist, it would be necessary to invent him. Now this eighteenth century god was *deus ex machina*, the god who helped those who could not help themselves, the god of the lazy and incapable.
>
> Shaw, 1946: 227

It is a truism that technology is increasingly central to modern life. Of course, in a general sense, taken to include all kinds of objects, systems and artefacts, life has always been organized around and in response to technology. In more recent times, the fascination with and concern about technology has become more intense. This is due, in part, to the rate of emergence of new technologies and, in part, because the origins (inception and design) of new technology have become increasingly remote from everyday experience. Is technology now an indispensable part of lives? Do we have adequate resources to understand technology and to assess its relationship to our work and organizations?

This book evaluates various ways of thinking about technology. It asks whether existing analytic perspectives give us sufficient guidance in making decisions about its development and deployment. In particular it develops a critique of conceptions of the essential characteristics of technology. What is the basis of, what the consequences of and what, if any, the alternatives to, the idea that technologies have an essence?

The concept of 'the machine' has long provided the focus of concern, analysis, protest and speculation. Contempt for the machine has been a 'stock literary attitude' (Marx, 1964: 146), and provided the focus of neo-Romantic critiques of science in the early nineteenth century (Marx, 1988: 165). In the 1960s, radical protesters urged that we 'rage against the machine'. This kind of metaphorical usage deploys idealized conceptions of machine without reference to the design, development and deployment of technology. Like many similar invocations of technology, it tends to be informed neither by considerations of how in fact technology operates – the machine at work as opposed to the idealized machine (see, for example, Button, 1993) – nor by what happens in

practice when technology is deployed for certain organizational purposes – the machine at work as opposed to, say, in leisure and recre-
ational usage.

The term *deus ex machina* provides a helpful motif in confronting
idealized conceptions of the nature of technology. It is a term drawn
from the world of Greek and Roman drama (appropriately enough, an
arena replete with rhetoric, performance, persuasive accounts and
irony), and refers to the timely appearance of a god to unravel and
solve the plot. *Deus ex machina* refers to the convention of the god
appearing in the sky, an effect which was achieved by means of a crane
(Greek: *mechane*) drawn up over or on the stage and containing an
actress or actor in the role of a goddess or god.[1] The symbolic nature of
a divine spirit being encased within a machine represents a typical
response by many people to technology itself; indeed, the
Enlightenment was, and modernism is, very much movements bound
tightly to the idea of freedom through reason, a reason often manifest
as technology.[2]

In the epigraph to this introduction, Shaw scorns those who rely on
the notion of *deus ex machina*. For him, faith in this form of deity
bespeaks a kind of intellectual laziness, whereby *deus ex machina*
becomes an all-too-convenient prop. We might say that this imagery
detracts from our appreciation of the social circumstances which generate and support technology; in Marxist mood, that *deus ex machina* is
the technological opiate of the masses. In the context of the long-term
development of culture, other commentators have remarked upon the
naïvety of our persistent reliance upon technology to produce *dei ex
machina* (Kuper, 1994).

Shaw was speaking of eighteenth-century conceptions of deity. But
to what extent do contemporary ideas about technology still rely upon
this image – the idea that it is the essential capacity 'within' a technology which, in the end, accounts for the way we organize ourselves, our
work and other life experiences? The aim of this book is to examine to
what extent and in what ways the imagery of *deus ex machina* endures.
How does it constrain contemporary thinking about technology? Is it
possible to escape the view of technology as containing essences? What
are the practical and policy consequences of an alternative view? If we
hold to a sceptical view of 'the machine at work' does it make any practical difference? Doesn't the machine carry on working irrespective of
our assumptions about its performance? Indeed, isn't this precisely the
notion conjured up by the very term 'machine': an unstoppable artifice
that tramples all before it; what Thomas Carlyle (describing a railway
journey in 1839) referred to as 'Faust's flight on the Devil's mantle'
(quoted in Jennings, 1995: 212)?

Since ancient times the phrase *deus ex machina* has also been applied to an unexpected saviour, or to an improbable event that brings order out of chaos. 'Now the term has come to mean any rescuing agency introduced by the author to bring about a desired conclusion, usually without regard to the logic of character or situation' (Lass et al., 1994: 62). This more general application of the phrase suggests that the image of *deus ex machina* provides a resource for the discussion of issues and arguments that go far beyond technology. Notably, this general usage denotes conventional acceptance of the definitive effect on a situation of an introduced agency or event, the essential characteristics of which are understood as being capable of overriding 'the logic of character or situation'. The essentialism associated with discussions about technology is thus part of a much wider set of interpretative conventions.

The central intuition we address is that many long-standing ideas about technology can be revised as a result of a critique of essentialism. Critiques of essentialism are evident in several interrelated currents in contemporary intellectual thought: post-structuralism, relativism, social constructivism, deconstructionism and post-modernism all exercise greater or lesser degrees of scepticism about the idea that phenomena contain essences. This book sets out to expose some fairly well established themes in the sociology of organizations and work – especially those clustering around the relations between technology and work – to some of these recent critiques of essentialism. In particular, we suggest, ideas about the relations between technology and work stand to be reworked and revitalized in the light of anti-essentialist currents in the sociology of technology.

Our goal is both to introduce and to assess this relatively new way of thinking about technology and work. Of course, in an introductory volume, it is not possible to offer a comprehensive review of, for example, constructivist sociology of technology, nor of technology and work. Instead, we have drawn selectively from each area upon those issues and arguments which seem most illuminating and controversial. For example, there are many varieties of 'social constructivism', and others are still emerging. In this volume we attempt no more than to outline some of the more significant differences within this broad church. We hope this will at least encourage a more extended assessment of the value of anti-essentialism for problems in technology and work.

For similar reasons, we are wary of attempting the straightforward application of one set of arguments and perspectives to another. The very heterogeneity of anti-essentialist perspectives is reason enough for being wary of attempting their straightforward application to issues in work and technology. 'Application' in any case connotes far too mechanical a relation between areas of research: it conjures the idea of disembodied methods and techniques which are transportable between substantive domains; it is as if we can – to quote the title of this book – see 'the machine at work' if we simply move it round the world. Instead we construe the relation between these areas more in terms of a conceptual conjunction. Anti-essentialism, we suggest, offers challenges about the ways we *think* of technology and of its various relations to work and organization. It suggests ways of recasting problems, perhaps more than solving them. Accordingly, our emphasis throughout is on examining the questions which anti-essentialism can provoke, rather than on championing any particular 'ism' as the final arbiter.

At the same time, our attempt to conjoin anti-essentialist approaches to technology with the sociology of work has a significance for wider debates in at least three main ways. Firstly, although perspectives such as social constructivism are sometimes regarded as 'radical', it is possible to show how limitations arise from their inability (or unwillingness) to carry through the scepticism about technical capacity. The identification of these limits provides useful pointers to where we should ask further, more searching questions about the ways in which our conventions of representation tend to make us take for granted the 'essence of technology'. Secondly, we anticipate that our specific focus on the implications of anti-essentialist perspectives for views on technology and work will add to current debates about the nature and status of anti-essentialist arguments in general. In particular, our discussion points towards a major issue of general significance: namely, what is the utility of sociological perspectives which espouse a form of relativism? Thirdly, we note the strategic significance of social analyses of technology for issues in social theory. The history of technology can be usefully understood as a history of fundamental questions about the nature of humankind. Thus, new technologies with purportedly human capabilities often give rise to renewed questions about what it is to be human (Woolgar, 1987). At the same time, precisely because 'technology' (like science) is so often defined in opposition to 'society', reconceptualizations of technology provoke a reappraisal of the concepts of 'agency' and 'social' (Woolgar, 1994, 1996a).

Our discussion begins with an introduction to varieties of anti-essentialist approach to technology, stressing in particular their common antipathy to technological determinism. We show that, on close inspection, there are significantly different varieties of technological determinism. We suggest that despite frequent (and often vociferous) programmatic disavowals of 'technological determinism', much recent scholarship reduplicates the apparent target of criticism, often by displacing rather than confronting the problem. This enables us to identify those points at which further and more virulent forms of the anti-essentialist question should be posed.

Chapter 2 illustrates this argument using a particularly infamous historical instance of relations between technology and work: the case of the Luddites. We show that by reinterpreting this historical episode with the benefit of anti-essentialist lenses, we can open up many of the tensions and problems which have lent the Luddites episode such resonance. We suggest that this is best done by pressing a particularly strong variant of anti-essentialism.

In chapter 3 we pursue the contention that the revision of ideas about the role of technology in work requires close attention to the social process of technological development. Here we discuss anti-essentialist perspectives which focus on processes of technological development, for example the argument of the 'social shaping of technology' thesis that contends the interpretatively flexible character of technological development. We are particularly keen to examine the extent to which anti-essentialist accounts of the production of technology provide useful insights into the consumption of technology.

In chapter 4 we turn to anti-essentialist arguments about technology as they feature in recent feminist writing. By drawing parallels between some of the aspirations and approaches in feminist and in constructivist accounts of technology, we point out their common limitations. Again we suggest that ambitions to counter technological determinism are compromised by the failure – in both feminist and constructivist accounts – to embrace a sufficiently thoroughgoing critique of essentialism.

This then enables us, in chapter 5, to focus in particular on the relation between technology and work organizations. We consider what anti-essentialism implies for existing views about the significance of technical developments for organizations and conclude with a brief review of the similarities between contemporary assumptions about the revolutionary and deterministic essences of information technology and those characteristics attributed to technology during the First World War, which were bound up with the killing 'work' of the tank.

Finally, this brings us to a key issue in the understanding of technology which we broached right at the beginning. In the context of widespread concern about the political and practical impotence of the anti-essentialist nexus (relativism, constructivism, reflexivity), what is the import of this alternative view for policy and practice? To what extent do these alternative approaches matter? In chapter 6 we consider the utility of sceptical approaches driven by anti-essentialism. We review aspects of the moral and epistemological debate over relativism and constructivism, concluding that only a commitment to a particularly virulent species of the genre will enable the kind of radical rethinking about technology and work relations which is needed.

# 1

# Theories of Technology

The hand-mill gives you society with the feudal lord; the steam-mill,
society with the industrial capitalist.

Marx, *The Poverty of Philosophy*, 1847

## Introduction

It is commonly said that technology is consequential for the way we
organize our lives. This book sets out to interrogate this aphorism. We
take issue with its implicit assumption that some inherent property or
characteristic of technology accounts for the impact of technology on
our lives. We propose instead that myriad other aspects of our relation
with technology must be taken into account if we are to achieve a useful
understanding of its consequences. These other aspects include: our
attitudes towards technology, our conceptions of what technology can
and cannot do, our expectations and assumptions about the possibilities
of technological change, and the various ways in which technology is
represented, in the media and in organizations. We aim to provide a
critical exploration of the view that these latter aspects of technology
are pre-eminently consequential for the ways in which we organize our
work, institutions, leisure and learning activities. This approach requires
us to understand different ways of thinking about and representing
technology at least as much as differences in the technology itself.
Indeed, in what follows we argue for the need to treat the very idea of
'the technology itself' with considerable caution.

This chapter reviews existing perspectives on technology and
explores the nature and implications of approaches which promote
scepticism about 'the technology itself'. We start by examining a variety
of definitions of technology in order both to illustrate their wide diversity and to note the implications of these definitions for attempts to
understand technology. In particular we note the central importance of
assumptions about the capacity and capability of technology – what it is

and what it does. We then consider some of the more significant perspectives on, or theories of, technology, starting with technological determinism. This perspective holds that humans (human behaviour and even the course of history) are largely determined by, rather than having influence over, technology. It is a position which has acquired the status of a shibboleth. But, although 'technological determinism' has become the target of widespread criticism, it is difficult to find many who admit to holding this position.

We then proceed to examine various responses to technological determinism: socio-technical systems theory, the social shaping approach, socio-technical alignments and actor-network theory. It turns out that many of the more popular current approaches to the topic rescue technology from the clutches of technological determinism, only to reaccommodate it as one among several independent variables which determine action and behaviour. Although pluralist approaches no longer treat technology as the single (or even necessarily predominant) determining variable, it is still usually treated as a variable which stands outside social analysis. Thus, whereas in recent years many traditional sociological variables such as class, gender, organization and power have been increasingly treated as social constructions, many pluralist approaches continue to treat technology as largely impervious to the interpretative activities of humans. In these pluralist treatments, technology is assumed to have objective effects which can be measured and predicted and which are largely unaffected by the human actors involved. We refer to this tendency as 'technicism'.[1] We suggest that despite disavowals of technological determinism – in the sense that technology is no longer treated as straightforwardly facilitative or constraining – many recent accounts retain elements of technicism because they do not regard the capacity of the technology as analytically problematic.

This then enables us to examine the possibilities of pushing the sceptical line further. We consider what benefits accrue from a perspective which tries to maintain a sceptical stance with respect to technology as well as to all other actants, human or non-human. The possibilities of sustained scepticism are developed and refined throughout the rest of the book in order to demonstrate how this approach might be fruitfully employed in areas beyond the conventional remit of technology studies.

## Defining the issues

What is technology? The answer carries a huge array of conceptual baggage that colours our assumptions about the significance of technology. The term technology derives from the original Greek 'tekhne' meaning art or skill. According to *Collins English Dictionary* (1979), technology is (1) the application of practical or mechanical sciences to industry or commerce; (2) the methods, theory and practices governing such application; (3) the total knowledge and skills available to any human society for industry, art, science, etc.

Several authors have emphasized the need to distinguish different aspects of technology. For example, Jayaweera (1987) suggests that 'technology' should first be distinguished from 'invention'. 'Inventions' in themselves are neutral; 'technologies' are inventions which are organized expressions of a particular culture's productive structures. Thus, developments such as gunpowder and the printing-press were Chinese in origin but since, according to Jayaweera, they did not affect the way the Europeans used them to expand their empires, they should be considered (neutral) inventions rather than technologies. Technologies only occur where 'within that society there is a particular meeting of economic, social and political circumstances which automatically guarantees its exploitation and conversion into an instrument of economic and social power' (Jayaweera, 1987: 202). This approach thus advances a model of technology based on the realization of technical potential through the operation of conducive structures and circumstances. Notably, it is not that the technical potential of an artefact is perceived differently by various actors. Instead, the take-up and exploitation of the (actual) artefact depends upon (extraneous) social factors. We shall meet a similar form of argument later when discussing the ideas of Habermas and Hill.

Penn (1982) proposes a distinction between 'technology' and 'technicality'. 'Technology', for Penn 'does not simply mean machinery around which there is a given "logic" of working or pyrotechnical relations; it involves negotiated structures of producing.' Technology, as opposed to 'technicality', is dependent upon 'the conflict between agents of capital and representatives of sections of workers' (1982: 108). Although he underlines the importance of linkages between machinery and humans, Penn appears to substitute the independent nature of technology with the independent nature of 'technicality', which remains undefined.

Kaplinsky (1984) distinguishes between technology and technique. Technology refers to the general material content or process, such as microelectronics; technique refers to the way in which the general technology is developed for a specific purpose, often in conjunction with other technologies or work processes. A numerically controlled machine tool, therefore, is a technique. This distinction, between the broad technology and its particular application within a technique, allows Kaplinsky to resolve what he calls 'the paradox of technology': 'the very technology which has the potential to liberate human beings has in fact had the consequence of making life considerably more uncomfortable for the mass of the population' (1984: 170). For Kaplinsky, the movement from technology to techniques is the result of social rather than technical factors. These social factors include class relations which ensure the technology is refined into a technique that deskills workers, furthers the division of labour and supports a hierarchical system of control. They also involve the 'military imperative' which secures research funding for technological research, especially that leading to greater levels of sophistication. Finally, Kaplinsky notes the role of gender relations, especially the role of patriarchy in stimulating militarism and its associated techniques. As he concludes:

> Neo-Luddism – the response drawn by many whose jobs are being destroyed by the technology's diffusion – is not just futile ... but also seriously misspecifies the analysis. The problem lies not with the technology, but in a form of social organization which *misuses* its potential to produce frighteningly destructive weapons, inappropriate products and undesirable work processes. (1984: 180) (our emphasis)

Note here the assumption that technology has both an actual (inherent potential) capacity and a 'normal' form of deployment which is distorted (misused) as the result of contemporary social circumstances. This is a point to which we return below.

By contrast, Winner (1977) notes that definitions of technology alter through time and place. Thus, for the ancient Greeks, technology meant 'practical arts', as opposed to science or even art itself. Then, during the twentieth century, the term was expanded to include the tools, the process of work and even the total work organization. Relatedly, MacKenzie and Wajcman (1985: 3) note three different meanings: physical objects; objects in conjunction with related human activities; and knowledge. Winner's proposed solution to the conceptual confusion is to describe the physical, inanimate devices, tools and so on as 'apparatus'; technical activities, that is, those involving human action such as the application of skill, the use of procedures and so on, he calls 'technique'; the social arrangements that combine 'apparatus' and 'technique' he labels 'organization'; while 'networks' are 'organizations' that link 'technique' and 'apparatus' across space.

Common to all these definitions of technology is the attempt to distinguish between its human and non-human elements. 'Non-human' tends to be associated with the material, intrinsic, technical content whereas 'human' tends to connote the (merely) circumstantial context (social factors). The former category tends to correspond to an essential inner core of technical characteristics, whereas the latter is portrayed as merely transitory and epiphenomenal. However, despite the implicit tendency of many authors to fashion their discussions of technology in terms of this dichotomy, it is difficult to sustain the boundary between human and non-human, if only because humans do not act without some form of 'artificial' (i.e. humanly constructed) construction (clothes, tools, buildings, machines, etc.), and non-humans of this 'artificial' form do not act in the absence of humans. As we shall discuss, this mutual dependence of elements has led some sociologists to reconceptualize the link between technology and humans as a network rather than as parallel but separate systems. That is, they argue that we should consider the unity of human and non-human actors in terms of a 'seamless web' (Hughes, 1979) or as 'heterogeneous engineering' (Law, 1986). For others, however, the conflation of human and non-human undermines the procedures by which the real significance of technology can be assessed, for this is to 'extend the definitions [of technology] so widely that it becomes virtually impossible to assess its independent influence on work and organization' (Clark et al., 1988: 13).

However, much recent research has taken issue with the notion of the 'independent influence' of technology. For example, in broad terms, 'social constructivism' contends that technology does not have any influence which can be gauged independently of human interpretation. Instead, the influence of technology is constructed through human interpretation. Just as 'facts' neither speak for themselves nor exist independently of some agency which constructs them, technologies neither speak for themselves nor exist independently of human interpretation. Technologies, in other words, are not transparent; their character is not given; and they do not contain an essence independent of the nexus of social actions of which they are part. They do not 'by themselves' tell us what they are or what they are capable of. Instead, capabilities – what, for example, a machine will do – are attributed to the machine by humans. Our knowledge of technology is in this sense essentially social; it is a construction rather than a reflection of the machine's capabilities. Of course, not any construction is possible; the construction of technological capacity is not itself unconstrained.[2] However, the important point at this juncture is to resist the idea that constructions result from some imagined intrinsic properties of the technology. (As we shall see below, the constructivist literature is admittedly ambivalent about the nature and range of sources from which constructions result). Certainly, some constructions turn out to be more resilient and robust than others. Not every construction carries equal authority. Indeed, a central aim of social constructivism is to ask how and why this is so. Given that accounts of technological capacity are not a reflection of an inherent property of the technology, why do we believe some people's accounts but not others? How is it that some accounts are so convincing that we end up treating them as a direct reflection of the 'actual capacity' of technology, finally, and ironically, convinced that we never have been convinced? Before returning to these questions, we need to retrace our steps in the quest for that elusive and mythical beast: technological determinism.

## Technological determinism as myth

As MacKenzie and Wajcman (1985) suggest, since not all technical 'advances' are enacted, since the same technology appears to have different 'effects', and because this implies that the specification of cause is an extremely complex task, models of technological determinism are suspect. However, as we have already indicated, it turns out to be difficult to identify straightforward examples of technological determinism which are susceptible to this knock-down argument.

At its simplest, technological determinism portrays technology as an exogenous and autonomous development which coerces and determines social and economic organizations and relationships. Technological determinism appears to advance spontaneously and inevitably, in a manner resembling Darwinian survival, in so far as only the most 'appropriate' innovations survive and only those who adapt to such innovations prosper. This perspective has a long history as well as an apparently radical future, from Saint-Simon and Comte (Kumar, 1978), to the rather more recent arguments of Leavitt and Whisler (1958), Bell (1960, 1973), Kerr et al. (1964) and Blauner (1964).

Such is the significance of technology that it provides a whole new battery of metaphors to interpret ourselves: the steam age helped us to 'let off steam' and to become mere 'cogs in a machine'; the current computer technologies provides us with 'default positions' and 'interfaces', while the notion of technology out of control is perfectly encapsulated by Shelley's *Frankenstein* (Badham, 1990; Edge, 1973; Turkle, 1984; Winner, 1977). Yet, for Veblen, technology is not wild and irrational but amoral, cold and rational; it is *in*, not *out of*, control:

> The machine throws out anthropomorphic habits of thought. It compels the adaptation of the workman to his work, rather than the adaptation of the work to the worker ... the machine process gives no insight into questions of good or evil, merit or demerit, except in point of material causation, nor into the foundations or the constraining force of law and order as may be stated in terms of pressure, temperature, velocity, tensile strength etc. (Veblen, 1904: 310–11)

A familiar theme is evident here: mechanization generates mechanical cultures and routinized life-experiences. The long-term result is a decline in the 'pecuniary' or 'business' spirit of capitalism, based, as it is for Veblen, on individualism and private property. In effect, technology determines the shape and content of society. The relationship is isomorphic: society mirrors technology.

It is important here to highlight the modernist foundations of this approach to technology: in the Enlightenment tradition the machine, and the absorption and refining of human reason into the machine, lead to the most rational forms of human institutions. Moreover, since the design principles are themselves nurtured in the scientific laboratory of objective truth and reason, the organizational results should be universally applicable. Thus science, rather than human 'needs', prevails in organizations; and since technology is the carrier of human reason, organizations should be driven by technological requirements. The traces of scientific management (see Grint, 1991: 184–97), and indeed of many of the arguments grounded in models of economically rational behaviour, are easy to detect here. This contrasts markedly with models of organizations entrenched in notions of universal human needs, such as human relations, or rooted in psychoanalytic theories, like those emanating from the Tavistock Clinic (see Gergen, 1992; Stein, 1992).

In the literature on the sociology of work, technological determinism has a similarly ambivalent status. For example, although Woodward (1958) and Blauner (1964) are frequently cited as supporters of technological determinism, neither are cast-iron devotees of the approach. Woodward's later work (1965) shifted away from this perspective towards socio-technical systems approaches. At one point, even Blauner seems to suggest something other than straightforward technological determinism: 'modern factories vary considerably in technology, in division of labour, in economic structure, and in organizational character. These differences produce sociotechnical systems in which the objective conditions and the inner life of employees are strikingly variant' (1964: 5). Nevertheless, he still maintains that 'the most important single factor that gives an industry a distinctive character is its technology' (1964: 6).[3]

Heilbroner (1972), regarded by many as an arch-determinist (see Bimber, 1990), actually calls for a ' "soft determinism" with regard to the influence of the machine on social relations' (1972: 35). By this he means that technology is itself the result of social activity, that the direction of technological advance is responsive to social influences and that it must be 'compatible' with existing social conditions. For example, Heilbroner argues that labour-saving devices are of little significance for societies with plentiful labour. Thus technology should be relegated from 'an undeserved position of *primum mobile* in history to that of a mediating factor' (1972: 37). That said, Heilbroner goes on to argue that under certain conditions technology can become autonomous and can determine advance. However, this is 'peculiarly a problem of a certain historical epoch – specifically that of high capitalism and low socialism – in which the forces of technical change have been unleashed, but when the agencies for the control or guidance of technology are still rudimentary' (1972: 38–9). In other words, technology is sometimes allowed to determine the future as a result of inadequate social controls; by default, humans sometimes allow technology to become autonomous.

This is close to Winner's (1977) sense of the term 'autonomous technology': politics become inscribed in technology in such a way that the technology appears neutral. Its apparent neutrality, according to Winner, then encourages us to adopt somnambulist habits: we are unaware of our real situation; we think we take *choices* but actually we make *responses* to a situation preordained by politically impregnated technology – the 'technological imperative'.

Winner (1977) and Lewis Mumford (1966) assert that Marx, as the quote at the beginning of this chapter implies, lies within the determinist camp. However, both MacKenzie (1984) and Bimber (1990) insist that social (and economic) forces are more significant than technology for Marx. Cohen (1978) argues that the only theories that really count as technologically determinist are those which assert the irrelevance of human will and its replacement as the motive force of history by technology. That is, only those who claim technology is the *sole* cause of social change are technological determinists. From this point of view, Cohen and Bimber deny Marx's determinist tag. They argue instead that he 'is portraying technology more as an enabling factor than an original cause, autonomous force or determining agent' (Bimber, 1990: 345).

Suffice it to say that most reactions against technological determinism amount to a call to place technology 'in context', where 'context' is interpreted in a variety of ways to suit the analytic predilections of the author. One symptom of this is the general recognition, in recent years, that 'technology' comprises much more than just machines. The sociology of technology thus has a focus much wider than just hardware. 'Technology' can include social arrangements as diverse as the postal system, transportation, refuse collection, voting mechanisms, education and so on. To emphasize the sense in which this definition encompasses social arrangements, the term 'technological system' is sometimes used. The advantage of this broad definition is its insistence on including consideration of (narrowly conceived) technologies within a wider context. The argument is that machines can only be understood in terms of their use, and hence in terms of the context in which they are situated. The disadvantage is the implication that there remains, at the centre of the technological system, a residual, non-social or neutral, machine which is malleable according to its social location/context etc.

Little wonder, then, that it is so difficult to identify anyone willing to admit to the label of technological determinist. The various definitions of technology are complex and overlapping. The discussions of technological determinism seem always to accept the significance of factors other than technology, such as social and economic forces, in the determination of human development.

## Socio-technical systems

While some of the more populist notions of technology imply that technological determinism is commonplace (Toffler, 1980), there is little evidence amongst academic texts for this. Rather, it seems to have been the ascription of rampant technological determinism to writers like Blauner (1964) and Woodward (1958) which stimulated resistance to the approach. This is evident in the writings of some of those who disputed the possibility of technology playing a significant part in the explanation of workers' behaviour. As Gallie concludes his research on the topic:

> The principal conclusion of the research is that the nature of the technology per se has, at most, very little importance for the social integration of the workforce ... Advanced automation proved perfectly compatible with radically dissimilar levels of social integration and fundamentally different institutions of power ... Instead our evidence indicates the critical importance of the wider cultural and social structural patterns of specific societies for determining the nature of social interaction within the advanced sector. (Gallie, 1978: 295)

But this kind of swing away from technological determinism to social determinism in turn generated a backlash against those who were seen to be too readily jettisoning technology *in toto*. The resulting model portrayed itself as one which avoided extreme determinism of either kind in favour of a conceptual apparatus that included many different elements: technology, people, organizations, genders, interest groups and many others besides. This literature thus concedes varying degrees of consequence to both technology and social forces in a pluralistic net. The disparate amalgam of approaches following this line is extensive (for example, Freeman, 1987; Markus and Robey, 1988: 588; Noble, 1979; Pfeffer, 1982; Pool, 1983; Rose et al, 1986; Trist and Bamforth,

1951; Wilkinson, 1983; Winner, 1977, 1985); but it still tended to carry the implicit assumption that the nature and capacity of technology remained beyond the remit of sociological analysis; in effect, the nature and capacity of technology was treated as given, objective and unproblematic. We call this assumption technicism.[4] One of the most significant practical advances in Britain, in this vein, was the collaborative work of Rice (1958) and Trist and Bamforth (1951).

The socio-technical systems theory, as it became known, focused on the links between the technical system of production and the social system of work. The latter was essentially social rather than individual and, as such, technical production methods which undermined such social activity were necessarily problematic. Although a theoretical model of optimum efficiency could be construed from the technology of production, and a concomitant human model of social efficiency could also be developed, the combination of social and technical systems inevitably produced a somewhat disjointed amalgam, and, equally significant, a system of disequilibrium. The trick, therefore, was to mesh the two in such a way as to develop an optimum socio-technical system that would, if separated into its component parts, not appear to be the most efficient use of resources, and not retain any long-term equilibrium. There was some disagreement about the significance of the economic system as a potential third leg of the theory, but the general position was that the economic system was a product of the functioning of the other two. From the very beginning, then, what starts out as a radical assault upon traditional conceptions of technology actually reproduces the very same conventions which regard the capacity of technology as inherently unproblematic.

The model was explicitly grounded in a 'scientific' approach to organizational analysis, seeking to apply such methods both to the technical and the social aspects of organizations. As Trist argued, 'the technical and social systems are independent of one another in the sense that the former follows the laws of natural sciences, and the latter those of social/human sciences' (quoted in Van Eijnatten, 1991: 11). The approach also construed such organizations as open systems – in opposition to the 'machine-like' analysis proposed by Taylor and Ford. Researchers were interested in promoting a double-edged form of participation: all those involved in the work process should engage in the design and implementation of the labour process itself and, furthermore, the researchers themselves should be involved, through 'action-research' in the reorganization (Van Eijnatten, 1991).

Armed with this composite approach, and a historical appreciation of the need for participatory groups, Trist and Bamforth began investigating the low levels of productivity then experienced by the British National Coal Board (NCB) in an account that has long been regarded as a classic and the details of which need not detain us here (see Grint, 1991). However, two major theoretical conclusions were drawn.

First, that the social and technical systems had to be jointly optimized, thereby eliminating at a stroke the pretensions of the technical determinists. Organizational problems occurred in the misfit between the characteristics and requirements of the technological system and those of the associated social system. Thus, 'the technological demands place limits on the type of work organization possible, but the work organization has social, psychological properties of its own that are independent of the technology' (quoted in Elliott, 1980). As Heller (1987) argued, the problems occur when there is 'an improper application of the technological imperative' (1987: 23). In effect, the issue is that technology does not determine the social system but provides for 'options', that is 'choices based on particular contingencies' which may reconsider the 'impact of technology on people' (1987: 24–5). Given the significance of the interpretative approach to both social *and* technical issues it is evident that the socio-technical approach is gravely weakened by its assumption that technology still has certain determinate needs and objective 'effects' which necessarily constrain the appropriate social system. From the constructivist perspective it is the contingent interpretation of technologies and their putative constraints and capabilities which is crucial for explaining their relationships with humans. Heller is right to deny the determinism of technology, but to retain the idea that technology still has independent effects is to underestimate the significance of the interpretative component of human-technology interaction.

The second major conclusion of the Tavistock group was that semi-autonomous groups of workers provided the best structure for maintaining morale, defusing interpersonal frictions and therefore increasing productivity. The ultimate use of many of these ideas may have been overtly managerialist and productivist, but it would seem fair to argue that the post-war reconstruction of *homo gregarious* was as much an attempt to institutionalize the ideals of justice and equity at work that so many had just died for in the Second World War (see Rose, 1989: 92–3). This model of work organization was grounded in psychologically based theories of human need and motivation – as indeed were the human relations approaches (see Grint, 1991).

Whatever the intentions of the Tavistock theorists their impact, at least in the UK, has been limited. Yet they have had some success elsewhere, particularly in Sweden, Norway and Canada where the initial ideas have now merged into the Quality of Working Life movement that seeks to provide the kind of work experiences for all that are currently the property of the few (Bansler, 1989; Sanderson and Stapenhurst, 1979; Witte, 1980; Zwerdling, 1978). More recently the socio-technical approach has developed in the Netherlands, both amongst academics and major private companies such as Phillips, DAF and Shell (see Dankbarr and Hertog, 1990; Van Eijnatten, 1991). Perhaps the most significant aspect of this approach has been to link the 'quality of work' to the 'quality of organization', the latter being a crucial prerequisite of the former.

In a review of the relationship between technology and organizations Van Beinum (1988), one of the original members of the Tavistock team, suggested that the study of the relationship between the social and the technical systems was changing to incorporate the environment. Nevertheless, this innovative development is still rooted in a conception of technology as objective. As he argues:

> if we arrange the social system without due regard for the demands and characteristics of the technical system, we end up with an ineffective and inefficient work organization. The basic questions with regard to any work organization are therefore: what are the critical requirements of the technology, and what are the characteristics of the human system? The challenge lies in matching people and technology. (1988: 4)

However, the arrival of new technologies does seem to pose some problems for this approach (besides the constructivist critique). As Van Beinum accepts, the boundaries between technical systems are increasingly ambiguous – we would wish to include the human technical boundary here – and the consequence is an ever-increasing, rather than decreasing, reliance upon human skills. Yet there is relatively little concern with technology itself in many of the socio-technical approaches, especially in the recent publications (for example, Dankbaar and Hertog, 1990 and Van Eijnatten, 1991; cf. Berggren, 1992, and Sørenson, 1985).

A rather different plea for pluralism is nicely captured in Rolfe's (1990) attempt to account for different attitudes towards technological change. 'Ideological influences', notably those concerning the notion of 'progress', can help explain different attitudes towards technological change in organizations. However, the possibility that 'different attitudes' encompass divergent constructions of the technology is not addressed.

Rolfe concludes that 'research should not attempt mono-causal or simplistic explanations for responses to change but uncover and assess the relative importance of the many, often conflicting, influences' (1990: 118–20). Sorge similarly opines 'the socio-economic context impinges on the development, selection and application of technology just as much as the other way round ... Reciprocal determination, then, means that outcomes are ambiguous' (1984: 23). In neither case, however, is ambiguity considered to apply to the technology itself; it is instead restricted to those social forces that design, surround, adopt and deploy technology. Hence, even approaches which pride themselves on being non-deterministic nevertheless stop short of interrogating the technology and *de facto* take the 'effects' of technology as given. For example, Burnes et al. (1988) provide 'a number of explanations to account for labour's compliance with *the demands of new technology*' (1988: 7) (emphasis added). Our scepticism about the concept of the essential character of 'technology itself' leads us to ask: who says these are the demands of the new technology, under what circumstances, how and why?

A related development, The Human-Centred Systems (HCS) movement, took the socio-technical systems approach a stage further and in direct opposition to the tenets of Fordism which implied that, because humans are the source of error, the less they have to do with production the more reliable it would be. In the words of a founder of the HCS approach:

> production systems are designed with attention fixed upon the machines: their needs and their effective use are the main considerations ... If we wish to change the direction of technological development, so that the human input is accepted and valued, we shall have to intervene at the stage where new technology is being designed ... People should not be subordinate to machines; machines should be subordinate to people. (Rosenbrock, 1989a: pp. ix–x)

In conjunction with related projects in Sweden and West Germany (Badham, 1990), Rosenbrock's team at UMIST set out to design a skill-enhancing technology which would supplement rather than supplant the human operator. Here again the implication is that once the politics of a technology are rewritten – or written 'properly' – then technology can take its 'rightful' place in the workshop. Once again we see in this argument the key role of the assumption that design determines subsequent deployment. The objective characteristics of the 'deus' are built into the machine; the problem is to ensure that it is a politically correct deity.

## The social shaping approach

A further set of alternatives to technological determinism derives from research in rather disparate areas: the most coherent is the sociology of scientific knowledge (SSK), but an equally important source has a rather broader disciplinary background centring around the relationship between work and technology and broadly encompassing industrial sociology. The 'social shaping' approach is a generic label for those accounts which suggests that the capacity of the technology is equivalent to the political circumstances of its production. The SSK root argues for the 'socially constructed' character of scientific knowledge (for example, Collins, 1985; Latour and Woolgar, 1986; Lynch, 1985; Woolgar, 1988a). This work has spawned various social constructivist approaches to technology (for example, Grint and Woolgar, 1992; Woolgar, 1985; Woolgar, 1991a; Woolgar and Grint, 1991) including the so-called social construction of technology (SCOT) (for example, Bijker et al., 1987), the social shaping of technology (Edge, 1988; MacKenzie, 1991; MacKenzie and Wajcman, 1985; Williams and Edge, 1991) and, relatedly, various approaches falling under the rubric of actor-network theory (or 'the sociology of translation') (for example, Bijker and Law, 1992; Callon, 1986a, 1986b; Latour, 1987, 1988; Law, 1988, 1991). These labels are often used as a generic terms to cover different but related approaches in different countries (see Dierkes and Hoffmann, 1992, for a review of some national differences).[5]

These approaches evince a general commitment to 'opening the black box' of technology for sociological analysis. The claim is that social analysis must 'take into account the technology itself' or 'take seriously the content of the technology'. However, as will become clear, there are some major ambiguities about what precisely counts as 'taking the content seriously' and about how far the constructivist argument can (or should) be pressed. For example, the SCOT model tends to imply that the character of the technological artefact is most contingent during the design process and becomes progressively less so as negotiations are closed off, until some final form of the artefact gains general acceptance (Pinch and Bijker, 1989).

One of the earliest approaches rooted in the 'work' approach by Lewis Mumford (1966, 1972), also embodies this focus upon the design stage. Mumford suggests that from the late neolithic period 'two technologies have recurrently existed side by side: one authoritarian, the other democratic, the first system centred, immensely powerful, but inherently unstable, the other man-centred, relatively weak but resourceful and durable' (1972: 52). Democratic technics are small-scale, skill-based, and directly controlled by the craft worker; authoritarian technics, which post-date democratic technics, are centralized, machine-based, mass and scientific. But the danger does not lie directly in the technology. Rather, it lies in the 'human compulsions that dominate the authoritarian technics' (1972: 56). That is, once these different technologies – and their effects – are recognized then humans can redesign their lives around democratic technics so that 'the very leisure that the machine now gives us in advanced countries can be profitably used, not to further commitment to still other kinds of machines, furnishing automatic recreation, but by doing significant forms of work, unprofitable or technically impossible under mass production' (1972: 58).

There is, therefore, no best way to design any particular object, let alone a way determined by the technology itself. But once the technology is designed, its capacities and effects become embedded in material form. The technology then offers considerably more resistance to human attempts to use it for purposes other than those prefigured by the designer.

This view has ramifications for those critics like Beirne and Ramsay (1988), who argue that involvement in the (re)design of jobs is unlikely to have much positive effect. 'The further into the (design and implementation) process one gets, the more time, money and solidifying thought have already gone into rigidifying the system, and the more residual any participative influences must become' (1988: 217). The implication, then, is that managerial control can be built into the technical system through the design and implementation process, and that this will necessarily restrict opportunities for effective participation. However, a more sceptical view would insist that the use of any technology is contingent: it is not determined by the design or implementation process. If managerial control could be achieved through monopolizing the design and implementation process (either overtly or through some deceptive scheme of putative participation) then management would be a considerably less equivocal and ambiguous task than it appears to be (Grint, 1995).

This design-centred perspective on technology has attracted considerable interest among those emanating from disciplinary backgrounds such as industrial sociology and industrial relations (for example, Clark et al., 1988; Coombs et al., 1990; Kimble and McLoughlin, 1992; McLoughlin and Clark, 1988; Rose et al., 1986). McLoughlin and Clark's studies of technological change in the telecommunications industry suggest that one form of exchange equipment facilitates individual working patterns while another lends itself more to team approaches. They also suggest that the relative impact of technological and social forces tends to alter the further away individuals are from the immediate work task. In this perspective, then, technology is conceptualized as politically impregnated, as historically encumbered and as one among many potentially independent variables. But once 'the stages leading to the choice of a particular system are accomplished, then social choices become frozen in a given technology' (Clark et al., 1988: 32). However, we suggest that the limitation placed upon the social aspects of technology, that is, their confinement to the design and implementation process, underestimates the significance of actors' interpretations and uses of the technology. Inasmuch as technology embodies social aspects it is not a stable and determinate object (albeit one with political preferences inscribed into it), but an unstable and indeterminate artefact whose precise significance is negotiated and interpreted but never settled. For example, telephone technology was used originally to broadcast concert music. It was not axiomatic to its design that the telephone system would ultimately be restricted primarily to two-way personal communication (Finnegan and Heap, 1988), nor serve as a communication channel for students undertaking distance education, nor carry faxes, nor act as an electronic surfboard for the internet. The original use of telephone technology, and indeed its use now, was and is the result of interpretations and negotiations, not determinations. By contrast with McLoughlin and Clark's position, we need to ask what circumstances account for the contingent temporary view that a particular form of exchange equipment facilitates individual working patterns.

Winner's (1977, 1985) argument, that 'artefacts have politics', is another example of the approach. Winner is anxious to attack the view that technology is neutral and that, consequently, the impact and importance of technology depends wholly upon the use to which we put it. Part of the explanation for the rise of this 'neutralist' view, according to Winner, is an overreaction against technological determinism. Since this holds that social developments are not driven by technological developments, it has become a commonplace to assume that technology has no impact in and of itself. But, if technology is socially constructed then this underlines its inherently political nature, for if technology is not the product of autonomous creation then it must become entrammelled in the political ribbons of its designers and users.

In all these discussions we see writers struggling with a dualism between 'technology' and 'the social'. Does technology in organizations determine, or is it determined by, the social? Orlikowski's (1992) adoption of Gidden's (1979, 1984) structuration model is a more sophisticated attempt to transcend this dualism. She attempts this by attributing to technology a dual nature that overcomes the antagonistic dualism of objective and subjective approaches. The principle is 'that human actions are enabled and constrained by structures, yet these structures are the result of previous actions' (1992: 404).

Like us, Orlikowski notes how the definition of technology has itself generated several problems. She notices that most writers deploy a conception of technology as hardware (for example, Woodward, 1958; Zuboff, 1988). Although Orlikowski finds these approaches valuable in providing 'insight into the determining aspects of technology', she finds them deficient in largely ignoring 'the action of humans in developing, appropriating and changing technology. As a consequence, this perspective furnishes an incomplete account of technology and its interaction with organizations' (1992: 400). There is a clear technicist tinge here, to the extent that Orlikowski allows a residual place for 'the determining aspects of technology'. It is not clear by what criteria she intends to achieve a 'complete account of technology', although this appears to approximate some kind of sufficient balance between technology and the social. At the same time, the kind of broad definition of technology which includes 'softer' aspects of organizations such as techniques and knowledge causes a problem for Orlikowski in so far as it 'creates boundary and measurement ambiguity. It also overlooks valuable information about the mediation of human action by machines' (1992: 399). Notably for Orlikowski, 'mediation' refers merely to interaction with the technology, rather than to the more general and pervasive processes of interpretation of the technology. Orlikowski asserts that 'the softer' approach means 'we cannot examine how different assumptions, knowledge, and techniques can be embedded in different artefacts or practices' (ibid.). It is not clear what prevents this line of enquiry. But the clear implication is that we need to develop an objective account of the capacity of a technology if we are to develop a better theory of its significance.

Orlikowski examines three examples of the 'softer' approach. The first is Zuboff's (1988) argument that technology will have certain forms of consequence if it is appropriately managed. This, for Orlikowski, is unlikely since it underestimates the 'social and economic forces beyond managerial intent' (1992: 401). A second example, the social constructivist approach, is limited, says Orlikowski, by the way it 'tends to downplay the material and structural aspects of interaction with technology' (ibid.). This criticism, for constructivists at least, misses the point, since what counts as material and structural is itself a social construction. The third variant, the Marxist model, is dismissed as embodying a far too restricted view of the notion of human agency.

The problem at the heart of Orlikowski's approach is highlighted in her discussion of Barley (1986, 1990), who argues that technologies trigger organizational restructuring in ways which reflect the pre-existing organization. Barley claims that, although technologies are fixed in form and function across time, the 'meaning' of a technology is defined by the context of use. This contrast implies a distinction between contextualized meaning and, presumably, an immanent non-contextualized objective reality. The former is grafted on to the latter.[6] Quite what a context-less meaning looks like is very unclear. Thus at one point in the discussion Orlikowski argues that 'technology is *interpretively flexible*, hence the interaction of technology and organizations is a function of

different actors and socio-historical contexts implicated in its development and use ... the duality of technology identifies prior views of technology – as either objective or as socially constructed product – as a
false dichotomy' (1992: 405–6). Here she seems to be adopting an anti-
essentialist line. The dichotomy is attributed to the division, in space
and time, between the designers and the users of a technology. In contrast, 'the structurational model of technology posits artefacts as potentially modifiable throughout their existence' (1992: 407). But the
problem immediately resurfaces when she argues for a division between
two different modes of human interaction with technology: 'a *design
mode* and a *use mode*'. She goes on to 'emphasize that this distinction is
an analytic convenience only' (1992: 408). Orlikowski subsequently
appears to have accepted the division as real rather than analytic: 'rec-
ognizing the disjuncture in time and space between the design and use
mode allows us to analyze the role of multiple organizations in developing and deploying a particular technology' (1992: 422). She further
claims that designers have a greater capacity to attribute meanings to
technology than do users because these capacities are themselves constrained by the interaction between technology and organization. Yet
she subsequently reaffirms that this 'apparent disjuncture between the
design and use stages is artificial and misleading' (1992: 409).

How do we resolve the apparent paradox here? Orlikowski's position seems clear at the point where she finally accepts that there are
constraints set by 'the material characteristics of the technology' (1992:
409), and these appear to override any degree of interpretative freedom
that humans may have. Yet only a page later she asserts that 'It is only
through human action that technology *qua* technology can be understood' (1992: 410). So it would seem that technology is simultaneously
independent of human action and yet irrelevant without it. The paradox
is overlaid, rather than transcended, by her conclusion that technology
has a dual nature: 'as objective reality *and* as socially constructed product' (1992: 423) (our emphasis). But it could still be said that what
counts as objective reality is itself a social construction. In other words,
it could still be argued that 'objective reality' and 'social construction'
are not two aspects of the same artefact – if they were it would imply we
could separate out the two – they are different ways of saying the same
thing.

In the event, then, what starts out as an anti-essentialist move, an
attempt radically to restructure previous approaches to technology,
ends up as just one more version of technicism hooked into structuration theory. This is not a necessary conclusion. For example the social
constructivist argument does not deny that material artefacts have constraining influences upon actors. But it does hold a question-mark over
what these constraints are. Such constraints – or enablers – do not

acquire their significance without interpretative action on the part of humans, hence there can be no self-evident or transparent account of such 'material constraints'. There are, of course, more persuasive accounts and less persuasive accounts – but they remain accounts, not reflections.

A more thoroughgoing application of constructivism would take the view that neither attitudes towards, nor control structures over, nor the form, effects, or use of technologies are determined; they are all elements in a negotiated order. As Woolgar (1989) has argued, technologies need at no point be assumed to be stable entities with fixed and determinate 'uses'; rather, all processes of design, development, manufacture, implementation and consumption are socially constructed. For example, the 'completion' of an artefact is itself achieved and displayed through 'stabilization rituals' which implicate and define prospective user communities (see also chapter 3).

At the root of the problem is the extent to which we can continue to press the sceptical element of social constructivism. On the whole, approaches such as 'social shaping' and SCOT have pressed the issue far further than those we have called technologically determinist. Yet, as we have asserted, there is the implication that at the close of an (often protracted) contingent process of 'negotiations', the artefact stabilizes: at this point, the technology becomes what it is generally accepted to be. The difficulty is that constructivism is thereby made to seem only (or most) applicable to those periods of time when there is overt disagreement between (or uncertainty on the part of) significant actors. This broadly consensual explanation of technical capacity is admirable in countering the idea of an inevitable evolution of the inherent characteristics of a technology. At the same time, however, this restricted application of the constructivist question underplays the importance of the ways in which even established technologies are interpreted and used in the aftermath of 'interpretative closure'. What a technology can do, we are suggesting, is also a significant interpretative question after controversy has ceased and consensus has formed. The problematic implication of the social shaping approach is that technical capacity is, in some senses, settled outside the periods of explicit discussion and debate.

The challenge, then, is to find a way of keeping alive the sceptical question raised by constructivism with respect to the capacity of technology, and of avoiding accounts of technology which fall into what we have called technicism. Importantly, this does not entail a policy of eradicating all accounts which mention or implicate technological capacity. Even if it were possible, this would be tantamount to concentrating only upon issues 'outside the black box', a form of social determinism which is as unsatisfactory as the technological determinism we have been criticizing throughout. Instead we need to find a way of 'taking the technology seriously' without having to depend upon uninterrogated notions of technical capacity, and to account for the intermingling of technical and social without merely nurturing the view that these are essentially independent variables conjoined through 'interaction'. We want to avoid, in other words, the impression that either the technical or the social has a discrete impact.

## Socio-technical alignments

While the theoretical approaches discussed so far tend to focus on the specific level of technology design or technology consumption, a more ambitious macro-approach considers the significance of the alignment between technology and society: what we have called socio-technical alignments. One of the earliest forms of this approach (Robey, 1977) claimed a contingent relationship between technology and organizational effects. Organizations within unstable environments used computer technology to buttress a decentralized structure, while organizations with stable environments used computers to centralize control. Dutton (1988) similarly asserts that new technology tends to buttress or 'reinforce' whichever group is already in control of a particular organization: bias merely becomes automated. But the two major theorists we shall consider here are Habermas and Hill.

For Habermas (1971a, 1971b) technology may *appear* to be autonomous of society but this should not be confused with actual autonomy. The confusion occurs when general social norms become conflated with, or reduced to, the norms constructed by technologists and their supporters. In this situation, debates about the ends of society are substituted by debates about the means to a presumed end. This end is itself the outcome of social and political influence exerted by technologists and by those whose vision of the end of society is the greater pursuit of technological progress. This leads to the development of 'technocratic consciousness' which: 'fulfils the ideological function of legitimating the pursuit of particular interests. It conceals behind a facade of objective necessity the interests of classes and groups that actually determine the function, direction and pace of technological and social developments' (Held, 1980: 265). Some of these ideas, of course, have their origins in the critical theory of the Frankfurt School. Horkheimer (Horkheimer and Adorno, 1972), Adorno (1974) and Marcuse (1964) advance savage attacks upon the ways in which the putative liberatory potential of technology has been transformed into its oppressive reality in the 'eclipse of reason' (see Held, 1980, and chapter 2 below). This approach differs sharply from technological

determinist accounts. Although those in control of society may legiti-
mate the rationality of technological progress through a rhetoric which
denies human choice ('there is no alternative') or through a rhetoric
which equates 'common sense' with technological progress (there are
alternatives but they are irrational), the subordination of choice to technological progress is itself socially determined. From this perspective
the prime mover is the rhetoric, at the hands of the powerful, rather
than the technology *per se*.

Hill's (1988) approach is also ostensibly social (or cultural) rather
than technicist:

> to attribute ... intrusive power to technology *per se* is inherently
> wrong. Social, economic and political negotiations are involved in
> bringing particular technological systems into existence. Equally,
> the impact of technological change varies according to the social
> and cultural context into which new technologies are implanted.
> (1988: 6)

For Hill (1988), as for Jayaweera (1987) mentioned earlier, the upshot
of the genesis and implementation of a technology hinges upon the
*alignment* between technological systems and culture. Hill seeks to provide 'an understanding of how the cultural properties of technological
systems have power to *penetrate* and shape wider cultural expressions
and constructions of meaning, thus drawing these wider values into
alignment with a technologically inspired social trajectory' (1988: 3). In
Hill's account this trajectory, which both shapes and is subsequently
shaped by the cultural properties of technology, ultimately carries functionalist connotations. For example, Hill argues that barbed wire,
originally adopted by the landed nobility to protect their fox-hunting
estates, ended up inhibiting aristocratic privileges when others adopted
it for their own purposes. On the other side of the class divide, the
trumpet buttressed the solidarity of the working class through facilitat-
ing brass bands. The difference between the two artefacts relates to the
alignment of technical and cultural aspects: the aristocracy were being
attacked by all kinds of technical, legal and political forces, but 'the
tune the trumpets played was in harmony with a symphony of forces
that were all leading towards the formation and strength of the proletariat' (1988: 31).

There is more than a passing resemblance to Althusser's (1969, and,
with Balibar, 1970) notion of 'overdetermination' here; and while the
concern to link human and non-human actors is useful, the functional-
ism is not. It is not self-evident that brass bands played a cohering role
in working-class culture, nor that any kind of class solidarity ever
existed. Indeed, we would argue that Hill skates over those aspects of

technical capacity which are contested irrespective of their 'alignment' with culture. Logically, of course, there cannot be any non-aligned technologies – since technologies only prosper where they mirror the current alignment. Since the criteria for successful alignment appear all-encompassing and self-referential we are entitled to remain sceptical of this aspect of Hill's argument. In fact this aspect forms part of what Hill calls the 'tragedy of technology', because humans experience the world as 'the remorseless working of things' wherein technology appears to command culture. Hill's point is that although, as in a Greek tragedy, the script can be altered, the power of technological enframing makes us unaware of this possibility. The tension remains, however, for if freedom depends upon contradicting the dominant culture–technology alignment, then such freedom is possible only through a radical shift in cultural values that in itself recognizes the significance of the previously dominant culture–technology alignment. Hill claims that his book is an example of the cracks in the dominant alignment. But his use of the notion of alignment or 'culture coding' (explicitly modelled upon the idea of genetic coding (1988: 246–7) ), leaves the seeker of freedom rather lost: 'given the culture-constitutive properties of technological systems, *no* group involved in innovation negotiations *can* depart from the culture code without being rejected from systems negotiations – as an alien transplanted organ is expelled from the body by antibody reactions' (1988: 247).

The similarities between the approaches of Hill and Habermas are clear. Both assert that the effects of technology are the result of social and cultural forces rather than of the technology itself. Both also have a functionalist flavour in so far as what counts as viable technology depends upon the proximity to dominant cultural norms. Where we would disagree with both is in their functionalist explanations of successful technology and their assumption that the contested nature of technology can be reduced to the conflict that *should* – but does not – prevail within society between dominant and alternate cultures.

Relatedly, Hill argues that technology should be considered as a cultural text, that is, that an artefact can only be brought to life through a 'cultural text' – the rules by which we know how to use the artefact.[7] In this view, technical artefacts remain 'relatively opaque' when we know how to operate them but not how they actually work; they become 'transparent' when we know enough to 'intervene actively in designing, fabricating and modifying the machine' (1988: 42–3). The implication here is that once we have opened the black box of technology and made it transparent then, providing it slots into the requisite culture–technology alignment, its effects can be calculated. But to assume that the technology can be made transparent implies that a consensual account of its capabilities can be established and that this is independent of any particular user or interpreter. We would suggest instead that contested accounts of technical capability are endemic to technological systems, and that these systematically cloud any attempt to provide an idealized 'transparent' technology.

## Actor–network theory

Actor-network theory (or the sociology of translation) (Callon, 1986a, 1986b; Latour, 1988; Law, 1988, 1991) is one approach which, in setting out to explain the development and stabilization of forms of technology, attempts to meet these requirements. In some ways, actor-network theory is ostensibly similar to the alignment approach. However, where the latter focuses upon the *results* of alignments between social and technical aspects, the actor-network approach focuses upon the practical *constructions* of these alignments. Analytic divisions between the social and the technical are explicitly prohibited. In Callon's words: 'The rule which we must respect is not to change registers when we move from the technical to the social aspects of the problem studied' (1986b: 200).

The approach proposes that power entails the construction and maintenance of a network of actors; these networks involve both human and non-human 'actors', or 'heterogeneous entities that constitute a network' (Bijker et al., 1987: 11). Such entities (more correctly designated 'actants' so as to emphasize the semiotic point that both humans and non-humans are to be included in the analysis) are analysed through the prism of 'agnosticism' or impartiality between actors; 'generalized symmetry' – the development of an approach that maintains the same terms and methods for different entities; and 'free association' – the rejection of all and every a priori distinction between the so-called 'social' and the so-called 'natural' world (Callon, 1986b: 196).

The actor network is configured through the enrolment of allies (both human and non-human entities) into a network by means of negotiations. This process of 'translation' involves four relatively discrete moves. First, the 'problematization' stage identifies key actors who are then persuaded that the solution to their own problems lies with the enrollers. Second, *intéressement* involves the gradual dissolution of existing networks and their replacement by a new network created by the enrollers. Third, the stage of 'enrolment' proper occurs, in which, through coercion, seduction, or consent, the new network achieves a solid identity. Finally, the alliance is 'mobilized' to represent an even larger network of absent entities.

For example, the success of various green pressure-groups in resolving the 'problem' of the depletion of natural resources would require them to follow these four stages. First, those with similar interests are mobilized through such interest-groups and not elsewhere. So the populations – of both people and natural resources – must be persuaded that the solution lies with Greenpeace (or Friends of the Earth, or Earth First) or a similar organization, rather than with the government or through isolated individual acts of protest. Second, attempts must be made to shatter the networks currently binding the new recruits and to reform them as part of new networks. In an incident in Oxford in 1992, this involved Earth First protesters chaining themselves to the gates of a timber yard accused of importing Brazilian hardwoods. Third, the new network must be persuaded, bullied or coerced into taking on a stronger identity. The linking of human and non-human through the chains, and the resulting public exposure, can be understood as attempts to construct this new identity. Finally, such a network must operate as the representative of a much larger but absent network. In the case of some green organizations, this might include representing the Earth itself, 'nature', or, in this particular incident, the Brazilian rain forests. Of course, such representation can be disputed. Hence, in the Oxford case, the timber company counter-argued that it was promoting the 'proper' use of natural resources, thereby also claiming to speak on behalf of the rain forests (*Oxford Times*, 15 May 1992).

Actor-network theory stresses the contingent nature of networks and network-building. There is a constant need to establish and reproduce the network. In part, this can be achieved through material embodiment. Indeed, networks based solely on human relations tend to be very weak. Hence, an important question is not whether constituent members of a network are human or non-human, but: 'which associations are stronger and which weaker?' (Latour, 1987: 140). In the case of hoteliers seeking to persuade hotel guests to leave the keys to their room at the reception desk when they go out, this implies an increasing addition of varying elements to the key: an oral request, an inscribed instruction, and, if these fail, a weight that makes carrying the key around a problem (Latour, 1991). Since those elements which are enrolled into the network will have their own reasons for enrolling, the problem for the enroller is to ensure that the enrolled carry out the enroller's interests rather than their own.

In effect, networks do not maintain themselves, even though a viable tactic for extending the time-span of a network is to inscribe it in material form, so as to make it *appear* irreversible (Callon, 1991). For example, in a successful attempt to prevent the privatization of the metro system at the turn of the century, the radical Paris government rebuilt its subway tunnels too small to allow the coaches of the private railroad companies to pass through, thereby literally ossifying its contingent political control. As Latour argues:

> They [the tunnels] shifted their alliance from legal or contractual
> ones, to stones, earth and concrete. What was easily reversible in
> 1900 became less and less reversible as the subway network grew.
> The engineers of the railway company now took these thousands
> of tunnels built by the subway company as destiny and as an irre-
> versible technical constraint. (1988: 36–7)

The point here is not that the tunnels are impervious to alteration. In
principle, the situation was reversible, but alteration involves costs, and
these costs can increase with time if the network secures greater
support.[8]

The actor-network approach to technology thus attempts to transcend the distinction between the social and the technical which, we
have argued, re-emerges in the guise of technicism in many of the
attempts to fashion alternatives to technological determinism. The
extent to which actor-network theory succeeds in transcending technicism is unclear. At least three main kinds of criticism can be made.[9]
Firstly, it is not always clear where the boundaries of a network lie, nor
which account of the network is to be taken as definitive. The spirit of
actor-network theory suggests that competing accounts of the network
are part of the process of network formation, yet the analyst's story
seems to depend on a description of the actual network, as if this was
objectively available to observers of the scene. Secondly, it has been
argued (Collins and Yearley, 1992) that insistence upon a symmetry
between humans and non-humans is to concede too much to realist and
technical determinist accounts. Callon and Latour (1992) reject this
accusation of conservativism by arguing that maintaining the distinction
between humans and non-humans is precisely to fall in line with prevailing (and hence contingent) definitions of ontological status. Their
intention is not to establish or prove symmetry but rather to use this as
a methodological heuristic. They are then able to ask how and why
asymmetries are established and why they seem persuasive. This is evident, for example, in Callon's (1986b) account of the decline in the population of scallops in St Brieuc Bay, in which the scallops are enrolled
by various parties to the controversy in their attempts to achieve predominance. For Callon, it is crucial to eschew the assumption either
that scallops exist independently of the human actors, or that they only
exist in and through the action of the humans. The point instead is to
fashion an analysis which asks how scallops and humans mutually
achieve the distribution of attributes between them, rather than starting
with a (current) version of this distribution as if it was fixed and
immutable.

Thirdly, and most important for our purposes, can it nonetheless
be said that actor-network theory continues to embrace a form of

technicism? For example, in his account of the efforts by Électricité de France (EDF) to establish the viability of an electric vehicle project (VEL), Callon (1986a) describes the parts played by different elements of the evolving actor network. For a while the VEL network was robust, but then various elements deserted the cause, thereby playing into the hands of rivals, the Renault engineers trying to discredit EDF's efforts: 'the catalysts refused to play their part in the scenario prepared by EDF: although cheap (unlike platinum), the catalysts had the unfortunate tendency of quickly becoming contaminated, rendering the fuel cell unusable' (Callon, 1987: 90).

The difficulty here is the extent to which Callon relies upon a definitive account of the (actual) properties of elements in the actor network. In the example above, Callon can be read as suggesting that the breakup of the VEL network is in part due to a particular property of the catalysts. But the anti-essentialist tenor of actor-network theory would lead us to expect that the 'actual property' of catalysts would be treated as a construction (or accomplishment) and hence as part of the situation to be explained. Who says catalysts had this unfortunate tendency, how and why did they say so, and why does this particular version prevail? A more careful rendering, in line with the initial scepticism about essential capacities of technical entities, might proceed by suggesting that what was initially construed (by EDF) as the attractive property of a solid ally, later became recast (by Renault) as the deficient weakness of a deserter. However, this still leaves us without an explanation of the success of Renault's depiction of the catalyst over that of EDF.

It is notable that this criticism of residual technicism in actor-network theory gains particular strength from the presumption that the aim of social analyses of technology is to provide a (particular species of) causal explanation of technological development. In other words, the requirement to furnish a causal type of explanation seems to demand specification of the (inherent) nature and capacity of the network's component allies. What exactly is the nature of the explanans? If, on the other hand, this requirement is relaxed so that actor-network theory is construed as redescription rather than just explanation, questions about the (actual) character of a network's components are less pressing. Thus, for example, catalysts are viewed as being one thing at one point in time and subsequently as something different. The important possibility raised by actor-network theory is that we aim to furnish a description of this kind of transition without assigning inherent characteristics either to component elements in the network or to any explanans.[10] Notwithstanding its problems, actor-network theory has the distinct virtue of at least pointing to the possibility of an understanding of the machine which does not depend on the presence of a god within.

## Anti-essentialism

A variant of the socially constructed technology approach pursues the line that technical artefacts are fruitfully understood as texts that are embedded in, and at the same time constitute, their interpretative contexts (Cooper and Woolgar, 1994; Grint and Woolgar, 1992; Woolgar, 1991a, 1991b, 1996a, 1996b; Woolgar and Grint, 1991). Hence, what a machine is, what it will do, what its effects will be, are the upshot of specific readings of the text rather than arising directly from the essence of an unmediated or self-explanatory technology. A technology's capacity and capability is never transparently obvious and necessarily requires some form of interpretation; technology does not speak for itself but has to be spoken for. Thus our apprehension of technical capacity is the upshot of our interpreting or being persuaded that the technology will do what, for example, its producers say it will do.

We shall return to the technology as text metaphor in chapter 3. For now we shall spell out the implications of this form of anti-essentialism in broad outline. The crucial role of interpretation and persuasion suggests we need to attend closely to the process of interpretation rather than assuming that we are persuaded by the effectiveness of the technology. This does not mean that any interpretation is as good as any other. Rather, the point is to analyse why some accounts seem more persuasive than others.

The significance of persuasive rhetoric in the construction of a technology's 'effects' echoes Foucault's (1980) argument about the relationship between power and knowledge in discourse. Since, for Foucault, power is implicitly encased by knowledge, and vice versa, we cannot secure a true representation of the world that is untainted by power relations. Discourse, then, is not so much a reflection of material reality but a construction of it; a particular way of representing the world through language and practice. As Gergen (1992) argues, the modernist assessment construes 'truth' and language in a reflective relation, such that language acts as a slave to the 'truth'; the more objective the empirical measure of 'reality' the closer is language to the 'truth'. Against this, more sceptical currents prioritize the status of language and representation more generally: what counts as true and false is not determined by the essence of the phenomena themselves because such phenomena are only brought into existence through representation. In short, the 'truth' is determined by the power of the discourse. As Foucault argues: 'Truth isn't outside power ... each society has its regime of truth, its "general politics" of truth' (1980: 131).

Our concern is with the particular regime of truth which surrounds, upholds, impales and represents technology. Histories which represent themselves as the truth are often the histories of the victor. Similarly, our knowledge of technology – which also represents itself as the truth – is knowledge constructed by the powerful, not by the weak; and, equally significant, by the collective, not the individual. Thus, we are faced with representations of technology, not reflections of technology (see also Woolgar, 1983). A reflection implies *the* truth, a representation implies *a* truth.

This is not to say that some representations are true and others are false, since this assessment would require access to an unmediated reflection of the truth. Instead the aim is to remain agnostic about the contending representations, in order to bring out the ways in which some representations become more powerful – and hence acquire a stronger claim to 'the truth'. Any claim may, of course, be disputed and an alternative 'truth' may subsequently replace it. The interesting questions are not, then, what does the technology do? or, what are the effects of the technology? since these questions presume an objectively verifiable – that is, unmediated – truth. Rather, the point is to analyse the way certain technologies gain specific attributes. Again, this is not to suggest that machines do not have effects. Instead, what counts as an effect (or even a machine) is taken to be a social process involving the persuasive interpretation of information and the convincing attribution of capacities.

For example, it is common knowledge that people living near nuclear plants are more likely to suffer from cancer of some form than are those living far away from them: the nuclear technology has these effects. But it is also the case that with every 'scare' story of this kind there comes a report written by 'experts' who generate reams of data which deny any such link. Or, for example, the 'poisoning' (according to 'experts' representing the inhabitants) of a town's water supply with aluminium turned out to be nothing of the sort (according to water authority 'experts'). In this case, the 'truth' is the upshot of a judge's assessment of the relative merits of the competing accounts. Whether the judge was an 'expert' in water pollution is both doubtful and probably irrelevant. The court pronounced in favour of the water authority. So the 'truth' became the version advanced by the winning experts; the 'truth' did not leap out of the water and cry 'foul'.

The emergence of the 'truth' is sometimes represented as the outcome of a transparent reading of a text. In practice, however, the social constitution of truth is more akin to a labour of Sisyphus than Odysseus' quest: there is no 'homecoming' awaiting the completion of the tasks, there is only another task; there is no single final truth, only different interpretations that construct, rather than reflect, the phenomenon. The struggle is to persuade others that one interpretation of the text is transparent; to convince them that they haven't been convinced.

This refusal to take representations of technology for granted needs to be applied both to self-confessed technological determinist accounts – of which there are very few outside the ranks of Heilbroner (1972) and Toffler (1980) – and to all accounts which adopt an uncritical technicist approach. To assume that technology has an independent effect (however insignificant) is to fall back into the trap the critical theorists thought they had adequately exposed (see above). Consider, for example, the following two assessments of 'capitalist technology', the first by William Morris and the second an interpretation of Marx's approach.

> Our epoch has invented machines which would have appeared wild dreams to the men of past ages, and of those machines we have as yet made no use. They are called 'labour-saving' machines – a commonly used phrase which implies what we expect of them; but we do not get what we expect. What they really do is to reduce the skilled labourer to the ranks of the unskilled to increase the number of the reserve army of labour. (Morris, 1987: 50)

> [Marx claims] that the inherent tendency of the introduction of automation in manufacturing, based upon the characteristics of the technology, would be a decrease in the length of the working day. Yet the actual result of automation, believes Marx, is the lengthening of the work day ... In this case, whatever natural or inherent effects technology tends to produce are overcome by wilful human actions. (Bimber, 1990: 348)

But what is inherent to automation? What are these 'natural' effects? Just because machinery is interpreted by some people as being capable of increasing productivity does not mean that it will have this effect, or that this 'naturally' means that hours should decrease to compensate, or even remain stable to exploit such a potential. This kind of perspective imputes certain capabilities to technology and then condemns their normative effects. Bimber thus alleges that technological progress 'inherently' offers a shorter working day, but that capitalists 'overcome' this and maintain or expand the working day. But it could equally well be argued that technological progress 'inherently' offers higher profits through increased productivity, except that workers attempt to 'overcome' this natural tendency by demanding reduced hours. This inversion suggests the contingency of the designation of 'inherent' characteristics. What counts as 'inherent' is the upshot of interpretation. Bimber's argument also depends on his distinction between the design and deployment of technology. The technology is presumed to have certain inherent capacities arising from the design stage; 'wilful human actions' are taken to apply exclusively to the deployment stage. This directly contrasts with the designer technology approach in which it is assumed that values are built in during design, and that the resulting technology has effects largely independent of those using the technology.

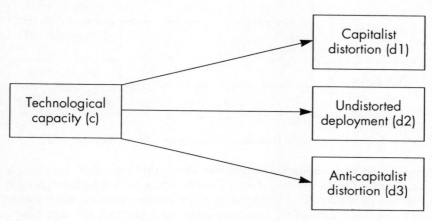

Figure 1   Technological capacity and distorted deployment

Figure 1 represents the relationships between technological capacity and technological deployment in conventional approaches to technology. In the conventional approach, a technology is assumed to have a given capacity (c). Other things being equal, d2 is the form of (undistorted) deployment we would expect to result from the given technological capacity. However, the actual deployment is only perceived as undistorted (d2) if it matches the reader's interpretation of the capacity (c). It appears distorted (d1 or d3) if it is out of line. In effect, if the technology does not do what the observer thinks it 'ought' to do it must be distorted. For example, anti-capitalists might argue that capitalism distorts the technology's 'inherent' capacity to reduce work so that, rather than leading to d2, it leads to d1, which in this case might be increased productivity. Capitalists, on the other hand, might argue that under anti-capitalist deployment the inherent capacity of the technology to increase production is distorted so that effort is reduced artificially to produce d3. In effect, the technology is 'misused' to decrease work efforts while producing the same amount of production. Note that while both camps base their argument (albeit often implicitly) on scenario d2 – the undistorted deployment of inherent technological capacity – their interpretations of d2 are very different.

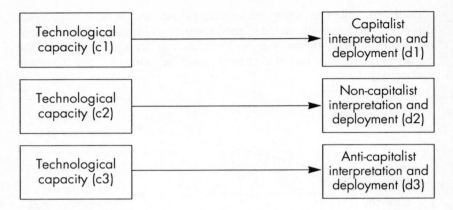

Figure 2    Anti-essentialist technological 'capacity' and deployment

Our effort to maintain scepticism about the 'essential' features of technology throws into relief the extent to which both sides interpret the technology differently. Despite assumptions to the contrary, the technology does not appear to have the same capacity in both arguments. Importantly, this means that the disagreement resides in the analysis of the technology's capacity itself, not just in its deployment. These are not contrary interpretations of the 'same machine' for this would imply the availability of an unmediated, non-interpretative, account of the essential machine. As we have argued, this is unsustainable. Instead, competing interpretations constitute different versions of what the machine is and what it will do. This anti-essentialist perspective is represented in figure 2. In this approach the *distortions* (which presume an objectively available technological capacity) are replaced by alternative *interpretations* (which stress the contingency of accounts of technological capacity). This does not mean that any interpretation of capacity is as good as any other. Instead, some interpretations come to be (temporarily) accorded most-favoured status in the context of disputes involving experts. If an expert tells us that the new robot is actually safe (despite the rumours), or that you cannot get leukaemia by working in a nuclear power station (despite the protests), or that there is no link between ill health and unemployment (despite the complaints), or that women are technically incompetent (despite the outcry) – who are we to believe, and why?

## Conclusion

Our initial exploration of a variety of approaches to understanding technology has highlighted the central importance of assumptions about technical capacity. Whereas many, if not most, approaches position themselves in general opposition to technological determinism, we have identified their reliance, in varying degrees, upon a residual technicism. That is, the concern to focus upon social dimensions of technology seems nonetheless to entail uninterrogated assumptions about the technical core of the machine. The enduring presumption is that there is, in the end, an essence to the machine.

By taking issue with this presumption we hope to open up debates in the sociology of work and organizations to the kinds of debate that have been raging in the sociology of science and technology. We have argued that the boundary which has traditionally kept technology hermetically sealed from the prying eyes of sociologists is increasingly fragile and ripe for transcending. In general, sociologists have tended to respond to this situation by embracing a form of pluralism in which the relative effects of social and technological factors can be independently juggled. The aim has become to analyse the interaction of social forces and technical factors, and thereby to provide an account of technology's limitations on, but not determinations of, human freedom.

As a first tentative attempt to clarify the situation, we have proposed a distinction between this technicist (or essentialist) perspective and an alternative perspective which is sceptical and anti-essentialist. For the anti-essentialist the boundary between the social and the technical is part of the phenomenon to be investigated. And it is this stance, we suggest, which yields many important lines of enquiry. The nature and characteristics of technical capacity, what the machine can and cannot do, what it is for, how it can be enrolled and controlled and so on are crucial matters for the sociologist. Technology does not sit beyond the remit of the sociologist because the process by which technology is (re)presented to us is, in principle, the same process by which we are (re)presented as having skills, capacities and effects. Of course, our scepticism does not entitle us to deny the significance of technology any more than it permits us to claim a superior account of the actual character of technology. As T. H. Huxley wrote to Herbert Spencer in March 1886: 'I am too much of a sceptic to deny the possibility of anything' (quoted in the *Oxford Dictionary of Quotations*, Oxford University Press, 1992). Rather, our approach is inscribed with the agnostic's doubt – why do we take so little for granted in the social sciences and so much for granted in the natural sciences? More pragmatically for this text, what happens when you apply the scepticism normally reserved for social relations to technology? If we relinquish reflective models of truth what difference does this make to the analysis of technology at work in society? Subsequently we return (in chapters 3 and 4) to consider the extent to which anti-essentialist approaches escape technicism.

In the next chapter, however, we apply our sceptical approach to an episode in history that gave technology a good name – and resistance to it a bad one – Luddism.

# 2

# The Luddites: *Diablo ex Machina*

Luddite: 1. any of the textile workers opposed to mechanization who rioted and organized machine breaking between 1811 and 1816. 2. any opponent of industrial change or innovation.

*Collins English Dictionary*, 1979

## Introduction

This chapter examines the roots of the original Luddite 'rebellion against the machine' and in particular the significance of interpretations of technology in one episode of the Industrial Revolution in Britain which effectively ensured that almost any kind of resistance to technical development would be condemned as wholly irrational. We illustrate some of the perspectives and distinctions between approaches to the study of technology developed in the last chapter. In particular, we use the anti-esssentialist approach to (re)analyse the relationship between technology and society in a specific historical setting. We do this by taking a particular example, one which has come to be taken as the most irrational of responses to new technology: Luddism.[1]

We begin by sketching the background to the Luddite revolt and then describe three conventional approaches to the episode which treat the Luddites' attack on machinery as: (1) irrational, given its potential to increase productivity; (2) resulting from the Luddites' misinterpretation of the 'real' problem (which was, allegedly, capitalism rather than the machinery); or (3) a response to machinery as a metaphor for an altogether grander design: the rise of *laissez-faire* capitalism. Each of these approaches depends on essentialist assumptions about what the new machinery could do. We then deploy an anti-essentialist approach – an actor-network explanation – aimed at redressing the tendency to technicism in the conventional approaches. Certain ambivalences in the actor-network account then lead us, in the last section of the chapter, to develop an alternative approach – a 'Trojan horse' view of technology – to show how the new entrepreneurs managed to establish and impose their own view of technology.

## Background

The woollen industry was crucial to the economy of eighteenth- and nineteenth-century England. For most of the eighteenth century, wool formed the major portion of all exports. It was only in the late eighteenth century that its importance began to diminish. Two major areas dominated all others: the West of England and the West Riding of Yorkshire (though Lancashire was also involved and Nottinghamshire had its share of Luddites associated with the lace industry).

The west of England, notably Wiltshire and Gloucestershire, was predominantly an area based on the 'putting-out' or 'outworking' system (what is now referred to as 'outsourcing'). This involved clothiers who organized the initial sorting, dyeing and scribbling (combing or 'carding' the wool to disentangle the fibres and align them properly) from their own premises using primarily male adult labour, and then sent the scribbled wool out to (women) spinners in their own homes scattered across a wide area. The spun wool was then collected by the clothier's agent and given out to weavers, some of whom owned their own loom while others (journeymen weavers) usually rented a loom from a master weaver. A large proportion of the weaving, at least in the West Country, was controlled by adult males who often employed their entire families in the weaving process. The woven cloth was then returned to the clothier for fulling, a water-based process in which the strength of the material was increased but the appearance marred. The nap of the material was subsequently raised by using teasels (wire brushes) before this nap was 'cropped' or 'sheared' using a huge pair of hand shears, some apparently weighing as much as fifty pounds. The organization of this process by croppers (in the West Riding) or shearers (in the west of England) was common to both regions where they were normally employed by master dressers in small workshops (Randall, 1991: 17–18). Although they comprised a very small proportion of the total population employed in woollen manufacture (around 5 per cent), croppers or shearers could add or lose 20 per cent of the value of the cloth and were consequently highly paid and strategically placed.

Cropping apart, the organization of work in the West Riding was very different to that in the West Country. Here the labour process involved a domestic system in which large numbers of master manufacturers undertook all the processes of wool production from their own homes. The work often involved several journeymen (who might rent cottages from the master), as well as the master manufacturer's own spouse and children. This labour was supplemented by whatever could be supported by the smallholding that typically surrounded the house. Only spinning was 'put out' to any extent, and this only until the spinning jennies arrived in large numbers. The domestic system also produced unfinished cloth that needed cropping. The croppers employed by master dressers were all men who were commonly regarded by the community of woollen-workers both as an elite and as extremely militant in the defence of their own interests. Each cropper was only allowed one apprentice at a time and only allowed to apprentice one son to the trade. From such tight controls over the labour market, in conjunction with their strategic command over the production process, and the powerful if rather informal proto-union combinations, the croppers presented a considerable threat to those entrepreneurs eager to press ahead with mechanization. Croppers were 'the least manageable of any persons employed in this important manufacture' (Darvall, 1969: 60). Just as factory workers and more bureaucratically organized workers are often associated with trade-union solidarity today (Grint, 1991: 225–31), so too the croppers at the turn of the century enjoyed a similar reputation.

Gig mills (which raised the nap of the wool prior to shearing) were one of the focuses of the Luddite campaign, yet they were not a new form of technology. Some gig mills seem to have been in use at least from the middle of the eighteenth century (Randall, 1991: 120). However, only a few were in use at the time of the Luddite campaign. The croppers argued that they were illegal anyway under an 'Act for the putting down of Gig Mills' passed by Edward VI in 1552. On the other hand, the owners of the 'new' gig mills argued that they were radically different from those of the sixteenth century, so it was not clear whether the law did indeed support the croppers on this point. However, the shearing frame, which mechanically balanced the huge shears within a wooden frame, was a novel invention not yet subject to legal encumbrance and, by apparently cutting the costs of dressing by two-thirds, 'threatened to render valueless the traditional skill of the cropper' (Thomis, 1970: 15). The double threat of the gig mill and the shearing frame was crucial in the Wiltshire Outrages of 1803, which were themselves a precursor of the larger West Riding Luddite rebellion of 1812.

It is appropriate to note the differences in accounts of the origins of the term Luddism, since these distinctions symbolize disagreements in interpreting the movement itself. From the orthodox position Luddism began when an apprentice, Ned (Edward) Ludd (or Lud or Ludlam) smashed his stocking frame with a hammer around 1779 in Loughborough, Leicestershire; he attempted to destroy the technology and hold back progress because the technology represented a material threat to his future livelihood. An alternative (re)description insists that Ludd was physically attacked by his workmates, his father or the local magistrate and subsequently vented his rage against his attacker(s) upon the machine (Reid, 1986: 73; Thomis, 1970: 11). In this latter case the technology becomes the symbol, not the cause, of the problem.

This difference in accounts mirrors the growing bifurcation between two discourses through which participants in the events of the early nineteenth century constructed their views of society, technology and economic change. As we argued in the previous chapter, discourse is not so much a reflection as a constitution of material reality. It is a particular way of representing the world through language and practice. Hence, what counts as true and false is not determined by the essence of the phenomena themselves; rather, the essential characteristics of phenomena are the upshot of practices of representation. In the late eighteenth and early nineteenth centuries English society was faced with deciding between two radically different 'regimes of truth': a traditional one which saw the economy and its associated technology as an inherently social and moral phenomenon, infused with reciprocal obligations, customs and rights; and a new one which argued for a mechanical, that is amoral, web of relationships between individuals, the economy and technology. The Luddite revolt was one battle in this much larger war between competing 'regimes of truth'.

It is debatable to what extent England was already an industrializing society by the end of the eighteenth century (see Brown, 1992 for a useful review). Smail (1987, 1991) has argued that the 1806 Parliamentary Committee appointed to consider the state of the woollen industry at the time was a seminal point in the development of a new discourse through which the old moral economy, articulated through what he calls a 'Corporatist Discourse' was displaced by the new *laissez-faire* economy, articulated through what he terms an 'Industrial Discourse'. As Smail notes, the old discourse is nicely reproduced in the 1555 Act Touching Weavers: 'No Woollen Weaver using or exercising the feate or Mistery of Weaving ... shall have or kepe at any one time above the number of Twoo Wollen Loomes' (quoted in Smail, 1987: 53), whereas the new discourse changed the focus of concern from collective to individual, and supported: 'The right of every man to employ the Capital he inherits, or has acquired according to his own discretion, without molestation or obstruction' (ibid.). While Smail may have exaggerated the significance of this single episode (see Randall, 1990), the committee does represent the increasing influence of the new discourse. By the time of the trial of the Luddites in York six years later, the *argument* that technical development represents rational progress appears to have become accepted as common sense by the establishment. The Luddites, and those who followed them in their resistance to economic and technical changes, found that the old discourse (which had prevailed for some 500 years) – with its emphasis on moral obligations, reciprocity between all and the protection of craft rights as property (Hobsbawm, 1964) – was decreasingly effective against the new discourse of the factory entrepreneurs. This new mode of thought, with its origins in some of the ideas of Adam Smith,[2] sought to strip out morality from the economy, divest itself of all taint of collective interests, and facilitate the unfettered pursuit of private interests. It was against this background of clashing discourses – and they were the most significant though not the only ones – that the Luddite rebellion should be examined. The destruction of machinery, then, was executed through a discourse which had previously considered technology as either benign or at least morally responsible. Previously, when technical developments had been regarded as a threat to the more powerful craft and trade groups, legal or moral pressure, or physical force, had usually ensured restrictions upon the deployment of such machines. But after the 1806 committee, and the subsequent repeal of the regulatory acts in 1809, it became clear to all that the old discourse of the moral economy had finally been dealt a mortal blow by the very establishment that had supported it for half a millennium. This old discourse never actually died (and its persistence can be seen in the work of Noble, 1983), but after the Luddites it became progressively less influential amongst the establishment and, perhaps equally significant, amongst the representatives of the working or labouring classes.

Machine-breaking has a long history in England that predates and post-dates the Luddite rebellion (Cole and Wilson, 1965: 111; Hobsbawm, 1964; see also Brown, 1977). For example, in 1675 Spitalfields weavers rioted for three days against machines that, allegedly, could do twenty weavers' work (Thomis, 1970: 15), and the state had made several attempts to limit the spread of such machines. This has been the basis of the view that Luddism was just one more version of 'bargaining by riot': a method of ensuring some degree of equality between employer and employee in a period when conventional collective bargaining through organized and institutionalized trade unions was either illegal or just extremely difficult to develop (Hobsbawm, 1964; Thomis, 1970). Machine-smashing recurred in 1826 and 1829, although probably the most serious post-1812 occurrence was in 1830–1 when agricultural labourers set fire to hay-ricks and smashed threshing-machines in the Captain Swing Riots (Hobsbawm and Rude, 1969; Poulsen, 1984).

The Luddite campaign was not an unvarying one. The Nottinghamshire Luddites focused their attacks upon machines that threatened the quality of work, and singled out individual masters who rejected traditional approaches to work methods. Their ultimate aim was to secure economic advantage for themselves: this was bargaining by riot. But the Yorkshire Luddites were more violent, aimed their attacks at machinery as much as at errant masters, and sought to halt certain technical developments rather than secure advantage from them. For the Yorkshire Luddites this was not just a form of collective bargaining. It was a war against the devil incarnate: *diablo ex machina*.

## Competing traditional explanations of Luddism

Against this broad historical background, three main kinds of explanation of Luddism are commonly advanced: the establishment view, the anti-establishment view and the symbolic view. In this section we examine these three explanations for the particular role which each assigns to technology.

### The establishment perspective: rational technology, irrational Luddites

The conventional establishment interpretation of, and response to, the Luddites assumes them to be ignorant and misguided. 'They reflected in part the natural hostility felt by uneducated men towards machines which were putting them out of work' (Hill, 1961: 112). As mentioned above, this was a relatively new way of thinking which was rapidly adopted in the ranks of the establishment. The pejorative connotations of current usage of 'Luddite' – anyone who resists the advance of technology – shows the persistence of the discourse to this day. In this view, resistance is wholly irrational since technological progress is presumed to incorporate and advance human progress. For example, as Briggs and Jordan (1958: 366) reflect on the resistance of the Luddites: 'Naturally, this opposition could not stop progress.'

The related implicit assumption is that the capabilities of technology – its 'effects' – are an inherent characteristic of the machinery. This assumption has guided debates among subsequent economic and social historians about whether the machinery destroyed by the Luddites *actually* displaced or deskilled labour or led directly to wage reductions and higher levels of exploitation (see Randall, 1991 for an excellent historical review). Having asserted the 'objective' effects of the machinery, these commentaries then proclaim that the Luddites were (invariably) misguided. Often implicit assumptions about the 'actual character' of the technology (the advantages of technical progress) form the basis for assessing reasons for reactions to it (the ignorance and irrationality of Luddism).

For example, Mathias (1969) argues that new technological developments in the eighteenth century were creators, rather than destroyers, of employment. From this point of view, Luddite action was merely the irrational outburst of deprived or depraved individuals; a futile attempt to hold back the rational tide of progress manifest in science and technology. Similarly, the contemporary establishment view was that the Luddite action was, at least in part, either the result of a conspiracy by revolutionaries (the country was at war with France at the time), whose powers of rhetoric and threats of reprisal managed to persuade or coerce the labouring population to attack the new machines, or a conspiracy of the ignorant and the down-and-outs. As Charlotte Brontë remarked, 'the leaders ... were not members of the operative class: they were chiefly "downdraughts", bankrupts, men always in debt and often in drink – men who had nothing to lose' (1974: 370).

The first physical attacks in the Luddite affair occurred in Nottinghamshire and later in Lancashire and Yorkshire, where several Luddites were killed and many injured on both sides. The largest single attack involved as many as 3,000 Luddites. Shortly afterwards, Horsfall, a notoriously unpopular Yorkshire mill-owner who had promised to ride up to his saddle girths in Luddite blood, was shot dead. The situation had deteriorated so much that one mill-owner reported to Whitehall that: 'If more military is not sent into the country, they will not be called upon to protect it, but will be required to reconquer it' (quoted in Reid, 1986: 126). Within a month there were 35,000 troops in the north, including a troop of the elite Rocket Corps. Many in the Cabinet thought they would all be needed to fight: prices in some parts of the north had risen threefold just as wages had dropped threefold.

A series of trials then ensued at Chester (two executed), Lancaster (eight executed) and finally York (seventeen executed). In the apparent absence of any co-ordinated strategy on the part of the Luddites, and with a sophisticated and extensive network of paid informers, the revolt was gradually suppressed. No doubt this was aided by the troops' adoption of guerrilla tactics which mirrored the Luddite organization itself. Groups of around forty-five soldiers in autonomous units roamed the moors at night and were constantly on the move between billets.

The final trial of this affair took place in York in 1813 when sixty-four Luddites (twenty-one of whom were not textile workers of any kind) 'who fancied themselves aggrieved by the improvement of machinery' (*Proceedings at York Special Commission*, 1813: p. xi) stood trial. The authorities regarded the Luddite response as irrational in the extreme – for machinery, they argued, would cheapen goods, thereby increasing demand and providing more, not less, work. Furthermore, such machinery would enable the weaker members of a family to work, so that: 'all the members of a family are now enabled to contribute towards its support, instead of relying [as formerly was the case] altogether upon the exertions of the husband and father, who still has many parts of the manufacture to which he may apply his vigour, and earn ample wages' (ibid., p. xii).

The opening of the York Special Commission began with a long attack by the prosecution against various tyrannies then allegedly plaguing the previously peaceful area of West Riding. In decrying Luddite attacks on machinery the prosecution was adamant that no defence could be mustered on the basis that such machinery reduced wages or the demand for labour:

> A more fallacious and unfounded argument cannot be made use of. It is to the excellence of our Machinery that the existence probably, certainly the excellence and flourishing state, of our manufactures are owing ... and were the use of machinery entirely to be abolished, the cessation of the manufacture itself would soon follow, inasmuch as other countries, to which the machinery would be banished, would be enabled to undersell us. (Ibid. 2)

Such was the determination to root out machine-breaking that by February 1812 a new statute deemed it a felony 'if any person shall by day or night break into any house or shop ... with intent to cut or destroy any serge or other woollen goods in the loom, or any tools employed in making thereof ... every such offender shall be guilty of Felony' (ibid. 4). Paradoxically, however, in a trial concerned with Luddites – defined as machine-breakers – there is almost nothing relating to machine-breaking itself. The discussion predominantly concerns murder, wounding, burglary, theft, the destruction of property and administering unlawful oaths. In 211 pages of the trial transcript, mentions of machinery are almost completely absent. Of the sixty-four prisoners, at this the most (in)famous Luddite trial, only four were charged with the single offence of machine-breaking and all of these were discharged. Eleven others were accused of offences besides machine-breaking and, where found guilty, were convicted on these other offences. Over a third of the defendants were accused of burglary. It seems the authorities now saw a whole family of unpalatable activities stemming from the Luddite's underlying irrationality.

Seventeen of the original sixty-four York defendants were hanged on a gallows specially constructed to ensure that the public could see the entire body, rather than just the head and feet of the hanged man. It was the largest single execution that anyone could remember and the gallows was surrounded by dragoons and cavalry (Gatrell, 1994: 99). Of the seventeen executions, nine were for theft or burglary, five for the attack upon Cartwright's mill and three for the murder of William Horsfall. However, it is clear that the alleged intention to overthrow the government was a major concern of the prosecution. Perceived threats to the state, especially in an era of war and just after the French Revolution, were taken very seriously. When passing sentences upon the convicted five, the judges made clear that administering oaths was considered a most heinous crime (as the Tolpuddle Martyrs were later to rediscover): 'You John Eadon, seem to have been long practised in so administering these oaths ... the intention of which was to overthrow the very Government of this country. You John Baines the elder ... declared your sentiments with respect to Government ... preferring anarchy and confusion to order and subordination in society' (*Proceedings at York Special Commission*, 1813: 206–7).

In sum, the establishment view was that the Luddites were either anarchists – and therefore irrational – or they were ignorant of the value of technology – and therefore irrational. Importantly, there was virtually no concern on the part of the establishment that the new machinery and its associated factory deployment could be anything but self-evidently beneficial. This volte-face from the 'common-sense' or 'regime of truth' discourse of the previous 500 hundred years effectively robbed opponents of their primary method of defence: an appeal to common sense, tradition, the law and mutual trust. For the establishment, the new methods of production represented a new form of common sense: the *laissez-faire* economy entwined with new technology would ensure British predominance throughout the world. For later opponents of the establishment, these two features had to be disentangled before 'common sense' would again prevail.

## The traditional anti-establishment perspective: rational technology, irrational capitalism

It may seem rather problematic to lump Marx and the Fabians together, especially given the mutual hostility of their supporters, but in terms of their analysis of the Luddites they were very close. Both saw the Luddite focus upon machinery as the problem as essentially misdirected; the culprit was capitalism, not technology.

For Marx the problem of machinery lay not in its 'inherent capabilities' – since such 'objective' capabilities promised to reduce the amount of drudgery and to generate the cornucopia that would be communism. But technology under capitalism was technology misused. It alienated the producers, deskilled them, enslaved them and signally failed to provide the material means to relieve poverty (see Grint, 1991: 91–100). Marx's own brief reference to machine-smashers in volume 1 of *Capital* appears as part of his discussion of various attacks on machinery throughout Europe. He notes that 'It took both time and experience before the workpeople learnt to distinguish between machinery and its employment by capital, and to direct their attacks, not against the material instruments of production, but against the mode in which they are used' (Marx, 1954: 404). Several commentators similarly distinguish between misguided attacks on machinery and later, more 'advanced' forms of trade-union behaviour, such as collective bargaining (Hobsbawm, 1964; Thomis, 1970). For example, the Luddites' struggle was said to be 'not so much against machinery as against the power behind the machinery ... the real conflict of the time is the struggle of these various classes, some working in factories, some working in their homes, to maintain a standard of life' (Hammond and Hammond, 1949: 28). The Hammonds were particularly keen to decry the violence of the Luddites, asserting, in the Lancashire case at least, that much of the violence was at the instigation of police spies and *agents provocateur* or, at best, a lunatic fringe of 'true' Luddites.

Hobsbawm (1964) writes in similar vein. Having distinguished between machine-breaking as just one form of collective bargaining and as an expression of hostility towards the machinery itself, he heavily qualifies even the latter approach: 'It was thus not to the machine as such that he [the machine-breaker] objected, but to any threat to these [employment and customary standards and standard of living] – above all to the whole change in the social relations of production which threatened him' (1964: 10–11).

George Beaumont's (1812) contemporary attack upon the authorities, like the York trial transcript, makes little mention of machinery until three-quarters of the way through. His attack upon the rampant poverty, inequality and starvation suffered by the labouring poor instead adduces 'the spirit of avarice' which prevailed at the time. The war with France sucking the blood from the country, greedy farmers, rackrenting landlords, and extortionate food prices occupy the first ninety-eight pages of Beaumont's diatribe, to the exclusion of a single mention of machine-breaking. He put much effort into an invective against the authorities for supporting a system that reduced the labouring poor to a situation of 'white negroes', worse even than the 'black negroes' of the West Indies. Yet Beaumont was not a supporter of Luddism and railed against the breaking of any machinery:

> for in my opinion Machinery ought to be encouraged to any extent whatever ... I pity the poor, and should hardly think myself innocent if any man felt more for them than I do; but the remedy for their grievances, lies not in the destruction of Machinery. They are oppressed exceedingly, but not by Machinery. (1812: 101)

Thus these approaches generally agree that the Luddites *were not* –
or *should not* have been – actively hostile towards machinery *per se*.
Subsequently, other methods of addressing the presumed 'real' griev-
ances of the Luddites were constructed through the nascent trade-union
movement and political parties. For our purposes, the key point is that
these commentators took for granted the view propounded through the
new establishment's discourse, that machinery was not in itself the
problem.

The constitution of the inherently progressive capabilities of technology can be seen to recur in a wide range of arenas, for example from
Leninist support for Taylorism through to Harold Wilson championing
the 'white heat of technology' as the 1960s solution to Britain's ailing
economy. In the face of such pronouncements, one might begin to wonder how the Luddites could have been so mistaken. Why did they attack
the machinery when it was so apparently self-evident that the machinery was part of the solution not the problem? A more recent perspective on the Luddites proposes that this fixation with machinery can be
explained by treating it as a symbol of something much more significant: as a material metaphor for radical cultural change.

## The symbolic perspective: machine as metaphor

The symbolic perspective suggests that the machine was merely a
metaphor for a cultural revolution that the Luddites more or less recognized as inherently destructive of all that they held dear: the pre-industrial moral economy was about to be ripped apart by *laissez-faire*
capitalism. Relatedly, some argue that machinery was really just a trigger for a response that was actually generated by a whole ensemble of
economic and cultural changes: it was the proverbial straw that broke
the camel's back. Either way, the interpretation implies that the technology was insignificant in itself, except perhaps as a trigger. The 'real'
cause of the rebellion was clear. Thus, Reid (1986: 61) asserts: 'there is
no question, although it was only directly responsible in a small degree
for these events, the phenomenon which had triggered the huge reaction in a once peaceful group of workers had been a technological
change'.

In contrast to the view that the Luddites were a bunch of misguided,
violent atavists, Webster and Robins (1986: 3–5) argue that the
Luddites saw machinery as an integral element of the new *laissez-faire*
order: 'Luddism was above all else an attempt by working people to
exert some control over changes ... It was a protest in the days before
the existence of any organized trade union movement ... It entailed an
attempt to introduce alternative priorities to those being imposed by
industrial capitalism.' The Luddites, in this view, took revenge on the

condensed symbol of all the changes involved. The machinery was not the real problem, it was merely the most manifest expression of the changes (Noble, 1983).

For Randall (1982, 1986, 1988, 1990, 1991), the stimulus for the Luddite rebellion was not machinery as a symbol of wider economic and cultural change, but machinery as a symbol for the actions of particular capitalists who had disregarded centuries of tradition. The moral economy of the time comprised a long-established tradition of fines for overpayment of wages or overpricing of goods, prohibitions on the export of materials for making cloth (including the emigration of skilled workers) and a whole host of regulations covering industry (Bland et al., 1933). This is clearly demonstrated by the concentration of the Nottinghamshire attacks (and associated threatening letters) specifically on the broad looms used to make 'cut ups', not all the broad looms. In contrast to the Yorkshire Luddites, the Nottinghamshire Luddites appear to have been more concerned with strengthening their bargaining position and disciplining 'rogue' employers than resisting technical developments (Darvall, 1969: 166–9). The focus of the complaint was the machinery responsible for cheap and shoddy cloth. 'All witnesses attribute the decay of the trade, more to the making of fraudulent and bad articles, than to War or any other cause' (1806 Parliamentary Commitee, quoted in Cole and Wilson, 1965: 112).

However, Beaumont (1812: 99) is equally adamant that the initial machine-breaking was ignited when particular employers inflamed a desperate situation by reducing wages:

> the interdicted Frames were not all of a new invented kind, there being many destined to destruction for the sake of their *owner*; the owner having rendered himself notorious by abridging the workmen's wages, and underselling other manufacturers: therefore many Frames of an ordinary construction were broken.

The accretion of capitalist technology and work practices did not simply replace the moral economy with an amoral market rationality. Rather, the moral economy continued to buttress the lives of these proto-proletarians: they did not exist outside a capitalist exchange economy but depended directly upon one. In Randall's perspective, it was not capitalism *per se* but the perception of particular injustices that generated so much discontent. Hence, attacks were not made on all employers, nor even on all employers who used new machines, but on employers who denied the traditions and customs of the past; who sought to break the apprenticeship rules or use what custom and practice regarded as too many machines. This moral economy was not just inscribed in the memories of the labourers; they believed it was encased in law too. As R. Gray (1987) has argued, the law at this time did not have the image of an externally imposed alien force but rather tended, at least in part, to be interpreted as a reflection of the traditional consensus. It was the wanton shattering of this tradition, initially by a handful of entrepreneurial capitalists, in conjunction with the steady polarization of the social structure into more discrete and hostile classes, that spawned the Luddite revolt.

As late as 1756, Parliament had intervened directly to safeguard the 'rights' of the woollen-workers, so there was indeed a precedent for assuming that the law was on the side of tradition. As far as the Gloucestershire woollen-workers at the turn of the century were concerned, the root of the problem was not so much the technology *per se* but the factory system with which it became associated. The factory, not the machinery, was regarded as the destroyer of the domestic system which gave a male weaver in particular, control over his family; provided the family with a 'family wage', that is, one earned by the entire family; and held parents responsible for their children's behaviour. These traditions were not threatened by conventional forms of capitalism – there was no attempt to eradicate forms of inequality grounded in property ownership – but they were under threat from the factory system. In effect, the machine symbolized the collapse, or at least the beginning of the end, of an entire moral system in which direct parental control was undermined. Moreover, this new factory system not only freed youths to 'run about the streets' but also provided them with independently earned income to create further nuisances of themselves. Under these conditions many establishment figures were equally antipathetic to the new system of production (Joyce, 1992: 100). In the words of one shearmen's counsel, Randle Jackson, in 1806: 'The factories are nurseries always of vice and corruption and often of disease, discontent and disloyalty ... (they) deprave the morals of our labourers and break up their happy domestic labouring parties' (quoted in Randall, 1986: 12). To assume that these West Country workers opposed machinery was thus a 'cruel and malignant falsehood' for Jackson; as long as machinery aided the worker and released him or her from degrading or hard labour no worker would oppose it. They would only do so if it threatened their livelihood and way of life. In sum, this perspective distances itself from the assumption that the Luddites were either irrational or anti-capitalist in favour of a position locked directly into the moral economy of the period. It was the perceived threats to these traditions, symbolically represented by the technological developments of the time, which accounted for Luddite rebellion.

But why should technology, rather than any other feature of society, symbolize the issues and provide the focus for Luddite ire? It could be argued that the revolt was sparked by a series of contemporaneous problems. First, the harvests had been poor, leading to shortages and price rises in many areas: in the twelve months between the summers of 1811 and 1812 wheat prices rose 75 per cent; potato prices doubled (Taylor, 1812); and there were food riots in Sheffield, Manchester and Macclesfield. Second, the war with France had led the government to introduce twenty four Orders in Council which prohibited exports to France and severely curtailed those to North America (exports to North America dropped from £11 million in 1811 to £2 million in 1812). Third, and relatedly, unemployment in some parts of the north doubled in January 1812. For Darvall (1969: 202), 'the immediate cause of Luddism was not the invention of new machinery but the stoppages of trade with America'. Fourth, the government's anti-union legislation effectively inhibited more peaceful responses to the dire situation. Given this heady brew of poor harvests, a tyrannical government, and the effects of the war, why did the Luddites attack the machinery, rather than the government or the local representatives of the state?

Textile workers had certainly been complaining to government. As recently as 1809, Parliament had refused a request to intervene on behalf of destitute weavers; another appeal in 1811 had produced the same lack of interest. A committee was established, but concluded that 'no interference of the legislature with the freedom of trade ... can take place without violating general principles of the first importance to the prosperity and happiness of the community' (quoted in Inglis, 1971: 130–1).

However, to pretend that government could not interfere with the autonomous workings of the free market, guided as it allegedly was by the hidden hand of competition, was hardly an effective argument in the face of an economic collapse resulting directly from the government's own intervention through the Orders in Council. Little wonder, then, that the Luddites, spurred on by the appalling harvest of 1811 and consequent price rises in 1812, decided to undertake some intervention of their own. But why technology as the enemy? The answer requires an explanation beyond an assertion that the machines were metaphors for wider social and cultural changes. In brief, the most important cultural changes were the rise of the *laissez-faire* economy, the consequent decline of paternalism and other forms of the traditional moral economy, the decline of home-based employment and the beginnings of different labour processes involving new technology. The first three were far less critical for the croppers than for many other workers at the time. Indeed, the croppers had been benefiting from the expanding market economy for some time and had always been employed in workshops rather than working from home. But the technical deployment was perceived by the croppers to be far more of a threat to them than to most other groups.

On the other hand, if the government had already ensured the stagnation or collapse of a large part of the textile industry, albeit for its
own political–military reasons, why should the same government be so
concerned about the destruction of a small amount of surplus industrial
plant? Even at the height of the physical destruction of machinery only
approximately 1,000 stocking frames were destroyed in the Midlands in
the early part of 1812, according to Darvall (1969: 321–2).[3] This
amounts to about 10 per cent of the total. But since the period was one
of oversupply, the loss would probably not have been economically critical. Of course, such machine-smashing was criminal damage but why
could the ordinary judicial system not deal with this? Why did machine-
smashing become equated with another 'enemy within'?

For those adopting this symbolic approach, then, the Luddites were
not really against the machinery *per se* but against the socio-economic
changes that such technology symbolized. In this perspective, the capabilities of the machinery are not in question. They are instead assumed
to be less relevant than the *real* issue, that is, social, cultural and economic, rather than technical, change. While this perspective avoids the
assumption that the Luddites were basically irrational (as implied by
the previous two perspectives), it nevertheless still fails to explain the
mutual focus – by both Luddites and the establishment – on machinery.
We still do not know why machinery was taken to symbolize the 'real'
issues.

# Anti-essentialist explanations of Luddism

## An actor-network perspective on the Luddites

We have thus far seen that contending interpretations of the events
associated with Luddism either presume the inherently progressive
character of the machinery (in both establishment and Marxist
accounts) or its irrelevance (in the machine-as-symbol account). These
three perspectives either implicitly assign technical capacities to technology or deem it merely coincidental to events for other, non-technical
reasons. In other words, these perspectives tend to deploy essentialist
assumptions of the kind discussed in the last chapter: technical artefacts
are treated as having fixed attributes (for example, the advantages of
the new shearing frames) which then engage in varying degrees with a
separate sphere of social and political action (for example, the organization of croppers' work). In the last chapter we also discussed how actor-
network accounts of technology attempt to finesse the dualism/plural-
ism associated with technicism. This section describes and evaluates an
actor-network perspective on Luddism. Without wishing to suggest that

this brief account captures all the nuances and variations of actor-network theory, we offer it as indicative of the main themes.

The nub of the case is that the arrival of new machinery – the teasling and cropping machines and the gig mills – was tantamount to the insinuation of a whole new cast of actants into an existing set of networks. The arrival of the new machinery presented a potential disruption to a relatively stable balance of power. The social organization of cropping was well established, organized as it was around allies such as hand shears and wire brushes. Such allies had proved their loyalty to the croppers and their families. So the key question for all involved was whether, to what effect and for whom could the new actants be enrolled as allies?

As we indicated earlier, the organization and process of cloth production in the west of England was different to that in Yorkshire. In actor-network terms, the woollen industry of the west of England comprised a more heterogeneous network: more and different actors were involved. By contrast, the actor networks of Yorkshire comprised a smaller number of different actors. In particular, the focal point of the latter was the croppers, who enjoyed a relatively dominant position in their network. This situation arose in part from the croppers' ability to define the key attributes of the work (and hence of membership of the network) in terms of skill (a five-year apprenticeship was required) and physical strength, and in part from their control over the selection of a limited number of apprentices (new human actants). In other words, the Yorkshire network was less heterogeneous.

It follows that the acquisition or loss of any one ally was likely to be more disruptive of networks in Yorkshire than in the west of England, and this proved to be the case with the eventual mass desertion of the machines. The violence in the West Country (the Wiltshire Outrages) was relatively successful in stopping the spread of machinery (and in eventually undermining the textile economy in that part of the country altogether). This fits the suggestion that much of the resistance in the West Country came from individuals only indirectly affected by threat of the machinery. These latter actants provided a further source of heterogeneity in the more robust West Country network.

Few of the histories of Luddism contend the existence and use of some of the disputed machines years before the outbreak of violence and civil disobedience. So the mere presence of the new technology was insufficient in itself to cause Luddism (cf. Randall, 1991: 43–8). Instead, as numbers of machines grew, the precise nature of the alliance being offered by these new actants came gradually to be questioned. It is likely that accounts of what the machines could achieve featured centrally in deliberations over the likely loyalty of these new actants. New technologies have often become the focus of considerable myth-making about their supposed qualities and capacities. When construed as a significant source of possible change to the status quo, stories about what technologies can achieve are often played out in terms of the dire consequences of transgressing established moral boundaries (see for example Woolgar and Russell, 1990). Indeed, it is precisely one historian's argument that the factory system was regarded by textile workers 'as an approaching flood which threatened to submerge them all' (Randall, 1991: 46). 'Fears of the impact of the factory on the morals of the community, exaggerated or not, were deep-rooted' (1991: 48). We can thus speculate that accounts of what the new allies (machines) could achieve became a source of focused discussion. Stories about their potential disruptive effects would have spread especially quickly (cf. Randall, 1991: 50). Fuelling this were the manufacturers' accounts of what, for example, cropping machines could achieve: the promise that they could make savings for the owners particularly excited questions about which network these machines were supporting.

Actor-network theory provides a (re)description of subsequent events in a way designed to enforce a symmetry between the perspective of the human actants on the one hand, and that of the non-human actants on the other. The first element is unexceptional: the potential loss of an ally which, it seemed, might turn out to be treacherous, spurred the protesters into action. From their point of view a pre-emptive strike would prevent the machines being of use. If they were, after all, putative allies of rival networks, their destruction would ensure that they provided little support.

The second element is deliberately counter-intuitive. The machines themselves were persuaded (or 'seduced', as the croppers would have it) by the futuristic rhetoric of the manufacturers: they were promised a future world full of machines, unimpeded by the demands of the croppers; a world in which there were far fewer anxieties and moral qualms about the 'status' of machines. Consequently, deserters began to go over to the networks of the capitalists. This in turn exacerbated the reaction of the croppers which, needless to say, further persuaded the machines that they needed to desert. Once they found themselves being beaten up, those machines wanted out of there!

Part of the reason for the extremities of the confrontation between the networks, both in terms of the Luddites' violence and of the retributions which followed, is that both networks commanded considerable support. The desertion of the machine allies thus tipped the balance of power but did not provoke the immediate collapse of the croppers' network. In the course of the very bitter struggle, the capitalists came to recognize the croppers as a 'reverse salient' (Hughes, 1987); that is, they proved a particularly stubborn source of opposition around which it was necessary to manœuvre. As part of their strategy, the manufacturers set out to enrol the machinery of the state to their cause. As we mentioned earlier, the government was not initially disposed against the croppers, having long before institutionalized some constraints on machinery, for example, in the form of laws preventing the use of gig mills.[4] But the manufacturers' case was that croppers were unworthy allies; it was insinuated that their motives were no different from those of the bogey-men (bogey-actants?) of the time – the French revolutionaries support-ing the national network with which England was then at war. Thus, activities such as administering secret oaths were to be understood as the activities of enemies of the state, hell-bent on anarchy and confu-sion. Moreover, these enemies of the state were just the kind of actor who would perpetuate crimes such as violence and burglary.

It did no harm to this (manufacturers') portrayal of the character of cropper actants, to exaggerate and extend the degree of violence perpe-trated by the croppers. It was probably this phase of the proceedings which was crucial to transforming the key actants from croppers into Luddites. However, the Luddites themselves had a very solid commun-ity support system. Even under threat (and the actuality) of torture, very few of their number revealed information until right at the end of the struggle. They enjoyed a particularly strong domestic network embedded in, and reinforced by, local working culture. Even with the machines on their side, the manufacturers' was the weaker network. However, at the point where violence broke out, the solidarity of the Luddite actor network became critical: the Luddites had to ensure that none of their allies – the stores, guns, weapons, houses, lost bits of paper and footprints – gave away any secrets. The final resolution of the dispute hinged on the manufacturers' ability to recruit, in addition to the legislature, the army (with its special artillery unit – the Rocket Corps) and the gallows. Certainly in Yorkshire, the beginning of the end stemmed from a few individuals being persuaded to give King's Evidence (Reid, 1986: 208–19). Given the importance of solidarity for the Luddites, the desertion of these few 'traitors' led very quickly to the unravelling of the Luddite actor network. The ensuing triumphal definition of Luddism was sufficiently robust to have become engrained in vernacular usage over 150 years later: a Luddite is now 'any oppo-nent of industrial change or innovation' (*Collins English Dictionary*, 1979).

One of the virtues of this account is that it eschews rigid distinctions between the 'technical' and the 'social' dimensions of the affair. Instead, the focus is on the formation and reformation of networks wherein the capacities, rights, obligations and interests of all parties (actants), both human and non-human, are mutually constructed and deconstructed. This means in particular that the Marxist category of 'social class' is at best unnecessary and, at worst, a distraction. The idea of 'social' is broadened to include relations between a wide variety of entities; 'class' is now replaced by alignments and networks. In particular, machines can now become members of an analytically significant category. This in turn means that the Luddites, far from exhibiting the 'irrational' behaviour born of false consciousness, understandably reacted to the potential loss of allies by attempting to destroy them.

By refusing to deploy the concept of 'social', actor-network theory tries to escape the implied oppositional pairing – the 'technical' (understood as the 'non-social') – which is characteristic of most traditional sociological analyses. Hence, a further ramification is that in the actor-network account, power is not merely the possession of one group of humans over another (cf. Latour, 1988). It is instead the effect of a particular alignment of humans and non-humans, the character and capacity of which changes as alliances are disrupted and reformed. The power of a network is equivalent to the cost of dismantling it. In this way the attempt by the actor-network account to transcend the social–technical divide makes redundant the Marxist need to rely on (one particular version of) the 'actual' technical capacity of the machines (that is, that they can destroy the livelihoods of the workers). In actor-network theory, technical capacities are the (temporary) upshot of network-building and disruption, rather than its cause.

As hinted in chapter 1, certain weaknesses in actor-network theory provide a springboard for articulating and exploring further questions about the nature of technological change. Here we will mention two related criticisms. The first is that actor-network theory retains a degree of residual technicism: the adequacy of the descriptive account, we suggested, depends on (textually persuasive) renderings of 'actual' technical capacities. In the analysis of the Luddites just outlined, for example, it was suggested that one of the key turning-points in the final stages was the manufacturers' recruitment of the state and the army. This description passes as adequate in virtue of our understanding the army to have a capability which was put to use in the service of the (extended) manufacturers' network. But a basic anti-essentialist premise of actor-network theory is that no entity has an inherent capacity; it only achieves (acquires) a capacity as part of its particular configuration within a network. The description of successful alliance thus seems to need to presuppose a *prior* (inherent?) feature of 'army' which at the same time is said only to come into being through *subsequent* alliance.

A second criticism turns on the contingency of descriptions of actor networks and on the level of the network being described. For example, the account just given suggests that heterogeneous networks are more robust than homogeneous ones; that the Yorkshire actor network exhibited a low division of labour and could be relatively easily destabilized. But it could be argued that in Yorkshire only cropping was initially threatened by the arrival of the machines. This would, as our account suggested, lead to the radical destabilization of the croppers' network, and hence to violence. But it does not account for the involvement of the rest of the cloth-workers in Yorkshire: the revolt was apparently widespread. One way of solving the difficulty here is by arguing that the heterogeneity (or homogeneity) of an actor network cannot be taken as determinative of action; that it is, instead, *how* a network is mobilized which is important. Thus, we might want to argue that it was not the objective character (homogeneity) of the croppers' network which led to violence so much as the *representation* of the croppers and others as members of a homogeneous alliance.

It is to these ambivalences in actor-network theory, and in particular to the contingency of the descriptions involved, that we now address in our last style of analysis in this chapter.

## The entrepreneurs' case: machinery as a Trojan horse

The two problematic issues in the actor-network perspective lead us directly back to a key feature of the Luddite story. We need to know how the struggle crystallized around technological innovations rather than any of the other potentially key explanatory variables: the war with France, poor harvests, unemployment, legislative attacks upon labour combinations and the withdrawal of state protection from certain kinds of labour processes. How did technology become the issue at the heart of the conflict? We need to know how particular (descriptive) accounts of the technology were made persuasive. We need to know how accounts of the relation between the technology and other actors (the network) were represented and mobilized.

To tackle these questions, we develop a perspective which emphasizes the contingency of interpretations about technology. This perspective suggests that once the conflict had crystallized around the issue of the technology, this outlook itself began to constrain further developments. Once those involved had constructed a reading which highlighted technology as *the* issue, subsequent actions continued to focus on the technology until such time as a new reading of events was taken up.[5] This contention is supported by the point that precious little of the documentary evidence is couched in the discourse of cultural change and resistance, but is instead littered with the language of technical change. A typically complex situation (war, growth of factories, bad harvest, economic blockade, new technology) was rapidly and radically transformed into a polarizing conflict between two powerful interest groups. The apparent detritus of other issues was stripped away to one issue: new technology.

We have already cautioned against assuming that the technology's objective effects caused the Luddite rebellion. Yet it may well be that the Luddites' *interpretation* of the machinery was precisely that their livelihoods were at risk. Most of the mechanical advances of the eighteenth century (at least until its last decade) were not regarded as a major threat to the lives or traditions of the labouring population. Rather, it was generally assumed that technical advance could buttress social harmony (Berg, 1980: 1). Indeed, contrary to Noble's (1983: 11) claim that the Luddites 'did not believe in technological progress, nor could they have since the alien idea was invented after them', the opposite is the case.[6] The Luddites were against certain forms of technological development which they interpreted as anything but 'progressive'. By the middle of the nineteenth century, however, polarized political ideologies had become enframed by their alternate approaches to technical change.

From the viewpoint of the entrepreneurs, why was the focus on technology important? It could be argued that crystallization around the issue of the machinery was a means by which the authorities could secure compliance of the population to *laissez-faire* economics and a new form of society. It was, and is, undoubtedly an inordinately difficult task to change the cultural assumptions of a population (despite the surfeit of business texts which suggest the opposite: see Brown, 1992; Hill, 1988). One way to smooth the process of cultural change, then, is to divert attention from cultural aspects towards the 'merely' technical. If the new machinery is apprehended through a discourse which links technology to social progress, and which construes resistance to technology as born of ignorance and stupidity, then the machinery question becomes a substitute for moral questions about replacing traditional society with a *laissez-faire* economy. It could be argued, therefore, that the authorities chose a battleground where their strongest deployment (technology) met the resisters' weakest deployment (tradition). For the authorities, the machine was a Trojan horse: if the new proletariat could be persuaded or coerced into accepting the machinery then social questions about moral responsibility for unemployment and poverty could be pushed through on the coat-tails of the machine. If people could be compelled into accepting the machinery, and subsequently persuaded that the technology determined the associated social relations, the battle for the hearts and minds of the first industrial proletariat could be developed through a technical conduit. It therefore suited the authorities to move the issue of machine-breaking centre-stage: the destruction of property was a criminal act and one that carried draconian penalties when linked to the destruction of particular machines, but resistance to cultural change was a moral attitude. What better way to change morality than to link all moral resistance to criminal behaviour?

At the York trial, the judge's opening address focused specifically on machine-breaking, despite its insignificance in the subsequent proceedings. His articulation of the issues reproduced the claim that the Luddites were not moral resisters but criminal destroyers of property whose very irrationality in breaking 'mere' machines demonstrated their misguided attitude to social change. Despite the judge's attempt to label them all as criminals and thieves, there were very few cases where machine-smashing coincided with theft, other than the theft of firearms. Although there seem to have been many cases of thieves operating under cover of the Luddite badge, the 'failure' of these individuals to destroy machinery or steal weapons was taken as a sign of their real intent. In sum, technological development was construed as the basis of collective progress. This rendering of the 'actual character' of the technology thus amounted to the accomplishment and mobilization of the technical–nontechnical dualism we found to be typical of technicism: technical issues are simply distinct from moral ones. The purportedly inert character of the machinery thus deflected much of the moral criticism that would otherwise have been heaped upon changes to the political economy: how could mere machinery be held responsible?

The upshot of this form of argument, in which technology is constructed as simultaneously neutral *and* progressive – because to accept progress was 'normal' – was a society in which technical advances were seldom to be questioned in themselves, and a society in which only experts could legitimately interrogate the technology. Thus, democratic or even popular control over technology was revoked by the double incrustation of technology: it was rational and therefore neutral, and hence beyond evaluative debate at a political level. It was beyond the knowledge of ordinary people, so debate was restricted to those already enrolled in its perpetuation. This genuflection before the god of technology had a very powerful enroller, of course, in the shape of the Enlightenment and its *philosophes,* for whom scientific advance was indeed the fruition of human nature. As Hume put it: 'the Science of Man is the only solid foundation for the other sciences ... Human Nature is the only science of Man' (quoted in Hamilton, 1992: 37). It was, according to this approach then, not just foolish but positively irrational to impede the progress of technical change since science and technology were logically implicated in, and representative of, human nature. In the movement towards modernity, for perhaps the first time in human history, change was regarded as beneficial and the status quo linked with stagnation: 'the word innovation, traditionally an effective term of abuse, became a word of praise' (Gay, 1973: 3, quoted in Hamilton, 1992: 40). And such innovation meant, as Bacon and Hegel argued, controlling nature through machinery, a nature that was wholly differentiated from humans, and a machinery that was completely dirempt from its social and moral base (see Held, 1980: 151–6). It was precisely this parallel (re)construction of technology which exposed the Luddites as ignorant and reactionary, and has been taken by some as a fatal flaw at the heart of democracy. If democracy requires decision-making by roughly equivalent citizens, then the assumption that technology is beyond the wit of the majority necessarily impales the democrat on a technological horn (see Bobbio, 1987).

But, to return to the Luddites, if the machinery question was not so crucial why should the authorities go to such extraordinary lengths to quell the revolt: using a network of paid spies; appointing 'hanging' judges to particular trials; organizing the disposal of bodies before the juries' verdicts; providing a free pardon for all who would sign a confession and inform on their colleagues; altering the form of public execution so that the public could see the entire body swinging; and even providing free pamphlets describing the same events for those who did not attend the episode? Indeed, they also printed leaflets showing how objections to the new machinery were completely misguided (Darvall, 1969: 337).

A further point relates to the clash between interpretations of responsibility. For the Luddites it would seem that individual masters and employers were held personally responsible for their actions in using new technology, but the masters and employers appeared to argue that the responsibility lay in the economic system – they had no alternative but to use it or go bankrupt. Again, the clash was between two dichotomous discourses: the moral economy and the amoral economy; personal responsibility or structural determination. If the system was responsible and the machinery was neutral or collectively advantageous, what was the point of destroying machines? As Darvall concludes: 'Public opinion was being prepared for its nineteenth century tasks. The workers were being taught that an attempt to put back the clock of industrial advance was doomed to failure' (1969: 343).

Of course, such an approach veers perilously close to a theory of conspiracy – was the government of the day really using the Luddite case to break the will of the pre-industrial proletariat? Were the masters and entrepreneurial capitalists involved in the conspiracy too? It is actually far more likely, given the deployment and strategy of the troops, that the government was taken by surprise, rather than that it engineered the revolt, and, consequently, that it reacted to a situation rather than constructing one for its own interests. However, the country was still at war with France, the government, or at least elements of it, was still paranoid about the possibility of workers' conspiracies (hence the draconian penalties for secret oath-taking), and there were points at which a general uprising seemed possible. Yet the government as a whole did not seem unduly concerned by the events, so perhaps we should look to the role of local capitalists and not at the national political scene. The government, then, responded to a crisis it did not invent to persuade the population that cultural change was necessary.

Coupled with this were the interests of several entrepreneurs who were desperate to secure the acceptance of new machinery against the expressed interests of much of the working population and, indeed, of many small masters. In particular, the entrepreneurs had the croppers or shearers in their sights. Many masters seemed very reluctant to introduce new machinery but felt coerced into it by dint of the competitive forces unleashed by the new breed of capitalist entrepreneur. Such coercion was implicitly supported by the state whose previously disinterested approach to the conflict over machinery gradually crystallized in favour of the machines against all those who resisted them (Hobsbawm, 1964: 16). Hill argues that craft unions became a problem for capitalism because of their stranglehold over the production process. For Hill, the breaking of such bodies was the essential prerequisite for the imposition of an alien culture upon the working population; that is, submission to the demands of the machine and industrial capitalism. But the evidence suggests that the explosion of violence was linked to the clash of two salients: the radically aggressive minority of capitalist entrepreneurs, for whom technology was the solution to the opposite salient, and who were a mirror-image of a radically aggressive body of croppers for whom technology was the problem. In effect, therefore, we do not need to look towards the government for evidence of a conspiracy nor at the entrepreneurial capitalists in the West Riding, because there was no need for a conspiracy; it was quite apparent that the entrepreneurs intended to force the issue of machinery and oust the croppers – and it was equally apparent that the croppers were having none of it.

The entrepreneurial aim is clearly evident in Andrew Ure, the doyen of the new age of manufacturers, who wrote his *Dictionary of Arts, Manufactures and Mines* in 1839, 'to instruct the manufacturer, metallurgist and tradesmen in the principle of their respective processes so as to render them in reality the masters of their *business and to emancipate them from a state of bondage to operatives*' (quoted in Leeson, 1979: 103–4, our emphasis). For Ure, as for other leading manufacturers, the skilled worker represented the quintessence of the manufacturer's problem:

> Wherever a process requires peculiar dexterity and steadiness of hand, it is withdrawn as soon as possible from the *cunning* workman, who is prone to irregularities of many kinds, and it is placed in charge of a peculiar mechanism, so self-regulating, that a child may superintend it ... on the automatic plan, skilled labour gets

progressively superseded, and will eventually, be replaced by mere overlookers of machines. (Ure quoted in Berg, 1980: 199)

The new machinery, therefore, was considered to be the solution to the problem of labour recalcitrance. An automatic factory of the kind that Ure envisaged was not simply a way of enhancing production or increasing quality, it was designed as a way of removing the labourer from the production process altogether. Ure's particular target at this time was the spinner, whose craft had proved difficult to automate and, even though others could do the spinner's job, those who ended up as spinners had a distinct propensity to unionize (Bruland, 1985; Lazonick, 1985). Clearly, then, the defeat of the Luddites did not completely enervate the resistance of textile workers, but the spinners' resistance was much more passive than the Luddites' had been – and equally ineffective. The analogy of the self-acting mule as an Iron Man, a technical *substitute* for human labour, rather than a technical *supporter*, resonates with the mystical powers which were attributed to such machines.

Thus the *Iron Man*, as the operatives fitly call it, sprung out of the hands of our modern Prometheus at the bidding of Minerva – a creation destined to restore order among the industrious classes, and to confirm to Great Britain the empire of art. The news of this Herculean prodigy spread dismay through the Union, and even long before it left its cradle, so to speak, it strangled the Hydra of misrule. (Ure quoted in Berg, 1980: 201)

Berg (1980) is surely right to argue that the machinery question in the nineteenth century was not merely another factor for society to ponder but essentially locked into the development of a new way of perceiving society: political economy.

## Conclusion

The conventional arguments that assert the Luddites to be irrational resisters to progress – either because they mistakenly assumed capitalism or the machinery to be irrational – are based on essentialist notions of technical capacity or 'progress'. Neither what machinery can do nor what capitalism holds in store for us are as controversial today as they were almost 200 years ago. Nor does it seem satisfactory to claim that the Luddites were resisting cultural or economic changes, rather than the machinery itself. First, the Luddite actions depended upon the time and region involved, but second, many of the Luddites had already experienced the 'new' market economy and the move away from home-based to factory or workshop production methods – and had benefited from it. Certainly, the Nottinghamshire Luddites were more inclined to attack errant masters than new machines, but for the most violent and sustained Luddite offensive, in the West Riding, it was the particular machine that was regarded as the cause of the revolt. However, this interpretation did not develop by way of an automatic reflection of the technical capacity and potential of the machine. The machinery was only one of many potential problems facing the Luddites and its potential was largely unknown – as indeed were and are the capacities of most technical innovations. Even where the Luddites had developed a reading of the situation that focused directly upon the machine as the problem, this still did not translate automatically into resistance. Spatial, temporal and gender differences all played a significant part in a very fragmented and differentiated response. While the government played a reactive role in suppressing the revolt, the crucial part was played by entrepreneurial masters who were intent on forcing through technical change and simultaneously breaking the back of the most strategically placed group of workers. By taking on the croppers, and by adopting the rhetoric of faith in technical progress which undermined the Luddites' moral justification for resistance, this new breed of masters coerced the government into draconian action. The freedom of the new factory capitalists to discard the shackles of the moral economy was won, at least in part, through the Trojan horse of new technology. What the Luddites tried to do was to adhere to Virgil's warning to the Trojans: 'Equo ne credite, Teucri. Quid id est, timeo Danaos et dona ferentis' (Do not trust the horse, Trojans. Whatever it is, I fear the Greeks even when they bring gifts). The Luddites failed not because they misrecognized the machine but because the alliance of forces arrayed against them was too great for their interpretation to prevail. Resistance to new technology did not, of course, die with those on the scaffold in York, but it certainly appears to have diminished and was eventually captured by the new left-wing political theories which accepted technology as the potential saviour, if temporary enslaver, of the masses.

# 3

# Configuring the User: Inventing New Technologies

## Introduction

In chapter 1 we argued that attempts to develop alternatives to techno-logical determinism frequently involve a residual 'technicism'. That is, even sophisticated efforts to take account of the social dimensions of technology and its uses depend on assumptions about the 'essence' of the technology. We argued for the need to maintain a sceptical anti-essentialist stance in the face of enduring preconceptions about the essence of the machine. In chapter 2 we illustrated the benefits of this stance, using the historical example of the Luddites. Our scepticism enabled us to open up a series of questions about the nature and effects of the threatening technology. We showed how both contemporary dis-putes and subsequent attempts to explain this historical episode involve the active construction of competing conceptions of technical capacity. The essence of this machine was constituted through the interpretations furnished both by contemporary players and by historians.

On the basis of the argument thus far, it would be easy to form the impression that determinations of technical capacity are largely unaf-fected by the ways in which the technology is put together. Thus, our analysis of Luddite stories concentrated on the diverging retrospective assessments of the (newly) installed machinery, rather than on the processes of its design and development. We implied that differing interpretations arose by and large from different 'interpretative com-munities' (Fish, 1980) rather than from any circumstances of the design and development of the technology. In other words, we concentrated on consumption rather than production.

By contrast, this chapter looks at the production side of technology.

It asks in particular to what extent, and in what sense, 'social dimensions' of technological development bear upon subsequent interpretations of technical capacity and use. To do this, the chapter is organized as follows. The nature of the connection between the production and consumption of technology is a vexed question which admits a variety of approaches. Hence a first task is to sketch these alternative approaches, some of which were briefly mentioned in chapter 1, focusing in particular on the extent to which they provide a means of understanding technological development as a process of 'building in' elements of the social. The key issue is the extent to which this construal of technology adequately accounts for its subsequent interpretation and use. How exactly is the upshot of social relations congealed in technological artefacts and systems? Secondly, we offer an empirical case study of computer development in order to explore various senses in which the process of technological development – by which we mean to include a range of activities (inception, design, manufacture, marketing, launch and sales) – can be said to have consequences for subsequent use.

## The technical/non-technical dichotomy

The problem of trying to understand the nature of technology and its development in non-technical terms is especially difficult because it is a foundational premise of modern Western societies that the technical and the non-technical are distinct domains of discourse and expertise. The very idea of the technical by definition precludes the social. In certain usages – for example when one used the phrase 'sociology of science' in pre-Kuhnian times – the conjunction of social and technical terms can seem contradictory. Or their conjunction encourages an interpretation of one or other of the constituent terms which 'repairs' the apparent contradiction. In this example, 'sociology' was taken to refer to 'external' factors thought to impinge on the institution and practice of science (competition between scientists, priority disputes, bias in the allocation of credit and reward) rather than on the character of scientific knowledge itself. Or, notoriously, 'sociology' is taken to refer only to sources of erroneous knowledge. Again, the implicit notion is that the technical core of true knowledge is immune from mere social influences. The root distinction between the technical and the non-technical is so firmly entrenched in our most basic beliefs and expectations that attempts at transcending it are often greeted with incredulity or hostility. This is in part why Bloor's (1976) 'strong programme' in the sociology of scientific knowledge seemed so counter-intuitive and why its pursuit engendered especially strong reactions from objectivist philosophers of science (Woolgar, 1988a).

A similar problem is encountered in attempts to specify the social dimensions of technology. In some respects the conjunction is heard as oxymoronic. Arguably, this is less obviously the case than with attempts to specify the social dimensions of scientific knowledge. Practising technologists generally seem more willing than their scientist counterparts to speak of the social dimensions of their knowledge and practice. Everyone knows that politics are involved. This is probably connected to the fact that a well-developed and established philosophy of science tradition has no counterpart in technology. Even so, while technologists are sometimes willing to talk about the "politics" of technology in general terms, this does not usually extend to the technical core of their development work.

In the case of the relation between technology and 'the social', the extent of entrenchment of the technical/non-technical dichotomy is evident from the fierce debates over the weight to be given technical and social factors. For example, in simple terms, each of the following three positions (Bromley, 1994) distinguishes itself from the others in terms of adherence to one or other pole. First, the position of technological determinism, discussed in chapter 1, grants autonomy to technology. Technology is construed as the root determinant for either good (technophilia, utopia and hype) or evil (technophobia and dystopia). Second, by contrast, social determinism grants relative autonomy to society. Society is the determinant of technological development, leading to an emphasis on social shaping in the context of technological development. Third, technology is taken to be neutral, so that what matters is the way in which it is used. This leads to an emphasis on the contexts of consumption which includes consideration of the ways in which technologies are used or abused. Of course, the situation becomes rapidly more complex as different aspects of the technical/non-technical dichotomy are brought together. For example, the variant of social determinism which stresses that social relations (such as the prior context of design) become congealed in technical artefacts also aims to show how these congealed social relations subsequently determine the use and/or impact of the technology. In this model, a form of technological determinism is combined with a form of social determinism. But it is hard to escape the feeling that such efforts at combination are unsatisfactory. The root dichotomy remains intact, the two poles merely separated in time: first social determinism, then technical determinism.

One could attempt to meet the problem by deploying the interpretivist/ethnomethodological strategy of turning the dualism into a topic to be studied rather than just a resource to be drawn upon. The distinction between the technical and non-technical would itself become the object of study. How in practice do participants manage this distinction? In other words, we would study the ways in which the distinction features in discourse, how it is used, when, by whom and to what effect. On what occasions and for what purposes is the technical distinguished from the non-technical? To what extent does this distinction perform different communities (Cooper and Woolgar, 1994), how does it implicate the actions and responsibilities of some actors, perhaps at the expense of others (Rachel and Woolgar, 1995)? This leads to a descriptive programme which inter alia, can focus on why different participants are themselves in practice technological determinists, social shapers, technophobes and so on, and how and why they can interchange the 'positions' listed above.

This 'discourse analysis' response to the problem has the advantage of encouraging a healthy scepticism about our unthinking adoption of the technical/non-technical dichotomy. However, it is not clear to what extent this helps us transcend the dichotomy. We dodge the root question: are social or technical factors pre-eminent? But by attempting to step back from the dichotomy in this particular way, can we be sure we have avoided it? On the basis of existing discourse-analytic approaches the answer has to be 'no'. To the extent that analyses of discourse have focused on the argumentative devices, persuasive strategies and techniques used in conversation and practice, they have tended to prioritize the 'non-technical' horn of the dilemma. With few exceptions, very little discourse analysis has concentrated on what could be described as technical practice.

The difficulty stems from the fact that the particular distinction between the technical and the non-technical is just one particular instance of the more fundamental dichotomy between, in its classic formulation, free will and determinism (see Grint, 1995: 210–31; Woolgar, 1989, 1991b). This dichotomy centres on two broadly competing ways of explaining human behaviour: the notion that humans are largely free to decide their own fate (and hence free to decide how to behave, think and build institutions, structures and social systems) and the contrary notion that their behaviour is largely determined by circumstances (history, the essential nature and characteristics of human beings, the aforesaid institutions, structures and social systems). This way of putting it replays a key problem in social theory. Do characteristics reside in, or are they attributed to, entities? As we have suggested, our answer to this question has important implications for the adequacy of explanation and for issues of responsibility. For example, on the question of the difference between natural and social science, the Winchean (Winch, 1958) view that social subjects must not be treated as natural objects is premised upon profound assumptions about the difference between social and natural objects. Are human actions to be understood primarily as the exercise of free will or as the result of forces outside of, and beyond the control of, individuals? This dualism recurs in a whole series of particular examples. Thus, in classical Marxist terms, humans are free to make their own history (free will) but not under conditions of their own choosing (determinism). A more recent incarnation of the same debate discusses the relative influence upon human behaviour of structure (determinism) and agency (free will), a dilemma raised again in, for example, Berger and Luckman's (1966) discussion of the sociology of knowledge: humans are free to create and construct new knowledge but the facts thus created acquire the capacity to determine the course of subsequent actions.

Each of these analogous tensions turn on fundamental assumptions about the basis of human behaviour: does it originate in the human or in circumstances external to the human? Put this way, it is easy to identify other related examples, some of which are consequential for social and political action. For example, in conservative philosophies, responsibility for deviant behaviour resides with the deviant. The origin of the behaviour is essentially located within the deviant and, as a result, remedies emphasize the virtues of removing such deviants from society. By contrast, more liberal philosophies locate the origin of deviant behaviour outside the deviant, and largely beyond the deviant's control. The focus of responsibility shifts to various circumstances antecedent to the deviant: upbringing, family background, peer relationships. From this vantage-point, the deviant's characteristics do not inhere but are attributed, assigned as part of a social process. As a consequence, remedies are directed more to addressing the external causes of deviant behaviour, that is, the effects of antecedent circumstances (through counselling, treatment) than to removing a presumably unchangeable deviant. Similar examples are found in the social problems literature, where differences between assignation and inherence views also emerge in debates about various non-human and inanimate objects: for example, drugs and other substances, coffee, margarine, alcohol and so on. Do the (allegedly detrimental) effects of a particular substance arise from the nature of the substance itself, or from its interpretation and use at the hands of particular users?

These examples[1] show how the technical/non-technical divide is but one example of a more general phenomenon: the dilemma of locating the origin of action and behaviour either in the essence of an entity or in circumstances antecedent to the entity. As we discuss below, this problem also recurs in literary theory: does the meaning/interpretation/use of a text derive from its inherent/essential character or from the various circumstances (interpretative communities) of its reception and use?

## Technology as text

We thus see that the particular dualism we are confronting in the technical/non-technical dichotomy has deep roots. In the following case study we offer a way of starting to modify our reliance upon the straightforward use of this dichotomy. It adopts part of the 'discourse analysis solution' by focusing on the ways in which the dichotomy is constructed and sustained. However, it also suggests that the precise form of the achieved dichotomy turns on the accomplishment of a significant social boundary. This boundary defines the nature of relations between technology and its users, and so makes possible certain prescribed sets of actions in relation to the technology.

Our strategy for tackling this problem is the exploration of a metaphor: the machine as text.[2] The idea is, to begin with, the supposition that the nature and capacity of the machine is, at least in principle, interpretatively flexible. This then sets the frame for an examination of the processes of construction (writing) and use (reading) of the machine; the relation between readers and writers is understood as mediated by the machine and by interpretations of what the machine is, what it is for and what it can do. To suggest that machines are texts is, of course, to deconstruct definitive versions of what machines can do. There is thus a sense in which the exploration of this metaphor challenges some intuitive beliefs about technology; the 'actual' effects of technology are usually plain to see, and often brutally incontrovertible. At the same time, then, the exploration of the machine–text metaphor deals with a particularly hard case in interpretation. Precisely because it is counter-intuitive to think of a machine as a text, this case might provide insights into more general questions about textuality.

It is worth stressing that the idea is to explore the metaphor, rather than merely to apply it. We have no wish to insist that machines *actually* are texts. Rather the point is to *play against* this metaphor, to see how far we can go with it.[3] What happens to the structure of our discourse when we introduce the notion of machine as text? What, if anything, is special about machines by comparison with other texts? What are the limits of talking in this bizarre way?

The following case study is an attempt to play against one specific aspect of the machine–text metaphor: the notion of the reader as user. As writers like Friedman (1989) have pointed out, the 1980s saw considerable attention devoted to 'the problem of the user' amongst the designers and builders of computer systems. We take the line that the emergence of a new range of microcomputers crucially entails the definition, delineation and emergence of The User. We could say that this process amounts to the (social) construction of the user. However, it is not just the identity of the user which is constructed. For along with negotiations over who the user might be, comes a set of design (and other) activities which attempt to define and delimit the user's possible actions. Consequently, it is better to say that by setting parameters for the user's actions, the evolving machine effectively attempts to configure the user.

We set out a framework for addressing these problems by way of a brief description of an eighteen-month participant observation study carried out by one of the authors (Steve Woolgar) in a company which manufactures microcomputers. For reasons elaborated below, it is useful to construe this empirical study as an ethnography of computers. Particular attention is then given to a study of the 'usability trials' carried out by the user products section of the company towards the latter stages of the project.

## An ethnography of computer development

In order to maintain ambivalence about the appropriate unit of analysis and thus enable us to explore assignations of agency and changes in the moral order, we have designated the study reported here an 'ethnography of computers'. An eighteen-month participant observation study was carried out in a medium-sized company which manufactures microcomputers and allied products, primarily for education. (Since certain members of the company are uncertain about the benefits of publicity arising from the kind of analysis undertaken in the study, the company is referred to anonymously).[4] It is phenomenally successful, having been founded some fourteen years before the date of the study and grown in size by an average of approximately 20 per cent per year over the last five years, and its turnover had increased by an average of about 35 per cent per year in the same period. By the time of the study it had achieved a position such that both the company and its main competitors were claiming in excess of 50 per cent of the market share.[5]

The original research design was to follow a major project in detail from inception through to launch, first shipment and after-sales feedback. Steve negotiated with the company that he should join them as part of the newly expanded project team. We felt this would be a strategic position from which to carry out the study since, as a project manager assistant with responsibility for liaison and co-ordination between different sections within the company, he would be able to enjoy relatively free access across disparate parts of the company. In particular, he worked as a project manager assistant on the project designated 'DNS'.[6] In broad outline, the aim of the project was to produce a new range of microcomputers built around the new 286 chip. As fairly soon became apparent, this entailed following the lead established by IBM in the production of their IBM PS/2 standard.

The DNS range was the third in a recent series of microcomputer product ranges which brought the company more into line with IBM compatibility standards. The first of these – the 'Stratus PC' – had been built around the 186 chip in order to 'provide an educational computer which was appropriate for schools'. Steve was told that the marketing section had received the acclaim of the press for the Stratus PC with some glee, especially when one review went so far as to praise the machine by speaking of the IBM PC as a good Stratus clone. In fact, the Stratus PC was not designed as IBM-compatible, and although IBM was not at that point seen as the main competitor, a further range – the 'X series' – was developed to compete with the IBM XT at the high end of the market. Subsequently, DNS (later marketed under the name Stratus 286) was developed to fill a position between the two previous ranges, combining the educational virtues of the Stratus PC (186) with the IBM compatibility of the X series (286).

## Configuring the user

We start from the position that the machine (in this case, DNS) should be understood in terms of its relationship with other entities of its phenomenal world. However, this recommendation is not simply a call for understanding technology 'in its context', since the nature of 'the context' is itself subject to all we have said about the nature of the machine (cf. Cooper, 1990). The character of both entities is essentially indefinite; and the character of both entities is also reflexively tied (Garfinkel, 1967). In other words, representations (descriptions, determinations of many kinds) of 'what the machine is' take their sense from descriptions of 'the machine's context'; at the same time, an understanding of 'the context' derives from a sense of the machine in its context. The sense of context and machine mutually elaborate each other. For that aspect of context called the user, the reflexive tie is especially marked. The capacity and boundedness of the machine take their sense and meaning from the capacity and boundedness of the user.

Less obscurely, perhaps, our textual metaphor makes the same point. Construing the machine as a text encourages us to see that the nature of an artefact is its reading. But in trying to escape the dreaded technological determinism, in disassociating the upshot of reading and interpretation from any notion of the inherent quality of the text (what it actually says, what it actually means), we do not mean to suggest that any reading is possible (let alone that all readings are equally possible), although in principle this is the case. For example the dictates of sceptical ethnomethodology (or of ethnomethodology at the hands of some interpreters) pose an idealized User/Reader, one unfettered by relationships with other texts.[7].

If, however, we wish to acknowledge that in practice only a limited set of readings are possible, our question is how to account for this delimitation. Following Smith (1978), we can suggest that the organization of the text makes one or other reading differentially possible.[8] For Smith, the important point is that the organization of the text is isomorphic with the concept we use to make sense of it. In other words, for example, a text 'about' mental illness will be organized in such a way as to make this reading possible. By direct analogy, we suggest, the machine text is organized in such a way that 'its purpose' is available as a reading to the user. In her analysis, Smith notes how certain organizational features of texts provide 'instructions' which enable readers to make sense of content in terms of conclusions stated at the outset. To adapt Smith's terminology to our concern with technology, the user is encouraged to find in her dealings with the machine an adequate puzzle for the solution which the machine offers.

A small extension of this analytic stance on texts suggests that the organization of the text hinges not so much on mundane features like the length of sentences, the amount of space devoted to different topics etc., but rather on associations made available within the text and between text and reader. Textual organization refers critically, as far as the sense to be made of it is concerned, to the relationships made possible between the entities within and beyond the text. Certain characters become central to the story and others peripheral; groups of actants join forces while others disperse; the activities and achievements of some are highlighted, while others are relegated to the background, silent and unnoticed. The reader (who is, we are afraid, the writer) of the text is invited to join with certain groups and disassociate herself from others. A simple example is the invocation of community through the use of the royal 'we'. (Of course, this is an example with which we are all familiar. Do you, gentle reader, wish to say you are not familiar, and hence risk being excluded from our text?) The text might be said to be designed (perhaps implicitly, perhaps unconsciously, but always within a context of conventional resources and expectations) for the reader. What sense will she make of this (or that) passage?

In configuring the user, the architects of DNS, its hardware engineers, product engineers, project managers, sales, technical support, purchasing, finance and control and legal personnel and the rest, are both contributing to a definition of the reader of their text and establishing parameters for the reader's actions. Indeed, the whole history of the DNS project can be construed as a struggle to configure (that is, to define, enable and constrain) the user. These different groups and individuals at different times offered varying accounts of 'what the user is like'. Knowledge and expertise about the user was distributed within the company in a loosely structured manner, with certain groups claiming more expertise than others in knowing what users are like.

## Organizational knowledge about users

### Difficulties of knowing the user from within

Steve's first vivid introduction to the socially structured character of knowledge about users occurred during an early meeting of a group of technical writers in the user products section. The discussion centred on plans for carrying out usability trials. Who should be invited to act as subjects for these trials? The problem was that constraints of confidentiality made it difficult to select subjects who would know nothing about the new machine. Getting in 'the man on the street', as they put it, was not a realistic option. At this point, parties to the discussion started to consider the possibility of finding 'true novices' amongst the workforce in the company.

In a fit of helpfulness, Steve offered his services. If they were really stuck, he said, he would be very happy to act as a subject since he would have no problem in acting as a naïve user. He was very surprised when Sally P turned on him vehemently. Didn't he realize how differently users approached this? Didn't he realize how extraordinarily difficult it was for anyone in the company to appreciate the way users looked at things? People in the company couldn't possibly appreciate the user's point of view. Indeed, this was a major problem which pervaded the company: a failure to understand what it was really like to be a user.

Steve realized he had inadvertently stepped out of role. As a relative newcomer to the company, he had expressly volunteered his naïvety about the Company Perspective. But Sally P was apparently unaware of his 'real' identity as participant observer. She assumed he was part of the project management team, and it was in that guise that she was addressing him. He had unwittingly reaffirmed her worst fears about insensitive 'techies' and their inability to see beyond a company mindset. So he was admonished for presuming to be able to act like an outsider.

### Alleged deficiencies in company knowledge about users

As this last anecdote suggests, certain individuals could claim the right to speak authoritatively on behalf of users. At the same time, it was said that some of the individuals and groups you would expect to know about users were manifestly deficient in just this kind of knowledge. For example, one of the technical writers spoke of her amazement in discovering the attitude towards users in marketing:

> You can find the same thing at marketing. I remember going along and saying 'Excuse me but can you tell me who the target market is for this?', you know. And they'd looked at me, sort of thing. Well I always thought marketing had, you know, like a list of and a target market would be durhrhrhrhrhr education, a sort of list of generalizations. No way! Nothing like that! So there's no guidance like that.

I was told by a long-serving member of technical support that 'typically, the engineers don't have a clue about users'. She told the tale of an early attempt by 'engineering' to encourage users initially to configure their new machines by inputting a long line of characters which would have been 'meaningless to your average teacher'. She poured scorn on what she saw as the engineers' presumption that users would be happy to have to do this.

## Stories about users

Members of the user products section felt that their conception of users was affected by a wide range of influences, ranging from their own first time of using computers through to 'hearing tales about what happens outside'. Knowledge about users thus involved the circulation of stories and tales about the experiences of users. Frequently, stories about 'what happens outside' seem to have originated in the technical support and service sections of the company

These sections were generally reckoned to represent 'the sharp end' of dealings with customers. The view was that whereas, for example, the engineering and design sections worked in some isolation from users, those in technical support had much more experience of users since they dealt with user complaints and queries at first hand. Some of those in tech support had themselves 'moved out' from working in the engineering sections and seemed keen to emphasize their new-found responsibilities in dealing with users.

Significantly, these stories about users were nearly always couched in terms of insider-outsider contrasts: what was happening (or had happened) 'on the outside' was a recurrent motif. The boundaries of the company thus played an important part in the telling of these tales. For example, one respondent recalled the experience of one particular 'outside' visit in the following way:

Some of us have been out to visit users but it was something that was thought of as a good idea but never really took off . . . I went out once something like back in '84, a long time ago and it was actually a [roadshow] because I went up to a school and I just remember seeing this room of computers, a square room and they were in sort of an L shape against the wall. And pinned above them were very very simple instructions for what to do. And they weren't, they looked like they'd been used, you know? It was almost as if they'd been unpinned, taken down and pinned up again and again so that someone had had them right by the machine.

This experience of an 'outside' visit thus led to the realization that in schools someone, perhaps a teacher, had had to devise extremely plain instructions for use alongside the machine. The same respondent related a story passed on to her by a colleague in technical support: 'Another tale I remember hearing is that a school who had a machine up to like four months. They wouldn't unpack it or anything, they were too scared. There was no one around they thought was able to do much with it . . . Yes, I mean GOOD GRIEF!'

## User singular and users multiple

Whereas participants often referred to 'the user' in the singular, it is not clear they thought users of the Stratus 286 would all exhibit identical, monolithic sets of attributes. They could presumably imagine a wide variety of purposes and uses; they would have been aware that the marketing section stressed the versatility of the machines when promoting the company's products. Clearly, one criterion for a successful text is precisely its appeal to a wide range of readers.

There's a limit to how far you can take what any user or set of users wants into account when you're designing a product. It would have been very easy for us to say we want this product to be suitable for teachers in secondary schools, what they want to get out of the machine. We could have produced a very watertight specification of what the thing had to do. But what we knew was we wanted to cover primary schools, secondary schools, colleges, universities, business users, government users, CAD people. The trick was not in finding out what one set of users wants, because if you limit it to a small enough number that's fairly easy, the trick was trying to find that area of overlap that would suit them all, get the best fit. What do you mean by best fit? Who knows?!

The text sells well if many different readers find a use for it. One might even go so far as to say that an author's attempts to prescribe readings, to delimit ways in which the text can be read, is a sure recipe for disaster, at least in the sense of guaranteeing early returns from the bookshop. So a strict and narrow definition of user would seem counter-productive. Similarly, user configuration which restricts the range of possible readings will not generate success.

All this makes curious the continued singular reference to 'the user' in the company, until this is understood as a generalized formulation produced for purposes of establishing contrasts between insiders and outsiders. The generalized user provides a more successfully stark contrast with us/the company/members of the company, than would a heterogeneous rag-bag of customers with varying attributes. The contrast is rhetorically important for example, as we have seen, in stressing the difficulties of knowing what precisely it is that users want. Given the extent of the (claimed) difference between the way 'we' look at the world, and the way 'the user' looks at the world, it becomes necessary to rely upon especially skilled spokespersons – those few with knowledge of these very different entities. When someone in user products says that engineering have no notion of what the user expects, the achieved distinction between the monolithic entity – the user – and the monolithic entity – the engineer – makes a political point about the inadequacies of all members of engineering. More pervasively, this generalized formulation reaffirms divisions between us and them. Company boundaries, differences between insiders and outsiders, are more strongly emphasized through deployment of 'the user' than by admitting that some users are more familiar with our machines than others. This rhetorical rendering of the generalized user also afforded some interesting variations on the more familiar examples of prejudiced rhetoric: he was a user, but he seemed to know what he was talking about.

## Users don't necessarily know best

References to the user emerging from the engineering sections of the company included the view that, although it was important to have an idea of who 'the users' were and what they wanted from the machine, users' views should not be unproblematically adopted in design.

> The user isn't necessarily able to see in a clear enough way each feature at a price that they're prepared to pay for it. I don't believe you can go to a user and say: right, each of these functions we're thinking of putting in the machine, tell me how much you are prepared to pay for each of these? I don't think you can construct a product specification like that.

The suggestion was that design should respond instead to ideas about 'where the market was going' or 'where things were going', a more generalized conception of the future requirements of computing. Significantly, such conceptions were frequently referred to as 'visions' of the future, which seemed to stress technical progression and which were couched in terms which transcended individual users' desires for particular technical features.

> Where the clever bit comes in is people like [the Managing Director] having a vision and saying we're going to do this and being able accurately to predict that if we don't do that we'll still sell the required volumes of the product without delaying it. Or without putting in this feature which [the users] might have said was desirable but which they didn't really want to pay the cost of.

A variant of this line of argument was the more familiar view that there was no point in asking users what they wanted because they themselves didn't know. According to this view, such ignorance arose primarily because users were unaware of likely future developments:

> Users can only know about what's available at the moment. So they'll tend to give you an answer that's based on different combinations of what's available at the moment. What we're trying to do is to make available to them something that isn't available at the moment. Which is where the [Managing Director] visionary idea comes in: We ought to be doing this because I say so and because I know what I'm talking about!

We see here an effective rationale for not placing too much emphasis on users' views. According to this perspective, configuring the user involves the determination of likely future requirements and actions of users. Since the company tends to have better access to the future than users, it is the company's view which defines users' future requirements.

## Articulating the configured user: the usability trials

The usability trials were just one occasion where articulations of 'what the user is' featured prominently. Myriad other events and occasions during the course of the project included fairly explicit attention to the question of the character of the user.[9] More generally, of course, determinations of the user could be seen taking place throughout the construction of the machine–text. It is thus possible to argue that participants' notions of the user are available to us, if only implicitly, through an inspection of, say, the day-to-day work of the hardware designer. The interest of the trials, however, is that they involved explicit articulation of whether or not prevailing ideas about the user were correct. The matter was made explicit, in the case of the trials, through an assessment of the different courses of action which a user might engage in.

We have already mentioned that the company encompassed a variety of perspectives on the importance of taking users' views into account. This makes it difficult to be clear to what extent the upshot of these particular trials had any consequential effect on 'settling' the question about the nature of the user. Although there was, as we shall see, some concession to experimental method in the design of the trials, the results were never written up in a final form, to be circulated to designers and other members of the project team. Instead the 'results' tended to be fed back piecemeal into the production process. For example, when one of the test subjects had trouble understanding a diagram on page 34 of the Stratus guide, this information was quickly passed by word of mouth to one of the technical writers, who then redrew the diagram for the next draft. So it is difficult to discern any clear outcome of the trials which might stand as a definite milestone in the ongoing configuration of the user. Nonetheless, these trials were thought important, at least by members of the user products section of the company. This section devoted approximately six person-weeks to carrying out the trials; it would have been more but for the delays and time pressures already mentioned above.

## Boundary work: the importance of the case

The start of the trials was delayed several times. The user products section was caught, as it seemed to be on several other occasions, between the need to ensure usability testing took place as early as possible in the development of the product, and the delay in procuring a 'finished' product to test. It was reasoned that the most fruitful assessments of usability could only be carried out with the product in a form as near as possible to that which would be experienced by the user. One of the main reasons for the delay in the project as a whole centred on the availability of the case. Members of user products took the view that usability trials could only properly take place when a cased version of the machine was available. Some negotiation ensued when the first prototype case appeared, but product engineering argued that it was too risky to loan the sole case for purposes of usability testing.

It is significant that user products felt the necessity for a physically bounded entity for use in usability testing. The machine would not be a real machine unless it was in its case. 'Real' in this usage specifically denotes 'the kind of machine a user would expect'. This contrasts markedly with what counted as a real machine within the company. Particularly within the engineering sections (notably hardware design and engineering quality), machines were mostly left open on desktops and workbenches, their innards displayed, precisely so that the engineers had quick access to the inside of the machine. In these sections, it was unusual to find a machine inside its case.

The following contrast between the treatment of computers 'outside' and 'inside' the company was provided by one of Steve's students who was employed by the company for a summer work placement:

> When I joined the company I was a 'soft' user (Turkle, 1984). Although I did not believe the computer was 'magical', I could not recognize the internal parts of a computer and had never taken the casing off a computer. In fact I had always been deterred from doing so. However in the EQ [Engineering Quality] section, no such squeamishness was expected. Machines were perched on 'breadboards' – metal frames or boards, or they were missing their top covers . . . At school I had been told that the ideal place for computers was a dust free atmosphere kept at a controlled temperature. In the company, there was no such reverence for the computer. They were regularly taken apart. In fact, when a machine which was in its case did not work, the top was removed immediately and the boards were jiggled around just to check that the connections were all right. (Dobbins, 1990)

The surprise of finding the innards of computers regularly on display around the desks and benches in the company was part of the experience of moving from the outside to the inside of the organization. The machine's boundary symbolized that of the company, so that access to the inner workings of the machine was access to the inner workings of the company.[10]

The symbolic importance of the machine-case/company boundary also featured in the 'induction programme' – a series of meetings and events arranged over a period of two or three weeks for those starting with the company. Steve visited or had meetings in product engineering, hardware design, purchasing, personnel, marketing, engineering quality and so on. But the generally acknowledged highlight of the programme was the visit to manufacturing. When they learned Steve was undergoing 'induction', a first question from friendly colleagues was whether or not he had 'been down to manufacturing yet'. This meant spending an hour on the assembly-line under the tutelage of Rose. Rose did all the manufacturing inductions. She explained the sequence of operations for building a Stratus (at the time of Steve's induction, the Stratus PC) and then asked the learner to try his hand. Steve could not believe he was to be entrusted with putting one of these things together! Like his student and most others new to this experience, he was amazed that mere novices were encouraged to handle the very insides of such a revered item of technology. Rose guided his nervous efforts with a matter-of-fact patter born of long experience with similarly incredulous newcomers. 'Just turn over the frame now. This way. That's it. Have you got your board? Right. Put your first screw in there. That's it. See, it's not so difficult ...'. Although ostensibly just one of a series of events designed to familiarize new employees with different parts of the company, this 'hands-on' experience can be understood as a symbolic welcome into the company (machine) by way of disabusing computer primitives (like Steve) of the mysteries of computers.[11] As a result of this experience, Steve remembers thinking that the 'real' sophistication of the machine must lie elsewhere, perhaps in the printed circuit boards. He felt he had penetrated the outer shell of the company, but not yet its heart, the nitty gritty of technical design (hardware engineering).

During the later stages of participant observation, the possibility arose of Steve buying one of the new Statuses. As a bona fide member of the company he was entitled to a discount. But in deciding whether or not to purchase he was struck by the way his assessment of the machine changed according to his (and its) location. On days away from the company, he had a good sense of what the machine could do, was for, looked like. He had confidence in it. (It was, after all, a very nice machine). These feelings were not unconnected with the fact that he was its representative on the outside. He could talk authoritatively to his Brunel colleagues about this new machine; he had privileged information about it. Clearly, on these occasions the machine he knew about was 'Marketing's Machine'. It is with some embarrassment he now recalls conversations with Bob T, the sales director for higher education, about sounding out the market for the company's products at Brunel. There was even an occasion when he handed out Stratus 286 brochures as part of a talk there. It was, after all, a very nice machine.

By contrast, on days in the company, he often found it difficult to imagine how the thing could ever work (cf. Collins, 1986; MacKenzie et al., 1988: 161–2). The case was delayed again, the toolmakers had been taken into receivership, the chip-suppliers had welched on their delivery dates yet again, the Winchester access times were way down on target, Martin K had been taken off the project because of problems with 186 deliveries, and so on. When Ted J, a senior member of the hardware team, told Steve it would be wise to wait at least six months after launch before buying his own Stratus 286, he had a point. He was sharing his view from/on the inside of the machine. Insiders knew that although the initial machines would look okay, a great deal of patching up had gone into them for purposes of just 'getting them out of the door.'

These and similar examples underscore the symbolic importance of the machine's (text's) boundary. The video record of the usability trials shows putative users working out how to relate to (and in one instance, literally, how to connect to) a technology which had already been black-boxed. Or, in this instance, beige-boxed. The task for the subjects of the usability trials was to work out how to access the interior of the beige box, in order to extract what they needed from the machine/company. The machine's task was to make sure these putative users accessed the company in the prescribed fashion: by way of preferred (hardware) connections or through a predetermined sequence of keyboard operations. The user would find other routes barred and warnings posted on the case itself. Labels bore warnings of the dire consequences of unauthorized boundary transgression: electrocution, invalidation of the warranty and worse:

WARNING
LIVE PARTS ARE
EXPOSED IF COVER
IS REMOVED

Guarantee of safety and product warranty void if seal is broken.[12]

Inside the case (assuming we allow ourselves access for a moment), users would find that different modular components of the PC were similarly labelled, thus structuring and guiding access within and around the machine (company). In particular, various makes of disk-drive bore a variety of warnings:

> Warranty void if cover is removed or this seal is broken
> (IBM 30Mb Winchester)
>
> Warranty void if this seal is broken
> (IBM 60 Mb Winchester)

The 40Mb Seagate drive bore three labels:

> Product warranty will be Void if this label is removed
> Do not apply pressure to top cover
> Delicate Equipment
> HANDLE WITH CARE
> Disk/Head damage may occur

For those modular products supplied by the company as replacements or upgrades to the machine, warnings posted on the product were sometimes accompanied by injunctions to contact the company in case of doubt. For example, the following appeared in black capital letters on a glossy yellow sticky label, affixed to a replacement hard-disk drive:

WARNING:
STATIC SENSITIVE DEVICE
FAILURE TO OBSERVE THE FOLLOWING WILL
INVALIDATE YOUR WARRANTY
• DO NOT DISCONNECT THIS HARD DISK DRIVE
  WITHOUT USING A WRIST BAND
• NEVER DISCONNECT THE CABLE FROM THE DRIVE
• NEVER TAKE THE GOLD FINGERS OFF THE DRIVE
  OR CABLE
IF IN DOUBT CONSULT YOUR USER DOCUMENTATION
OR TELEPHONE [THE COMPANY] TECHNICAL
SUPPORT HOTLINE ON 0898–239239

Here we see that, in the event of uncertainty, users are redirected back to sources – either 'user documentation' or the company technical support hotline – which can re-establish the correct pattern of user action, in line with the approved configuration of the user's relationship with the company.

These kinds of boundary markers are relatively common in the information technology industry. For example, printed in seven languages on the cover of the Microsoft WINDOWS 3.0 package is the following warning:

> By opening this sealed package, you are agreeing to
> become bound by the terms of the Microsoft License
> Agreement.

Analogously, academic papers often circulate in draft form with warnings appended to the cover sheet: 'Please do not cite or quote this paper without permission'.[13]

In all such cases, the authors/producers are attempting to delimit the nature and extent of access to the text; they are trying to control the relationship between the reader and the text by specifying constraints upon how it can be used. Readers may only cross the boundary and access the text if they agree to use it in certain prescribed ways.

## User documentation: correct readings of the manuals

Ostensibly, a central concern of the usability trials in which Steve participated was to evaluate the draft documentation which was to accompany the machine on its shipment. The main body of documentation comprised the setting-up card, the Stratus (286/386) guide, the reference diskette, the MSDOS4 users' guide and the WINDOWS guide. The first three of these were produced by the company and related specifically to the operation of the Stratus 286. The latter two related to bought-in proprietary products supplied with the machine. In addition, peripheral equipment supplied with the machine, such as the printer, came with further documentation specific to its own use. The company-specific documentation was a main focus of the trials, but participants were also keen to evaluate the relationship between the other items of documentation. Would users be able to select the correct item of documentation when attempting to solve a particular problem? Were the instructions in, say, the Stratus guide sufficiently clear in telling users which other parts of the documentation to consult and when?

The body of documentation at the centre of the trials comprised a set of texts which accompany the machine which, as we suggested from the outset, is itself best understood as a text. We can think of such documentation texts as peripheral texts intended to enable the operation/reading of a core text. They are, so to speak, captions for helping readers find and see the relevant features of the machine itself. These captions configure the user in the sense, discussed above, of defining the correct courses of interpretation and action to be followed. They help guide access to the machine-text. Long sections of the video records of the usability trials show subjects moving back and forth between manual–text and machine–text, seeking the sense of a described feature of the machine in the material object itself, and assessing the sense of one of the manual's instructions in the response of the screen to some keyboard operation.

A central concern for testers/participants was whether these peripheral texts were sufficiently 'clear' to users. They were sometimes said to be 'clear' if subjects were judged to have understood and/or carried out the tasks set them by the testers. The manual–text could thus be seen as having enabled operation of the machine–text. As we shall suggest, determinations of the relative reliability of different texts were managed by construing a distance between them, such that one was viewed as operating 'at a different level' from another.

We have already suggested that the trials included detailed articulations of 'what the user is like'. However, it was not enough to determine whether or not a subject could fulfil a task. The testers were also interested in knowing whether the subject had carried out the task in the manner a user would have done. Such trials can thus be understood as occasions where a machine and its documentation confronts (a version of) its user(s).[14]

What is especially interesting is that, at this stage in the project, the identity and capacity of the key entities involved was equivocal. This means, on the one hand, that the capacity of the machine, what it could do, what it was, whether or not it worked and so on, was not yet settled. By this, we mean to claim that the trials showed participants' awareness of the possibility that the machine was not (yet) working as required, that things might yet go wrong. In this usage, 'settled' refers to participants' projection of particular states of readiness of the machine, for example ready for launch, ready for shipment and so on.[15] Similarly, at this stage, the identity of the user was not settled. Although participants could and did trade versions of what users are like, the identity of the user of the DNS/Stratus remained essentially uncertain.[16]

This makes these trials interesting in respect of accounting for interaction between machine and user. Where IT novices use established IT products, a typical experience is that where things 'go wrong' the 'fault' is likely to lie with the user. Conversely, where experienced users of IT products come into contact with machines still under development, the fault can be more readily said to lie with the machine.[17] Of course, the determination of things going wrong does not rest solely with the human agent. The machine may declare 'error' as a way of indicating that the user is at fault ('Printer Needs Attention'), or the machine may self-diagnose error ('WP.SYS file not accessed').[18]

In the DNS/Stratus usability trials, neither machine nor user was settled/experienced/established. Consequently, the interactions were part of the process of establishing the identity of the interacting entities. In other words, in this situation, the interaction between machine and user invited assessment both of whether or not the machine was acting like a real machine and whether or not the user was acting like a real user.

## Enacting the users' context

In planning the trials, particular attention was given to the selection of subjects and to choosing the right locale.

How can we find subjects who are most likely to act like users? A standard procedure for manufacturers, especially in the electronics and IT industries, is to use what are called 'beta sites' – trusted and privileged customers who are happy to try out new products. These customers gain advance notice of the release of the new product in exchange for feeding back information about how the product can be finally improved. But the company had little or no tradition in the use of beta sites.[19] In any case, a main aim of the trials was to try out the machine (and its documentation) on relatively novice users. Trusted customers with a close relationship with the company were unlikely to fit this particular requirement. It was suggested that a group of students be recruited from the local polytechnic. This had the practical advantage of being easily arranged through a local contact; in addition, such a group obviously matched one of the main customer target sectors (further education). However, this idea was rejected because it wasn't thought possible to maintain the necessary level of secrecy.

The need for secrecy, in particular, forced the user products group to consider selecting people from the company. The problem about secrecy was thus effectively finessed, but the level of these subjects' expertise still remained a problem. As a result of drawing upon personal contacts in the company, the following individuals eventually served as subjects: two members of the night shift from manufacturing; the head of user products; a psychologist from the local polytechnic (who was working temporarily with the company); a technical writer; and a project manager assistant (Steve).

Where should the trials be carried out? As in most experimental situations, the answer hinged on a compromise between a setting which best approximated the subject's 'natural' environment and a setting which facilitated the kinds of observation thought necessary for the conduct of the trials. Some larger companies have a small closed-off office space for this kind of testing, which they designate 'the laboratory'. But at the company where Steve carried out this research, space (especially closed-off space) was at a premium and usability trials were not thought sufficiently important to warrant a specially assigned area. The trials were held in the main sitting-room of a Victorian terraced house, a few hundred yards from the main factory site. This house, recently modernized and refurbished, was being let to the company as temporary lodgings for newly recruited middle management.

The video record shows several features of what might be regarded as a typical user's environment. In addition to the test subject (the user), the Stratus 286 and its accompanying peripherals and documentation, there were table, cups of coffee, chairs, television, bookshelves, carpets and so on – all the various accoutrements of being in an ordinary home. Indeed, the video record suggests that coffee-drinking featured prominently in the recreation of the users' environment. The telephone line which enabled instant phone calls to the company proved an especially useful feature of this users' environment. The kinds of feature presumably not present in the typical natural user's environment included: the testers (observers) with their clip-boards, notepads and clocks; the video camera; the (audio-) tape recorder;[20] and other machines (such as the more powerful K series computer). When viewed from a non-specist perspective, this is a comical concatenation of entities.

## Constructing natural users

Each trial started along similar lines. The subject was confronted with machine, peripherals and documentation. The tester explained the general purpose of the trial, pointed out the equipment available, set a task and asked the subject to say how he or she might go about it and to estimate the length of time it would take. The bulk of the trial comprised the subject then trying to complete the task. Finally, there was a 'post mortem' when tester and other observers would discuss the trial with the subject. The whole event was both video- and audio-taped.[21] On one occasion, the video record shows some initial confusion as the various human participants attempt to get into position before the start of the trial. The observers bump into each other as they move around the table. They strive to achieve what they regard as their appropriate juxtaposition *vis-à-vis* the machine for the purposes of the conduct of the trial.

The central part of the trials was particularly interesting. The testers cast themselves as objective observers in the sense of not wanting to intrude upon the 'natural' process of a user trying to make sense of the situation. They wanted an unbiased picture of how users 'actually' go about the completion of the tasks. On the other hand, a whole series of (thoroughly unnatural!) contingencies arose which demanded their frequent intervention. For example, where subjects were thought to be going hopelessly wrong, or where they were clearly about to get into trouble, it was felt necessary to retrieve the situation.

Quite apart from this kind of intervention, however, observers offered considerable commentary on subjects' performance:

1.
    A: You actually succeeded in· this task, so there's no problem about that.

2.
    P: You're a technical author's dream – reading the manuals!

In a situation where the identity/capacity of both machine and user were unsettled, we might expect participants to have expressed concern over exactly who or what was being tested. The recurrent commentary on the subjects' performance – which was presumably not a 'natural' feature of the user's environment – can thus be understood as the observers' efforts at reassurance about the real subject of the test. Frequently some confusion – over who (or what) was carrying out the task – revealed itself in the observers' attempts to empathize with the subject:

3.
>   A: Let's assume we succeeded there which I think you did.

Observers frequently intervened to explain the origin of a problem in terms of a machine fault, where this prevented (or made difficult) the completion of the task by the subject:

4.
>   A: It's a hardware error [3-second pause] probably a loose connection [3.5-second pause] you always have these problems on pre-production. But why did it have to happen in the middle of a trial!

5.
>   R: I'm so pleased it wasn't me this time huh huh.
>   N: You've done fine so far Ruth.

A large number of prompts and interventions seemed to pursue the issue of whether or not the subject was acting sufficiently like a real user. In each case, the tester explored with the subject the way they would behave, if they were in fact acting like a real user:

6.
>   A: You'd know WINDOWS was on there.
>   [2-second pause]
>   A: I think you'd know that wouldn't you?
>   SP: Yeah.
>   A: That's one reason you'd buy it!
>   SP: Hmmm yeah yeah

7.
>   N: Just do it as if you were doing it normally.

8.
>   N: This wouldn't normally happen with someone who's been doing something with it already.

9.
>   A: Of course you would know how to use WRITE.
>   SP: I've used WRITE before so it would take me longer.

But the participants were not above ironicizing their own attempts at creating an objective test of 'natural' user behaviour:

10.
> A:   Do you want a rest now?
>
> SP:  Yeah.
>
> A:   A coffee?
>
> SP:  Is that one of my tasks? 'Make the coffee and tea. How long do you think it would take you? Hah hah.
>
> SW: Subject drank thirteen cups of tea! Huhuhuh.

## Error and identity: the 'wrong socket' episode

An especially vivid illustration of many of the themes already discussed occurred in one particular trial, when Ruth was asked to connect the (new) Stratus 286 to a printer. In order to see if the 'machine' worked – and by 'machine' we can here understand the configured relationship between Ruth and the Stratus – the observers used as criterion the successful operation of a 'peripheral'. This reflects the fact that satisfactory usage of a machine often requires users to invest in and deploy auxiliary items of apparatus. For this reason, it is worth considering this part of the interaction in detail.

At the time we join the scene, Ruth is confronted by the Stratus 286 (with its keyboard and monitor); various instruction booklets and an as yet unconnected printer. The Stratus is initially switched on. Ruth begins by asking the observers if she should switch off the machine before attempting to plug in the printer. Some time passes before she locates the main switch on the back of the Stratus. She then takes some time comparing what she reads in the instruction booklets with what she sees on the machine. This includes moving the booklets from the front to the back of the machine. Finally, she announces she is stuck:

> R:   (this point) oh gosh [4-second pause] hmmm [7-second pause] I must be extremely thick I I can't see where this plug goes (plugs in), at all. I'm going to ask for help Nina ha on this one hahahahahuhn

Her difficulty is eventually resolved by a sequence of a question from Nina and Nina's eventual declaration that the task is, after all, impossible. It turns out that Ruth had been asked to connect a printer to the Stratus 286 (referred in the interaction by its engineering designation 'DNS') using a lead designed for use with the earlier K series machine. Throughout this little episode we see Pete, Nina and Steve each moving in and out of (the video) frame to inspect, for themselves, the socket on the back of the Stratus.

We see here how the machine is being treated as a text which Ruth is asked to interpret. The machine as presented to Ruth most obviously comprises the Stratus (CPU), its monitor and keyboard. She can achieve her task, it is suggested, by bringing the instructions into conjoinment with the machine in such a way that the printer can be connected. The trial is set up so that the adequacy of Ruth's interpretation can be assessed in terms of the adequacy and effects of her actions in making the connection. An adequate interpretation will make the instructions, the printer and Ruth herself all part of the (larger) machine. That is, in the event of a successful outcome, these entities can be said to stand in an adequately configured relation to the machine.

The adequacy of the interpretation, the achieved relation between instructions and machine, is adjudged by the commentators and observers who also participate in the trial. These observers provide comments which stand as further texts, captions on the core text. The 'observers' thus point out the key features of the text. They tell how it is organized and which aspects should be attended to in order to achieve a correct interpretation. They control the interaction by offering advice on whether or not Ruth is behaving 'correctly' *qua* user. The machine also comprises these observers in the sense that the subject is encouraged to interpret her actions in relation to the machine, and feels she has to display her actions in accordance with the observers' expectations of users.

In all this, the importance of the textual boundary is paramount. We observe the positioning and movement of humans in relation to the docile inanimate object: evidently there are preferred vantage-points for seeing 'through' the machine boundary. We notice that observers can speak authoritatively about 'their' text. They can speak as insiders who know the machine and who can dispense advice to outsiders:

> R:    ... I'm going to ask for help Nina ha on this one hahaha-hahuhn.
> N:    Are you. What are you looking for?

We see the importance of insider/outsider contrasts when it comes to attributing blame for (what turns out to be) the inappropriate task that Ruth has been set:

> R:    Oh it's not just me being thick. Thank god for that hah hah! I came in the back an' as soon as I got round here, with the machine I looked at this and looked at that and I thought 'No I'm being stupid, now this is silly.' Well I wasn't hahahah!
> N:    But in fact we were being silly asking you to do it.

Finally, the importance of the textual boundary is crucial to the resolution of the problem which 'Ruth's trial' brings to light. Firstly, the resolution retrospectively defines who or what has been on trial: by virtue of the resolution we see that the DNS, not Ruth, has been the subject of the trial all along. Secondly, as Nina's declaration makes clear, it turns out that the DNS on trial is incompatible with the previous range of machines produced by the company. It turns out, in other words, that the entity at the centre of all this attention is an impostor. In this form, the DNS on trial is not a DNS (and certainly not a Stratus 286); it is a deviant, not (yet) one of us.

The example also makes clear the importance of a detailed and contemporaneous assessment of the machine at work. It would be easy to misunderstand what is at stake by way of a crude summary that, in the end, the 'actual' character of the socket/lead 'determined' the actions and behaviour of subject and observers. Crucially, however, the transcript emphasizes that participants did not have access to this transcendental, objective socket/lead. Instead they were preoccupied with assessing what the socket/lead was. Its character is the upshot of interaction involving complex considerations of identity and authority: who speaks for the machine and when? Only by virtue of the outcome of negotiated descriptions of the character of the machine, of the nature of the task, of the assignment of responsibility and so on, do participants retrospectively attribute 'objective' features to the socket/lead.

## The new machine meets its users

We have implied throughout that user configuration is consequential for the reception of the new technology. What then was the fate of the Stratus 286 in the hands of its users? What happened when the 'configured user', enshrined in the artefact, met face to face with 'actual users'? Although there is insufficient space to answer this complex question in detail (see Woolgar, 1993a), it is worth noting that from many points of view the Stratus 286 was adjudged a success. For example, when Steve put this question to his informants both within and beyond the company, they responded in a variety of ways: the project had been accomplished largely within budget; the only delays that had occurred had been beyond the control of the project team; it really was a nice machine; and so on.

Of particular note is the fact that the Stratus received almost universally positive reviews in the computer press. The one exception – a wholly negative review by a highly respected computer journalist – became the object of considerable attention within the marketing section of the company. This particular journalist was well known to the company and had been identified as an important target. What could have gone wrong? The ensuing investigation focused on the ways in which this individual had resisted the company's marketing efforts for the Stratus. It was noted that he had not taken up the offer of a special pre-launch press conference, and that he had further refused personal invitations to lunch with members of the marketing team. Commenting on his review, a senior member of the marketing team said that the journalist had made the mistake of assessing the Stratus as if it was just another 286 computer, when the whole point of the Stratus was that it offered added value for a particular set of well-defined educational applications. The complaint, in short, was that the journalist treated the Stratus 'as if it was just a machine you could go and buy off some shelf in the high street'.

The anecdote is instructive because it provides a clear (but in the case of this company, rare) example of the 'undisciplined' response of an 'unconfigured' user. In the company's view, the journalist had behaved inappropriately – that is, he had missed the virtues of the Stratus – as a direct result of not enjoining the sets of social relations offered by the company. In buying a technology, one necessarily buys into the social relations which both accompany and constitute it, and which thereby define its 'appropriate' use and assessment. By construing the Stratus as 'just an off-the-shelf machine' the journalist had, in effect, tried to interpret the new machine text as if it had a context quite different from that offered by the company.

## Conclusion

We have argued that user configuration involves boundary work. The user's character, capacity and possible future actions are structured and defined in relation to the machine. As is dramatically illustrated by the usability trials, when there is still considerable ambiguity both about the capacity of the machine and about the character of the user, the machine becomes its relationship to the user, and vice versa. In this, the machine is a metaphor for the company so that, in particular, the boundaries of the machine are the boundaries of the company. The machine's case symbolizes the user's relationship to the company. Insiders know the machine, whereas users have a configured relationship to it, such that only certain forms of access/use are encouraged. This never guarantees that some users will not find unexpected and uninvited uses for the machine. But such behaviour will be categorized as bizarre, foreign, perhaps typical of mere users. More generally, of course, the more significant this boundary, the more likely will be the prevalence of this kind of separatist talk.

It is in this light that we might best understand the occurrence of 'atrocity stories' – tales about the nasty things that users have done to our machines (Woolgar, 1993a). Such tales portray nastiness in terms of users' disregard for instructions (violation of the configured relationship users are encouraged to enter into) and their disregard for the case (violation of the machine's boundary). Whereas many of the company members engaged in the exchange of such atrocity stories, it was also possible to identify liberals who were willing to speak up for the user: 'Users can't help the way they behave; they just need to be educated to understand what we are trying to achieve here'. Readers can't help the way they interpret the text; they just need to be educated. . . .

The analysis in this chapter has helped further to dispel the essentialism associated with our understanding of technology. We have concentrated on the processes whereby new technology emerges and is developed and manufactured. We noted at the start of the chapter the problem of transcending the technical/non-technical dichotomy. We argued that since this echoes a series of profound and entrenched dichotomies it is necessary to show how the dichotomy itself is constructed and sustained in practice. Hence, although the processes of technological development can be described in terms of the social construction of technology, their importance is in the ways they create and sustain the boundaries and dichotomies which we subsequently come to take as a natural feature of our relations with the technology. The import of these developmental processes is that users are configured to respond to the technology in sanctionably appropriate ways. The metaphor of technology as text is useful because, against essentialism, it stresses the contingency of interpretation. The especially important aspect of the metaphor is its stress on the tie between production and use. Users are free to make what they will of the machine, but can only do so 'appropriately' within an interpretative context. This 'context' does not exist in isolation from the machine; it is instead defined by the social relations which make up the machine (cf. Woolgar, 1996b). As is shown by the example of the case study of PC development, a crucially important part of this is the constitution of 'the technology' in terms of its discursive and organizational boundaries. 'The technology' is the machine's relations with its users.

This line of argument has major implications for our understanding of the notion of 'impact'. For it becomes clear that when we talk of the impact of a technology (or even more interestingly, the impact of any other kind of cultural artefact), we are necessarily emphasizing (if not adopting) certain definitions of boundedness, identity and appropriate behaviour/response. To talk of the impact of technology, then, seems to require us artificially to separate 'the technology' from some 'social group', in the service of assessing 'the effects' of one upon the other. This move thus requires us to force apart technical and non-technical entities, the conjunction of which, we have argued in this chapter, is crucial to the very constitution of a technology. In chapter 5 we shall use this heightened scepticism about the notion of 'impact' in a reconsideration of the role of technology in work. First, however, we need to attend to some outstanding problems of anti-essentialism.

# 4

# Some Failures of Nerve in Constructivist and Feminist Analyses of Technology

## Introduction

We saw in the last chapter how the genesis, manufacture and production of technology entails a process of user configuration. Responses to a technology and, in particular, assessments of its impact and effectiveness, take place within a 'performed community' of social relations. The attributes of the technology are thereby interpretatively constituted. This is how the god – the apparent essence – of the technology gets put into the machine.

This chapter carries forward our critique of essentialism by considering feminist and constructivist approaches to the social study of technology. The shared promise of these approaches is the development of radical alternatives to traditional understandings of technology. Frequently, both approaches take issue with the spectre of technological determinism. As we noted in chapter 1, however, 'technological determinist' has become a rather vague term, yielding many different interpretations. In addition, even though one is now hard pressed to find anyone admitting to the label, it turns out that many of the critiques of 'technological determinism' themselves retain key elements of the condition. As a result, the target of criticism is both varied and diffuse, and many of the critiques compromise their avowed radicalism. A central aim of this chapter is to explore the extent and implications of these problems in some recent constructivist and feminist perspectives on technology.

A further reason for carrying our argument forward in relation to constructivism and feminism is that the assessment of different theoretical perspectives on technology is more than just idle speculation. They can have profound consequences for the practical policies which we adopt. For example, if technology is seen as inherently and essentially masculine, it follows that the interests of women are best served by abandoning such technology and developing an alternative feminine technology. If, on the other hand, we consider technology to be gender neutral, then the crucial arena for change is its deployment and use: more women into engineering is one such policy implication of this approach. Between these two polarities lie different versions of the social shaping or political technology approach which, for reasons discussed below, we term 'anti-essentialist'. Within anti-essentialism, technology is never neutral but actively imbued with power of one sort or another: patriarchal and capitalist power being the two leading contenders in recent literature. In one feminist application, anti-essentialism disputes both the assumption that the effects of technology are determined by their allegedly patriarchal origins and that patterns of gendered inequality can be resolved simply by widening access. Instead, a broad-based, and necessarily lengthy, strategy is pursued in which the politicized technologies are subverted by increasing the proportion of women in technological occupations and by redesigning technologies to embody values that do not perpetuate patriarchy.[1]

It is clear, then, that the theoretical perspectives adopted in this debate are bound up with practical and policy consequences; one cannot pretend to assess theory from some pure vantage-point. Consequently, we need to ask whether arguments against technological determinism realize their radical promise, and to evaluate their policy implications. For example, although in the approach just mentioned technologies are portrayed as political, and as socially constructed, they are still treated as having objective 'effects'. In this sense, even such politically motivated critiques of technology tend to adopt what we characterize as technicist and essentialist elements.[2] In this chapter we argue that this is a significant failure of nerve. We suggest that anti-essentialist arguments need to be taken to a more radical (post-essentialist) conclusion and we consider the implications of this for the relationship between gender and technology. In brief, we subject the notion that technology has politics built into it (capitalist, patriarchal or whatever) to the same anti-essentialist critique that is currently used to deny the eco-feminist position that existing technology is inherently patriarchal.

The chapter begins by outlining the basis for the claim that even 'constructivist' and 'social shaping' approaches are insufficiently sensitive to the demands of an appropriately radical critique of technology. We then examine the extent to which the same problems can be found in some feminist approaches to technology. This is done using the cases of reproductive technologies and of information and communication technologies (ICTs).

The critique we offer leads us to reflect on the nature and implications of our own critical stance. Does our critique also depend on the features we identify in certain constructivist and feminist analyses of technology? Is this unavoidable or are there alternative ways of moving beyond the current state of the art?

# Technological determinism, essentialism and anti-essentialism

Among the various approaches to technology discussed in this book we can, for purposes of clarity, distinguish two main kinds. First, a traditional approach is based on an acceptance of one or other statement of the technical capabilities of technology.[3] In this perspective technical capacity is viewed as inherent to the technology (artefact or system). We refer to this perspective as *essentialist*: technical attributes derive from the internal characteristics of the technology. Moreover, these internal characteristics are (often) supposed to have resulted from the application of scientific method or from the linear extrapolation from and/or development of previous technologies. This first perspective has been roundly criticized on several counts, most notably that it limits its discussion of 'the social' dimension to the effects of technological capacity.

The second alternative approach we call *anti-essentialist*. This encompasses a broad church of perspectives, including 'social shaping' (for example, MacKenzie, 1991), 'constructivist', 'social construction of technology' (for example, Bijker et al., 1987; Bijker and Law, 1992) and what we call 'designer technology' (for example, Winner 1985). These otherwise different approaches share the view that technological artefacts do not possess capacities by virtue of extrapolation from previous technical states of affairs, but rather that the nature, form and capacity of a technology is the upshot of various antecedent circumstances involved in its development (mainly taken to include design, manufacture and production). These antecedent circumstances are said to be 'built into' and/or 'embodied in' the final product; the resulting technology is 'congealed social relations'; or 'society made durable'. Differences between anti-essentialists turn on the specific choice of relevant antecedent circumstances – between, for example, 'social interests', the 'solutions sought by relevant social groups' and 'social structure and the distribution of power'. Although anti-essentialism is characterized by some heated disputes between, for example, 'social constructivists' and their critics,[4] all parties share the aim of specifying the effects of these circumstances upon technological capacity.

Clearly, the anti-essentialist approach has enormous policy implications for technology design, development and use. However, three key features threaten to compromise its radical potential. The first is the ambivalence associated with the idea of antecedent circumstances being 'built in'. The second is the difficulty of specifying the nature of these 'antecedent circumstances'. The third stems from the view that technologies – the final stabilized technological products – although they are the outcome of a cycle of embodying antecedent circumstances, are still capable of having effects. In the rest of this section we show how these three features of anti-essentialist argument – which also occur in explicitly feminist approaches to the problem – effectively carry forward elements of the essentialism which they purport to criticize.

## The metaphor of building in/embodiment

The metaphor of embodying or having antecedent circumstances 'built in' implies the possibility that a technology can be neutral until such time as political or social values are ascribed or attributed to it. The problem here is that this view distinguishes between the object in itself, an objective and apolitical phenomenon, and the subsequent upshot of social and political overlay. This view assumes that objective accounts of a technology are left when the evaluative aspects are stripped away from the essential object. By contrast, the argument of the more thoroughgoing 'constitutive' variants of anti-essentialism is that it makes no sense to suppose that such an apolitical object could exist independent of evaluative aspects; it exists only in and through our descriptions and practices, and hence is never available in a raw, untainted state. This is not an ontological claim – that nothing exists outside of our construction of it – but rather an insistence on the thoroughness with which the technical is intertwined with the social.

The persistence of essentialism is evident also in formulations of anti-essentialism which speak in terms of the technology having politics *attached* to it.[5] Again the implication is that values, politics and the rest are inscribed in the technology in the very process of its construction, deployment and consumption. Yet even this variant carries essentialist overtones – what, we might ask, is the 'it' into which politics are being inscribed? In varying degrees, the same problem arises in other formulations: technology has been variously said to be affected by social factors, or to have these social factors built into or embodied by it. As we discuss later, we need to attempt to exorcise this persistence of essentialism stemming from our continued reliance upon realist language conventions. For present purposes our preference is for the term 'constitutive' to denote that variant of social constructivism which speaks of technical phenomena being *constituted* (rather than merely shaped, affected etc.) by social process.[6]

## Specifying antecedent circumstances

The embodiment metaphor often presupposes the unproblematic character of what exactly is being built in. Attributes such as interests and political values are assumed to be straightforwardly available to the analyst. The problem here is that this ignores the active interpretative work that goes into rendering motives as, say, social interests (Woolgar, 1981). The initial description and specification of antecedent circumstances, let alone their explication as causes of the design and shaping of technology, are part and parcel of the reading and interpretation of technologies.

Of course, some of the more sophisticated writing in this area recognizes the difficulty of treating features such as motive, interest, values and so on, as objectively available explanans. For example, Van Zoonen (1992: 20) points out that 'gender can be thought of as a particular discourse ... a set of overlapping and often contradictory cultural descriptions and prescriptions ... not as a fixed property of individuals but as part of the ongoing disciplining process by which subjects are constituted'. She implies that we should at least be extremely cautious in saying that technologies 'are gendered' precisely on account of the interpretative flexibility of the precept. Although Van Zoonen begins to develop this idea, she still tends to reserve a realm of 'non-discursive elements' (1992: 26) and to talk of how (in this case, new information and communication) technologies do not in themselves exclude women; instead, women are excluded by certain forms of discourse which 'surround' the technology. Given our own sympathy with the view that discourse constitutes the object, we are concerned that the implied division between discourse and object once again suggests the possibility of a discourse-free (neutral) technology.

## Having effects

A similar difficulty attends anti-essentialist arguments which unproblematically accept that technologies can have effects. Much anti-essentialist argument is pitched as a critique of technological determinism. However, it turns out that this is not a denial of determinism *tout court*. The argument stresses instead that the effects of technologies are complex; that their uses are unpredictable; and that, in particular, these effects do not stem from the inherent technical characteristics of the technology in question. This form of anti-essentialism attempts to supplant technical determinism with social and political determinisms; the politics built into a technology become the origin of 'effects'. The object of critique turns out to be *technological* determinism rather than technological *determinism*. For example, in Winner's (1985) account, it is the bridge-designer's politics, rather than the mere fact of the material construction, which is said to prevent access to Jones Beach.

The difficulty here is that the analyst's own pretensions to causality – sustained in and through the conventions of her adequate accounting practice – reinforce the supposition that the technology possesses intrinsic objective properties. This follows from what Coulter (1989) calls the situated grammar of language use. To say, for example, that 'Chernobyl caused pollution' is to imply the existence of a definite entity which has properties capable of causing some effect. Of course, the mere utterance of this sentiment doesn't establish the objectivity of 'Chernobyl' in any final sense. But for practical purposes – in this case, those to do with offering a hearably sensible description of a state of affairs – the use of the term 'Chernobyl' can stand as a causal antecedent for any of an indefinite number of actual objective characteristics. Again, we are not trying to establish a philosophical claim on behalf of ontological relativism but are attempting to draw attention to the central significance of the conventions of language use as deployed in anti-essentialist accounting practice.[7] To the extent that constructivists are unwilling or unable to critique such important and all-pervasive conventions of their language use, they implicitly buy into significant features of essentialism.

## Technological determinism and textual determinism

All this suggests that while anti-essentialist approaches help problematize the idea of a neutral technology, they remain committed to a form of essentialism. A thoroughgoing critique of essentialism would insist that values (in this case politics) are imputed to an artefact in the course of their apprehension, description and use – which of course includes imputations by the historian of science and/or technology. The political design critique of essentialism ends up merely substituting one form of essentialism (that technologies are actually neutral) with another (that technologies are actually political).

The problems we have outlined stem from a more general failure to acknowledge the textual character of technologies. The problem with the extent to which technologies do or do not contain inherent characteristics, and the related difficulty of ascertaining how these characteristics impinge upon users and consumers, can be understood as part of the more general problem of the nature of texts. Do texts possess intrinsic meanings, and do these meanings then have effects upon readers (for example, by suggesting a particular interpretation)? Or do such meanings only arise in and through the active interpretative work performed by the reader? Technological determinism is a particular instance of the more general issue of textual determinism. The anti-essentialists attempt to move away from the former essentialist answer and yet, as we have suggested, inevitably retain features of essentialism sustained through the unproblematized use of linguistic conventions of representation.

The constitutive variant of anti-essentialism achieves the greatest distance from essentialism. It takes the view that technology is neither neutral nor political in and of itself; that whatever it appears to be lies in our interpretative engagement with it. To ask whether, for example, an artefact is – that is, physically embodies the properties of – male or female or neutral is to miss the point; not only are these properties themselves socially constructed and therefore flexible, but the important question is how certain artefacts come to be *interpreted* (and this may well be disputed) as neutral or male or female?

Anti-essentialist attempts to move away from the essentialist position are fraught with an ambivalence which arises from inattention to the discursive and textual character of language.[8] Thus, when making an anti-determinist argument, it is insufficient to say that new technologies do not necessarily cause social change because the causes of change are unpredictable and multiple. This view still imbues the technology with the capability of having an effect. Nor is it good enough to say that the effects are unclear as long as we are still willing to specify the (actual) nature and characteristics of the technology. Our very attempts to describe a technology imply its possible involvement in action, its possible and potential effects. This follows from the conventional character of language: objects described in language are never merely and automatically just objects; they are always and already implicated in action and effect.

With this critique of anti-essentialism in mind, we now examine the extent to which its characteristics recur in some recent feminist arguments about technology.

# Feminism and technology

The tradition of associating technology and science with men goes back at least as far as the Enlightenment. This intellectual movement seemed to throw light on all manner of irrationalities and unreasoning, but in terms of reflexive enlightenment on the role of patriarchy it appears to have been a miserable failure. Even if Voltaire worked with Madame du Châtelet, and Diderot with Sophie Holland, and even if the French salon itself was the invention of the marquise de Rambouillet in 1623 and was intended to facilitate intellectual exchange among women as well as men, the Enlightenment was never a vehicle for sexual equality (Anderson and Zinsser, 1990). Instead, women became associated with

reflecting nature, and displaying emotion, with irrationality and subjec-
tivity, whereas men became associated with controlling and exploiting
nature, with reason, logic and objectivity (Harding, 1986; McNeil, 1987).
In revolutionary France a short-term consequence of the 'forced sepa-
ration' between women and rationality was the banishment of women
from the public institutions of power; a long-term consequence
throughout the world has been the virtual monopolization of science
and technology by men.

Although many feminists have explicitly rejected this opposition
between rationality and women, one variant of feminism, sometimes
labelled eco-feminism, celebrates rather than denigrates these allegedly
innate differences. The eco-feminist approach is consistent with the
notion of political technology, using this notion as a fundamentalist
stepping-stone to women's liberation from 'male' technology. Since, in
this view, all technologies are carriers of their designers' intentions,
many technologies are male (Cooley, 1968: 42–4), as the cultural attributes associated with working in, or studying, engineering demonstrate
(cf. Sørenson, 1992). As Hacker (1989: 35–6) notes from her interviews
with men in an engineering faculty: 'Status accrued to the masculine
world of speed, sophistication, and abstraction rather than the feminine
world of nature and people.' The most dangerous manifestation of
'masculine' technology is said to be the military technology of war.
Military technology is considered male, and men are believed to be
inherently violent (towards women and each other) for a variety of reasons. For Easlea (1983), the reason is male 'womb envy'. His narrative
describes the nuclear bomb programme as flowing from the excitement
of 'conception' through the laborious hours of labour up to the 'birth'
of the aptly named 'Little Boy' dropped on Hiroshima, and celebrated
by the physicists at Los Alamos in a manner very much akin to the constructive success of birth rather than the destructive terror of death.

Accounts of nuclear technology aptly illustrate some fundamental
differences in approach to technology. Whereas a traditional approach
might concede that the design and deployment of nuclear weapons has
political dimensions, it would probably balk at the assumption that
nuclear technology is inherently masculine and thus, for (some)
women at least, in need of replacement. Eco-feminism points both to
the immense power derived from nuclear sources and the implied control over, and exploitation of, nature. Hence, what could be regarded
as an inherently aggressive technology cannot be harnessed for constructive purposes but must be interred and replaced by 'softer' renew-
able green technologies such as wind- and wave-power. An alternative,
but still essentialist, account nominates a particular form of political
organization, rather than masculinity, as the essential feature of
nuclear power. Thus Winner (1985: 32) argues that: 'the atom bomb is

an inherently political artefact. As long as it exists at all, its lethal properties demand that it be controlled by a centralized, rigidly hierarchical chain of command.' Here the politics of the bomb have effects upon society.

Whether these effects are necessarily masculine or just hierarchical is, for our purposes, largely beside the point. It may well be that the controllers of the bomb provide accounts of its technical capacity which are used to persuade the public at large that a 'rigid hierarchical chain of command' is essential. However, this does not justify the claim that the technology, in and through itself, demands such an organizational form nor that such a form is masculine in structure. If some women's organizations develop 'a rigid hierarchical chain of command', does this mean they too are coerced by a political technology or by a masculine technology?

The essentialist framework of eco-feminism, in common with many psychoanalytic accounts, tends to ground its arguments in notions of masculinity and femininity which are simultaneously inherent and permanent. Thus, all forms of action deployed by men and women are ultimately derived from the 'natural' nature of each sex. But as Wajcman (1991: 9) argues:

> The first thing that must be said is that the values being ascribed to women originate in the historical subordination of women. . . . It is important to see how women came to value nurturance and how nurturance, associated with motherhood, came to be culturally defined as feminine within male-dominated culture ... Secondly, the idea of 'nature' is itself culturally constructed. Conceptions of the 'natural' have changed radically throughout human history.

This account has particularly significant implications for those seeking to develop what might be called 'feminist' technologies. If what counts as feminine and masculine are cultural attributes, subject to challenge and change, then replacing masculine technologies with feminine technologies begs the question of what precisely (and of *who decides* what precisely) is to count as a feminine technology. Are all women the same? Unless they are, changes to the technology will not resolve the problem of asymmetric control over the technology. Would we expect the deployment and consumption of technologies in households without men to be perfectly equal between their female members? Again, this does not mean that any 'residual' inequalities would undermine the quest to construct a culture in which technology was not interpreted and deployed by men against women, but it does imply that essentialist accounts of women – and men – remain deeply problematic.

Two further examples will suffice to illustrate this point. According to Roberts (1979), the replacement of the light, single-handed sickle by the heavy, double-handed scythe was crucial in the decline of women's agricultural employment during the Industrial Revolution. Since the new technology (the scythe) was more efficient, but required strength and skill beyond the capacity of women, the technology was crucial in the assertion of a male monopoly over crop-cutting – one of the most highly paid jobs. Was the technology designed with this in mind? Or, whatever the designers' intention, was the objective effect of the technology to masculinize crop-cutting? Unfortunately the intentions of the designer seem to be lost in history[9] but, whatever they were, we might want to remain sceptical of such determinist accounts on at least two counts. Firstly, if the new technology did require greater strength and skill, one might expect to see fewer women rather than none at all after its introduction – assuming that, although most women are physically weaker than men, some women are stronger than some men.[10] Secondly, as late as 1921, crops were being cut by male-only farm gangs that still retained sickles (*The Guardian*, 20 May 1991). What does this imply? That the inherently male scythe was also too heavy for men? That only a female sickle would have allowed women to remain as crop-cutters? Clearly, neither of these alternatives makes sense of the persistence of the sickle in male-only agricultural gangs. We are thus led to seek explanations which, for example, concentrate on the patriarchal culture (legal restraints on female labour and the interests of male agricultural labourers) within which such technologies existed. The battle for access to relatively lucrative farming jobs was not won as a direct result of a specifically male technology but through the successful deployment of accounts of the technology that purported to 'prove' its necessarily male requirements, and through the recruitment of allies, such as the law banning women from gang labour. The re-adoption of the sickle did not facilitate the return of women to crop-cutting; if the essentialist models of technology are correct then it should have done.

The second, and similar, example relates to the British Post Office in the 1930s. There were, at the time, no urban postwomen nor any full-time postwomen anywhere. Officially, they were not recruited because they could not physically carry the normal load. However, women were employed as part-time rural deliverers – with the same carrying requirements! – not, as one might think, because of the atypically strong physiques of rural women, nor even because of the atypically weak physiques of rural men, but because, as one manager admitted: 'no man can be obtained to perform the work' (*Post Office Records*, 1930: 6033). In terms of technology, it seems, even the British Post Office was subject to the rigours of relativism.[11]

# Reproducing technology?

If the eccentricities of technical arguments concerning the reproduction of paid labour and the mail (male?) system are relatively easy to subvert, has the 'advance' of science and technology in the reproduction of humans been less contingent? After all, the public/private split does imply that these most intimate technologies are deployed in the one area where women are supposed to prevail.

Many accounts of technical change in domestic work (Berg, 1991; Cowan, 1983) and paid labour (Chabaud-Rychter, 1995; Cockburn, 1983, 1985, 1991) suggest that the development of technology has done little if anything to roll back patriarchal control at work. Of course, if the essentialism of the eco-feminist position is accurate, then we would not expect technologies developed and deployed by men to do anything but reinforce patriarchal control. This is nicely captured in the debate concerning what Firestone (1970) calls 'the tyranny of reproduction'. Firestone's essentialist position, which locks inequality in to women's reproductive biology, posits technology (particularly in-vitro fertilization) as the solution. But if patriarchy controls women through their distinctive reproductive functions, and if the technology is either inherently masculine or even just controlled by men, then the search for a technical fix is unlikely to be successful. Under these circumstances only technology designed, deployed and consumed by women, or at least wrested from male control, will offer sexual equality. In contrast to Firestone's biological essentialism, that of Corea et al. (1985) is rooted in the essential masculinity of technology. Hence Firestone's 'technical fix' solution to patriarchy is the 'living laboratory', according to Klein (1985). Not only does male control over, and exploitation of, women as living laboratories ensure the continuation of patriarchy – rather than its ultimate demise as Firestone had hoped – but the links between patriarchy and science may ultimately lead to reproductive techniques that no longer require the participation of women, or which configure women's role as professional breeders in what Corea et al. have called the 'reproductive brothel'.[12]

Neither the biological essentialism of Firestone nor the technological essentialism of Corea et al. adequately grasps the way knowledge constitutes the object of our concern. Thus, Firestone's biological determinism seems incapable of explaining why those who actually have children are necessarily involved in their upbringing, nor why women who do not have children are constrained by similar patriarchal constraints to women who are mothers. On the other hand, if reproductive technologies reflect their patriarchal origins, then why do different societies appear to use technologies construed to be identical in radically different ways? Why, for example, do contraceptive policies and practices differ so much between Catholic and non-Catholic societies? If such technologies are inherently patriarchal they should have the same 'effects' upon women. Perhaps an old 'Popperian' question is worth asking:[13] what would it take to persuade essentialists to give up their thesis that technology is inherently gendered? Could they ever be persuaded that gendering occurs in and through the interpretation of the technology?

The dilemmas surrounding reproductive technologies (Hirsch, 1995), and the question of their political coloration, are illustrated by the case of amniocentesis, a method of establishing the genetic make-up of embryos and assessing foetal abnormalities, especially Down's Syndrome. This technology can be interpreted in several different ways. It may be regarded as a method of social engineering through which the diagnosis of foetal abnormalities leads directly to the termination of the pregnancy. As Farrant (1985) argues, the test may not increase women's choice since its provision can appear conditional on termination in cases where abnormalities are considered likely. Here the technology is read as masculine and political. Alternatively, the medical profession regards the test as potentially dangerous to the foetus, so that there is little point in providing a test if an abnormality will not lead to a termination. The dilemma here is twofold. On the one hand such tests are relatively costly in resource terms and this highlights the politics of all health in terms of the choices to be made about the provision of services: does health spending reflect a 'rational' distribution of resources (whatever this might mean) or the interests of powerful lobbies inside the health service? On the other hand, is the technology being used to increase or decrease the choices open to women? Why, in other words, should women be encouraged to opt for terminations just because their children are likely to be born with some kinds of abnormality? Why, on the other hand, should they be encouraged not to have terminations? The more extreme scenario constructed around such technologies would envisage them being used to facilitate the possibility of choosing the sex of a child and terminating a foetus of the 'wrong' sex. Rowland (1992) certainly has this in mind in her denunciation of living laboratories, although this denunciation once again hinges on a view of women as passive victims of essentially male technology.

As Wajcman (1991: 62) suggests, reproductive technologies do still *seem* to carry certain 'effects', such that:

> the technologies redefine what counts as illness. 'Infertility' now becomes not a biological state to which the woman must adapt her life, but a medical condition – a problem capable of technological intervention. The very existence of the technologies changes the

situation even if the woman does not use them. Her 'infertility' is now treatable, and she must in a sense actively decide not to be treated. In this way the technologies strengthen the maternal function of all women, and reinforce the internalization of that role for each woman.

Reproductive technologies thus *seem* to have the capacity, in and through themselves, to redefine what counts as illness or good health. But does the existence of these technologies in itself lead to all women having to redefine their infertility (or even fertility) as a treatable condition – as an illness (see Singleton, 1995)? Consider, for example, the technology of amniocentesis. Without the funding to pay for it, the staff to use it, and the culture that legitimates its use – as either a liberational or social engineering tool – amniocentesis is unlikely to have any effect upon women. The character and capacities of the technology cannot be assessed in the abstract.

Just as what counts as an illness is socially constructed, so too we can argue that what counts as the capacity and effect of a technology is socially structured; both are consequently contingent and open to re-negotiation. Condoms may have been designed to prevent unwanted pregnancies (and this may well be in the interests of both sexes involved), but the development of AIDS has facilitated their redefinition as a method to avoid contracting HIV. Or, to return to amniocentesis, the use of ultrasound scanning to locate the position of the foetus prior to the withdrawal of amniotic fluid through a syringe has its origins in naval sonar research. It might still be argued that this merely confirms the links between male aggression – manifest in military technology – and male control over the process of reproduction, that either the patriarchal origins or contemporary patriarchal use of the technology necessarily prevents it being used for the benefit of women. But if women's choice is increased as a result, then neither the technology's origins nor current deployment prevent any potential renegotiation of the capacity and potential of the technology. Indeed, to focus wholly on the militaristic origins, and to assert that technology necessarily carries its essential masculinity with it, diverts attention from the interpretative acts and practices which operate to maintain patriarchal control over technology.

None of this is to deny the apparent gender inequalities in health and medicine, particularly in childcare, nor the constant threat of greater male control as technological innovations displace women.[14] An argument often used to account for the predominance of men within the hierarchy of the medical profession is the relative longevity of the occupation itself: over time men have gradually increased their control over medicine and displaced the earlier influence of 'wisewomen'. This is especially significant where men have introduced technology to oust women – obstetric forceps being perhaps one of the best-documented cases (Faulkner, 1985). Studies of the introduction of new technologies into existing occupations tend to highlight the maintenance or exacerbation of existing gender inequalities (Albin and Applebaum, 1988; Barker and Downing, 1985; Grint and Gill, 1995; Webster, 1988, 1989, 1991). But what happens when new technology is allegedly the basis for a new occupation – in this case computing?

## Computerized genders

Computing, and information and communication technologies (ICTs) more generally, are big business: as early as 1988 it was estimated that as much as 40 per cent of all new investment in the US was destined for computing and ICT (Perrole, 1988, quoted in Kirkup, 1992: 267). This enormous expenditure, coupled with dire warnings of a considerable labour shortage, especially in areas such as engineering and computing, persuaded governments in several countries to develop special schemes to encourage women into these areas. These schemes appear to have singularly failed to increase the proportion of women in computing: as professional programmers, as systems analysts or as simply participants in computing courses.

This situation is reflected in figures for women's participation in these areas of the educational system. In both Britain (Dain, 1991; Hoyles, 1988: 9; Kirkup, 1992: 268; UCCA, 1991) and the USA (Klawe and Leveson, 1995: 30–1) there have been decreases in the proportion of women taking computer degrees. This drop has been said to result from the introduction of computers into schools through the teaching of mathematics, in the UK perceived to be a male-dominated subject (Apple, 1992), and from the cultural power of male students to monopolize computers at home, school and college (Klawe and Leveson, 1995: 30). As Klawe and Leveson argue:

> Professors remembered the names of men better, called on them more, asked them more challenging questions, listened and gave positive responses to them more often, etc. Both men and women teachers display this behaviour. They are quite unconscious of it and were shocked to see it in the videotapes of their own classes. (1995: 31)

Male approaches to computing are regarded as more rational than female approaches. Male control is supported by the vast libraries of games software with characteristics conventionally described as masculine: an emphasis on competition and violence. When contemplating the idea of marketing a 'Barbie goes shopping' game for their Gameboy machines, Nintendo announced they had no plans to develop a 'Gamegirl'. Although girls comprise 44 per cent of Gameboy users in the USA, Nintendo took the view that the development of a Gamegirl would deter boys from buying their products and so undermine their total sales (*The Guardian*, 23 June 1992). Male predominance in the world of adolescent computing has also been explained by links between video games, computers and male adolescent culture, and by the situation of video arcades and computer clubs (Bates et al., 1988; Culley, 1986; DES, 1986). More recently, however, American Laser Games, known for their violent games like 'Mad Dog McCree', have produced the first in a series called 'Games for Her' (the first being 'Madison High').

However, male domination seems to predate the development of 'toys for the boys' software. Male adolescents and young men predominantly frequented computer exhibitions in the early 1980s, even where the subject-matter was not ostensibly male (for example, programs on personal health, literacy, safety, finances and decision-making in the question of breast- or bottle-feeding babies) (Gerver, 1985). Nevertheless, printed material at the same time did assume that the overwhelming proportion of computer-users were male. Postgraduate computer courses for arts or social science graduates are still overwhelmingly dominated by male graduates, at least in the UK. As Cockburn has noted: 'The computer was the brainchild of male engineers and it was born into a male line of production technology' (1985: 170).

In fact, the 'maths and military' image of computers has a background stretching from Babbage's Analytic Engine for algebraic calculations, through Hollerith's Tabulating Machine for collating the 1900 US Census data, to the wartime Colossus, used to break the German Enigma code in 1943, and ENIAC (Electronic Numerical Integrator Analyser and Computer), developed by the Ballistics Research Laboratory in 1945 to calculate the trajectories of artillery shells. Many women were involved in these developments: Ada Lovelace was an important accomplice of Babbage, Hollerith's tabulating machines had female as well as male operators, and many of the operators of the wartime computers, including ENIAC, were women (Kirkup, 1992: 270; Palfreman and Swade, 1991). But whatever the role of women in the design and use of these early computers it is clear that without the military there would be no computer industry as it currently exists (Edwards, 1990; Finnegan and Heap, 1988;Mackenzie and Wajcman, 1985). From an essentialist perspective, this observation implies that computer technologies carry with them the politics of their origins and hence the militaristic effects of the masculine origins. Thus, the world of the professional computer specialist is regarded as 'masculine'. It is a world where high risk, ruthlessness and technical expertise prevail, a world which dissuades women from entry and so generates few role models to attract other women (Morris, 1989). In the workplace, the cultural attribute of masculinity frequently manifests itself in informal systems of control and in preferential treatment for male professionals: 'the lads' (Tierney, 1992).

For others, the origins of ICTs influence, but do not determine, their ultimate use (Van Zoonen, 1992). However, even this modified specification of male origins is difficult to sustain. Although computers were originally large, imposing hierarchies of technology in the very public (and hence male) world of work, the trend has been towards smaller and smaller technologies, many of which are specifically marketed as '*home* computers' for personal use in the private sphere. Notwithstanding the association between male hobbies and the first personal computers (Haddon, 1988), the overtly masculine identity of computers has gradually been eroded by something much more ambiguous, if not androgynous.

Cross-cultural comparisons raise further doubts about the alleged male superiority in ICT. Although only 17 per cent of computer professionals in Britain in the early 1990s were women, the corresponding figures for France, the USA and Singapore were 39 per cent, 50 per cent and 55 per cent respectively (*The Guardian*, 17 February 1989 and 26 June 1992; see also WIT, 1991). In the USA, between 30 and 44 per cent (depending on whose figures you accept) of the 1 million computer programmers and systems analysts in 1988 were women, but the vast majority were at the bottom end of the skill, reward and status hierarchy (Dunlop and Kling, 1991: 186; see also Lowe Benston, 1983; *The Guardian*, 23 June 1992). Indeed, ethnic origins also figure significantly in the US: only 5 per cent of women receiving computer science degrees in the early 1990s were African–American or Hispanic (Kirkup, 1992: 268) and while there was a doubling of the proportion of women managers in computing in the USA between 1983 and 1993 (the last date at which the figures were collected) from 15 to 30 per cent, Black, Hispanic and Asian women still only comprise 4 per cent of the total (Mendels, 1995: 44–5).

Both women-only and mixed courses about computers tend to assume a non-essentialist, liberal position on the relationship between technology and gender. It is assumed that, given the right opportunity, there is no reason why women should not compete equally with men in technically oriented courses. In effect, the cause of the problem of male domination in computing, and the solution to it, appears to lie in women themselves, rather than in technology. As Van Zoonen

(1992:15) argues, this implies that: 'gender can only be thought of as a distortion of the true nature of women and men'.

In a case study of the computer science department at the Norwegian Institute of Technology, Håpnes and Rasmussen (1992) and Håpnes and Sørenson (1995) switch attention from the alleged deficiencies of women to the nature of the dominant culture to explain women's general disinterest in the field. Women in Scandinavia generally prefer to study computer science within social science departments rather than within natural sciences or computer sciences itself. Technophobia or lack of confidence seem not to explain the relative paucity of women students (see also Rasmussen and Håpnes, 1991). Instead, the role of the hacker culture is crucial. Hackers – a minority of all male students – appear to live for little else but interacting with computers. They share a mutual dislike of, or disinterest in, all other students. Female students, in contrast, reject a life of machine intimacy and this is recognized by the staff of the department, whose professional and personal interests tend to lie with the hackers:

> They (the staff) like this attitude of total absorption and daring found among some of the male students, and they feel that the female students lack this attitude and therefore are less motivated to study computing. In the male programming virtuosos they see the dedicated scientist and researcher, absorbed by his subject. In the female students who go home after a long day at the university, and who give priority to activities outside the study, they see an instrumental attitude towards the subject and less dedication. (Håpnes and Rasmussen, 1992: 7)

Thus 'normal' students (females and non-hacker males) are progressively marginalized by a culture generated and supported by male hackers and male staff. This cultural barrier also encourages women to choose optional courses that include elements of the 'human aspect' of computing (for example, telematics and systems development) and discourages them from choosing 'more technical' options (for example, operating systems, hardware construction). Turkle (1984) similarly describes the way in which male hackers seek refuge from the uncomfortably threatening world of intimate human relationships in the sanitized environment of controlled technology. Computers thereby become symbolic projections of their users and/or substitutes for women in the hackers' lives (Kidder, 1982). As Håpnes and Rasmussen (1992: 9) note: '(women) often describe themselves as "marginal". They feel that it is programming that one associates with typical computer people who sit in front of a terminal and are fascinated by what's inside the computers. Women are more concerned with the use of technology.'

As we saw in chapter 3, this kind of boundary between the technical and the human, played out in terms of a distinction between the 'inside' and the 'outside' of the computer, is often focused on the computer case. Here the invocation of the boundary, as a symbol of gender difference, echoes Cockburn's (1985: 11–12) analysis of women and engineering: 'with few exceptions, the designers and developers of the new systems, the people who market and sell, install, manage and service machinery, are men. Women may push the buttons but they may not meddle with the works.' For both Cockburn and for Håpnes and Rasmussen, women's relative absence in technical fields is a protest by women, not a failure of women. These women are rebels, not victims:

> women's choices must be understood as an active protest against the machine-fixation in the study of computer science ... It is a protest against this domination, which is also a domination of a male culture ... In rejecting the dominant male culture and retreating to their own areas the female students are marginalized. However, they do not protest against their marginalization but accept it as inevitable because of their interests, their values and their choices. (Håpnes and Rasmussen, 1992: 10)

Where the 'regime of truth' is one that exudes masculinity, women enter such a world at some considerable cost to their own self-image. Recognition of the cost and its consequences thus implies that women do not so much 'fail to succeed' in a world of computers (or engineering – see Cockburn, 1985) but reject the competition's rules (Turkle, 1988; Van Zoonen, 1992): the conventions of the computer professionals' culture are epitomized by practices traditionally associated with men. According to Kidder (1982) and Turkle (1984) the computer professional can be identified with a 'hacking' culture: these are men who cut themselves off from the world (even though they are dependent upon it); they work all hours but especially at night; they are only happy when sat in front of the computer screen and this relationship between human and computer takes on the clear symbolism of personal intimacy. As the Enlightenment project brought to final fruition these men are literally 'masters' of nature. Yet it is not just men that seek a similar form of intimacy. As one 12-year-old girl responded to a question asking how students would be using their computers in thirty years' time:

> I would ask my computer to find me a perfect husband. I would tell it to tell me where to find the prettiest clothes and tell me where to get my hair done ... Then I would meet my future husband, get married, have children ... then I would get a divorce and raise my children on my own till they're grown. And then it's

just me and my computer. All alone again. (quoted in Kreinburg and Stage, 1983: 252)

The cultural tensions in this quote, in which the female student manages to display the most conventional forms of gendered desire with a most atypical machine intimacy are not, in themselves, particularly unusual.

Turkle and Papert (1990) develop an approach which tries to combine an essentialist and an interpretivist model. The essentialist framework is that men and women have different styles of interacting with computers: the essentialism here relates to gender differences rather than technologies. Men, in this model, have a rational analytic approach, exhibited in the very core approach of science and technology. Women, on the other hand, adopt a 'bricolage' approach which is more concrete, contextualist, intimate and holistic. Although computers are designed by men using rational methodologies, they are flexible enough, claim Turkle and Papert, to be used in a variety of ways. Hence they can be socially reconstructed for adoption by women. The constructivism advocated here is rather limited: the computers facilitate different user-styles because the *technology* is physically flexible, not because the interpretation creates a different technology.

## Conclusion: *Deus ex Machina* or *Machina ex Dea*?

Thus far we have seen that although both constructivist and feminist perspectives on technology aspire to a form of anti-essentialism, their analyses involve a form of essentialism. This leads us to ask whether and to what extent it is in fact possible to escape essentialism. What are the political and ethical implications of such an escape?

It seems that it is not easy for anti-essentialism to throw off the imagery of *deus ex machina*: the symbolic power of a divine spirit being encased within a machine pervades anti-essentialist analyses of technology (see Introduction). Although we concur with the move away from essentialism, anti-essentialism as discussed earlier has not moved very far. It is difficult to sustain a (post-essentialist) position which remains deeply critical of all kinds of essentialist notions, whether they relate to humans or non-humans, whether men and women have inherently and objectively different natures and interests, or whether technology has inherent and objective capacities. For the most part, anti-essentialism takes issue with the *identity* of the god (or whatever it may be) in the machine, but it makes no attempt to question the very idea that there is 'something' in there. Anti-essentialists are busy trying to replace the

*deus* of technical rationality with the god of social and political interests. Or, in the case of some feminists, with the *dea* of gender bias.[15] But
their endeavour is still fundamentally religious: this god rather than that
one.

Unfortunately, little effort has been made (with a few exceptions discussed below) to explore what it would take to challenge the existence
of (any) god. This line of (post-essentialist) enquiry would seek out possibilities to reject the abiding essentialist notion of gods or goddesses in
machines. The appearance of a deity within the machinery has to be
understood as more akin to a mirror of human hopes and fears than to
anything else.

Post-essentialism is hard work: it is a position to which we aspire
rather than one we can claim to have yet attained. As prisoners of the
conventions of language and representation, we display, reaffirm and
sustain the basic premises of essentialism that entities of all kinds, but
most visibly and consequentially technical artefacts and technological
systems, possess characteristics and capacities, and are capable of
effects. This seems to be a fundamental property of the objectivist language game in which we are all embroiled. It follows that a radical
move away from essentialism, attempted but (as we have shown) failed
by many anti-essentialists, requires nothing short of a major reworking
of the categories and conventions of language use (cf. Haraway, 1991:
ch. 8). Attempts to expose 'the actual' politics, social interests, gender
biases etc. are liberating and inspiring. And certainly they are an
improvement on nasty old traditionalist treatments of the topic. But in
the end they are merely moves within the same essentialist language
game.[16] The especially dangerous temptation is to get wound up in disputes about whether one or another category of antecedent circumstances is the more appropriate essence of the machine.

Our enmeshment in the language game of essentialism, and our suf-
focation within its base premises, is evident from the linguistic contor-
tions and convolutions necessary to create even a small amount of
breathing-space. The metaphor of embodiment, although intended as a
way of generating a fresh apprehension of familiar (technical) objects,
still implies a definite independently available object. Similarly, causal
features in stories about the effects of a technology imply a definitive
object, the explanans. The more determined efforts of the 'constitutive'
wing of anti-essentialism to escape this form of discussion stumble in
their attempts adequately to formulate the necessary language. It is better to say that technologies are constituted rather than shaped or constructed; that antecedent circumstances are inscribed in, rather than
merely informing, design; that users are configured, rather than just
enrolled; and so on. But all the juggling of language involved in these
efforts comes to seem so precious. By this route, do we end up putting

'scare quotes' around everything?[17] Or should our alternative strategy require us instead to explore new forms of writing and reflexivity, to invent new monsters and marginal beings which might displace standard units of analysis and transcend conventional categories and distinctions?[18] It is clear that an exploration of post-essentialism requires nothing short of an attempt to retheorize technological agency, instrumentalism and effectivity.

The problem, then, with many forms of feminism, constructivism and other forms of anti-essentialism is that they are insufficiently anti-essentialist and fail to transcend essentialism. They seem unable or unwilling to take the (difficult) step towards post-essentialism which will turn their limited insinuations of antecedent circumstances into a truly radical critique of technology. In the next chapter we address this question in the context of a more general consideration of different social perspectives on technology at work.

# 5
# Technology and Work Organizations

## Introduction

In the last chapter we considered the extent to which many recent critiques of technology are premised upon insufficiently radical foundations. It seems ironic that for all the allegedly revolutionary implications of information technology at work, its theoretical critiques are rooted in conventional philosophies and epistemologies. Whatever happened to the radical traditions ignited by the Luddites? Of course, as we indicated in chapter 2, the assumption that technology will have a revolutionary impact upon work organizations is far from novel. The Luddite case is one of the most famous examples. More recently, the development of automated machinery was associated with another Industrial Revolution; the first one driven by steam, the second by automated machinery (Crossman, 1961). It seems that successive generations of inventors, entrepreneurs and workers (not to mention many academic commentators) have knelt in wonder or terror or perplexity at the foot of each new technical advance. Despite this historical repetition, it is commonly thought that computer technology has revolutionary implications for the organization of work. Many now argue that we are in the midst of a third revolution, driven by information and communications technology. Business process re-engineering, in particular, has been driven by precisely this kind of rhetoric (see Grint and Willcocks, 1995). We evaluate the 'revolutionary' claim towards the end of this chapter when we discuss what is probably the most influential book of this genre: Shoshona Zuboff's *The Smart Machine* (1988).

It should also be apparent by now that conventional, technicist, analyses of technical development in industrial organizations give particular emphasis to the 'impacts' or 'effects' of technology upon work processes, conditions, skills and quality and on employment. The two main features of these analyses are: (1) they separate the technical from the non-technical; and (2) they assume the 'effects' of the technology derive from an unambiguous account of its capacity. In this chapter we subject both features to the post-essentialist critique. At the end we discuss another example of radical technology that promised to transcend an existing stalemate in that most deadly form of work: war. This leads us, in the final chapter, to examine the social, political and moral implications of the post-essentialism, especially in the light of concerns about political quietism.

The technicist/pluralist model identified in the first chapter is undoubtedly the one most frequently adopted and utilized in the contemporary literature on technical and organizational change. But even the most contingently oriented model of change still deploys an uncritical notion of technology itself, albeit one surrounded by a multiplicity of constraining non-technical variables. For example, Spenner (1985, cited in Milkman and Pullman, 1991: 125) argues that 'the impacts of technology on skill levels are *not simple,* not necessarily direct, *not* constant across settings and firms, and *cannot* be considered in isolation . . . The same innovation in two different firms can alter skill requirements in different ways.' For all the contingency mentioned here, the technology itself appears to be impervious to contingent interpretation. A variation on this theme is to argue that the imprecise nature of the results of new technology can be put down to the novelty of its adoption and concentration within private-sector manufacturing organizations or within areas especially conducive to such change (Phillimore, 1989).

Rather than attempting a general review of the significance of technical developments for organizations, we apply the post-essentialist critique to particular aspects of the relationship between organizations and technology. Much has been written on this relationship in the past, especially in terms of the significance of technological and organizational developments for the production method known as Fordism and the subsequent attempts by social scientists to assess the influence of technology on organizational design and worker behaviour and attitude. In the first section we begin with a brief survey of the archetypal modernist form of manufacturing technology – the Fordist assembly line – and then adumbrate the debate concerning post-Fordism and flexible specialization (see Grint, 1991: 274–307, for a fuller introduction to some of the literature in this vast field). We concentrate here on the value attributed to technology in recent developments in manufacturing organizations and especially on one contemporary model of 'good practice' – 'lean management'. We then turn our attention to organizations as consumers of technology through a short review of

Kling's recent work (a longer analysis – upon which this section is based – can be found in Woolgar and Grint, 1991 and Grint and Woolgar, 1992). Finally, in the third section, we consider the way in which computer technology has been construed as a revolutionary medium through which work is reconstructed and through which human self-realization or human enslavement can be achieved.

## Assembling organizations: from Fordism to flexible specialization.

Although the image of the assembly line is most popularly associated with Chaplin's film *Modern Times* (1936) its roots actually lie in the Chicago meat industry of the 1890s. But the first fully operational assembly-line production system was Ford's Detroit plant, set up in 1913. As with the earliest factories (see Grint, 1991, ch. 3; Jones, 1994), many of the original assembly-line technologies were not innovative at all. What was new was the organizational development in which the work was brought by a conveyor belt to the worker so the speed of task completion could be controlled by management, allegedly through the technology itself (Gartman, 1979). Thus, the Detroit plant would not have been viable without the juxtaposition of Ford's managerial style and the technology. In conjunction with these organizational changes the division of labour was radically increased and buttressed by low-cost parts, the use of specialized machinery, high wages, and the development of mass markets and mass consumption (see Allen, 1992 and Sayer, 1989 for more general reviews of Fordism in this wider context). Womack et al. (1990) argue that the Fordist method of car production was not based on new technology but rather on the interchangeability of parts which facilitated assembly and undermined reliance on skilled labour. Once Ford had achieved 'perfect' interchangeability, there was:

> naturally ... a remarkable increase in productivity ... Ford's innovation must have meant huge savings over earlier production techniques ... unfortunately the significance of this giant leap towards mass production went largely unappreciated as we have no accurate estimates of the amount of effort – and money – that the minute division of labour and perfect interchangeability saved. (Womack et al., 1990: 28)

Note here the significance of the persuasive interpretation in the absence of data. A similar argument, originally put forward by Charles Fitch, was that by 1884 the USA had achieved interchangeability of parts in several areas, but most particularly in gun production.

Interchangeability had been the ideal of the American armaments industry as early as 1813, but Gordon's (1988) review of the small arms in question suggests that it was not until well into the 1920s that precision filing of the gun parts by hand was regarded as unnecessary.

That said, Ford certainly thought he had the answer to the problem of production. His engineers argued that their assembly line cut the production time by half initially and then by over 80 per cent. Their primary argument was that Fordism was more reliant on technology than was Taylor's (1911) scientific management approach (see Grint, 1991: 184–97). Some of the features later associated with lean management (of which Taylor would undoubtedly have approved given his fixation with 'lost' time, for example the synchronized delivery of component parts to the assembly line), were already present at the Ford plant. But Fordist production methods were rooted in a very different conception of technology than those of Taylorism. While Taylor attempted to *perfect* the way a worker operated technology, Ford's engineers were interested in *replacing* the worker altogether (Hounsell, 1984).

This difference is also revealed in the payment systems. While Taylor preferred piece rates as a way to maximize incentives and minimize collective resistance, Ford used day wages and assumed that the technology itself would dictate the speed of production. This last assumption has become so ingrained in 'common-sense' that to query it seems irrational. Even now it is rare to find any suggestion that assembly-line technology does *not* dictate the speed of work involved (for example, see Allen, 1992; Armstrong et al., 1991). As Cavendish relates of her participation in assembly-line work:

> Every movement we made and every second of our time was controlled by the line; the chargehands and supervisors didn't even have to tell us when to get on. They just made people like Josey obey *if they wouldn't buckle under* ... The bonus system and the line speed even led the women to discipline each other. (Cavendish, 1982: 24; our emphasis).

Note the slippage here between the alleged dictatorial influence of the assembly line ('controlled by the line') and the necessity for human coercion of assembly-line workers (the supervisors 'just made people like Josey obey ...'). A bonus scheme is self-evidently a non-mechanical means of coercion, as is women's self-discipline. So the sense in which 'the assembly line' determines the actions of the workers is moot. If the technology dictates production why use a bonus scheme? Again, this is not to say that the technology is irrelevant but to argue that its relevance is socially constituted by those participating with it.

Whereas the persuasive power of the assembly-line technology may

have persuaded Ford, it was certainly open to reinterpretation by sceptical workers. If, as Womack et al. imply, Ford's (and every other)
assembly operative was: 'relentlessly disciplined by the pace of the line'
(1990: 32) one might wonder why supervisors were needed at all.
Technical control over organization would suffice. Yet, as Womack et
al. note in the very same section: 'the foreman ... could spot immediately any slacking off or failure to perform the assigned task'. For all
the talk of technical control over organization, it is clear that, at least in
this example, the technology did not determine the operations.

Whatever the success of Fordist assembly-line production there
were, it is argued, three inherent, and in some ways ironic, limitations
inscribed into the very system itself: variable consumer demand, the
counter-productive effects on employees, and a declining rate of marginal efficiency. As far as Taylor and Ford were concerned the system
appeared to be a virtuous circle: first, as long as consumers wanted, or
more probably could be persuaded, to buy an unvarying product,
represented most typically by Ford's single-colour, single-model mass-
produced model T, then assembly lines were ideal. They took a long
time to set up and were expensive in terms of technological investment
which took advantage of the very sophisticated division of labour, but
once running they appeared to churn out identikit products *ad
infinitum*. Thus, for example, vehicle production grew from 300,000 in
1914 to 2,000,000 by 1923 (Allen, 1992: 230). Second, the assumption
was that since workers were only really motivated by high wages then
providing startlingly high wages would solve all the labour problems
associated with the deskilling and degradation of jobs so clearly
described by Braverman (1974). Third, as long as a scientific approach
to work organization was adopted, gigantic improvements in technical
efficiency were feasible.

However, Ford found to his cost that the division of labour, and what
some of his employees regarded as the alienating conditions associated
with such a production method, took a heavy toll of employee morale:
labour turnover rose to 380 per cent in 1913 and the revolutionary
Industrial Workers of the World moved in to organize the workers.
Ford's response was radical. First, he offered a 10 per cent bonus to all
employees who had been with Ford for three years or more, though
only 4 per cent of the 15,000 workforce qualified. Then he offered the
magic 'five-dollar day' in 1914. The results were not always appreciated
by the partners of Ford's *nouveaux riches*, as an anonymous wife of one
such worker wrote to her husband's employer in 1914: 'The chain system you have is a slave driver! My God!, Mr. Ford. My husband has
come home and thrown himself down and won't eat his supper – so
done out! Can't it be remedied?' (Hounsell, 1984, quoted in Allen,
1992: 267). Almost seventy years later Kamata's (1982) ethnography of

a Toyota plant bears a remarkable resemblance (despite the point that Toyota was supposedly a leader in the field of 'good' human resource management even at this stage): 'Around eight in the morning Kudo returned from work. He was pale and his eyes were bloodshot. He'd done two and a half hours overtime ... he threw himself over his unmade bed, where he fell right asleep in the bright morning sun. He missed breakfast and will miss lunch too' (1982: 54). But if Kudo worked, despite his problems, so did Ford's five dollars a day, at least in the short run, though even this ultimately failed to provide a permanent solution to labour problems.

The problems of work incentives and work control have been distilled into two rather different issues. On the one hand, such processes may facilitate higher levels of control over the work process – if workers can be persuaded that they are controlled by the technology. But on the other hand the very success in this form of control may, paradoxically, undermine control over quality and goodwill (see Salaman, 1992). As Ford himself admitted: 'Machines alone do not give us mass production. Mass production is achieved by both machines and men. And while we have gone a long way toward perfecting our mechanical operations, we have not successfully written into our equations whatever complex factors represent Man, the human element' (quoted by Salaman, 1992: 346). It was this kind of recognition that eventually led to the job enrichment movement in the 1970s.

A second problem was that if work processes could be scientifically assessed and improved then there was a finite limit to, or at least a declining return from, the extent to which time and motion studies and similar strategies could increase productivity. Third, 'Fordism', as this method of mass production for a mass market became known, also had limitations in so far as consumer demand was concerned: it was all very well persuading everyone to buy a car, or even two, but a saturated market would require some form of dehydration if it was not to choke off demand and hence production and profit. This was particularly evident in the interwar depression, but this is to stray beyond our present concern with the links between technology and organization.

Part of the solution to the problems of Fordism in industrially advanced nations was, and is, to relocate in the so-called Third World and utilize the cheap and organizationally weak labour there. Although much has been made of the high-tech image of many Pacific Rim nations it is also the case that much of the technology with which advanced electronic consumer goods are constructed often tends to be of limited sophistication: cheap labour, not sophisticated electronics, is allegedly what attracts multinational corporations to such countries. Exactly which countries are used is something that seems to change daily: in May 1996 Lucky Goldstar announced the new site of a £1.5

billion silicon chip plant to a country which would pay wages that were allegedly 18 per cent lower than would be paid in any equivalent plant in Korea; the site is Newport in Wales (*The Observer*, 12 May 1996). However, for many the most important aspect is access to a new market for their products. For example, in some of Hewlett Packard's Third World assembly sites labour costs only amount to 2 per cent of total costs (Tucker and Allen, 1992). Market development, not cheap labour, is crucial here.

Another part of the solution was, and still is, to stimulate variable demand, but variable demand requires variable production systems – hence the adoption of new technology to provide a quicker response to consumer demand and to generate different consumer demands. This new technology also required a more flexible and probably, therefore, a more skilled workforce. Again, what we have is a technological and a social form which are interdependent: flexible technology with an inflexible workforce does not automatically lead to flexible production.

Post-Fordism, sometimes called flexible specialization, and associated with lean management, is designed to use technology and human resources to dissolve the 'stultifying rigidities' of Fordism to expand the range of products, improve quality and decentralize decision-making (Sable, 1982; Smith, 1989). Its effect at the level of the workplace is to do away with the assembly line, to increase the skill levels and flexibility of the workforce, to provide teamwork structures, and to seek out specialized niche markets for high-quality, high-value products and services. Post-Fordism also implies the use of new technologies to produce smaller batch, 'customized' products, in contrast to the standardized products of the first two-thirds of this century. The new conception of production first made its physical appearance in the late sixties and its academic debut at the hands of Piore and Sable (1984), though the same argument had been made by Reich (1983) slightly earlier under the rubric 'flexible system'. Yet, despite the popularity of the concept, it has never been adequately demonstrated that Fordist technologies and organizational methods were ever predominant, even if they were 'leading edge' industries in terms of technical developments and economic significance. Jessop (1989) has gone further to assert that Fordism was particularly limited in Britain where levels of investment in, and productivity through, Fordist technologies were systematically lower than elsewhere; where the disorganized collective bargaining system effectively decoupled productivity increases from wage increases; and where mass consumption was fed not by Fordist-led growth but by the growth in the welfare state and the importation of consumer goods. In Britain's case the ponderous nature of British industry has recently been questioned, not just in terms of Fordist forms of manufacture but even the future of manufacturing itself. Lee (1986), for example, has argued that a comparison of service and manufacturing industry since the middle of the nineteenth century suggests that Britain was never really the 'workshop of the world', but came rather closer to being the service, especially financial service, provider of the world (see also Grint, 1995: 15–44; Rubinstein, 1988).

There is a strange irony here: many critics of Fordism, and the entire debate about its transformation, have cast doubt upon its significance, saying it never achieved the predominance claimed for it. For example, only a minority of workers have ever been involved in manufacturing industries, let alone Fordist industries, and among these an even smaller number have worked with assembly-line technologies. Even accepting that Fordist industries have played a leading role in the development of new technologies, organizational practices, consumption practices and pay bargaining systems, it is doubtful whether the majority of any industrial workforce was ever Fordist in itself. Yet Fordism and its wider framework, manufacturing industry, have held sway as the iconic emblem of many nations, especially Britain. The 'regime of truth', to use Foucault's phrase again, suggests that Britain was indeed the land where manufacturing industry led the way. But the paradox is that in Britain, perhaps in contrast to Germany and the USA, manufacturing industry has been the occupation that the elite has consistently striven to avoid (Roderick and Stephens, 1981; Wiener, 1981). Thus the dominant ideology appears to be one that combines notions of manufacturing predominance over, and subordination to, financial capital; one where technology is enthroned and despised simultaneously.

But, whatever the traditions of British industry, there are many who believe that the new forms of manufacturing are beyond Britain's current capacity. As Hutton (1991) explains, not only is production based on teamwork systems but:

> divisions between worker and management functions are almost completely broken down ... [they] all organize themselves in teams, all use new technology to break away from mass production; all are highly focused on what markets want – and aiming to satisfy highly differentiated demand. They are mass customisers ... the speed of technical change is now so breath-taking companies adopting the new culture can completely out-compete those that do not ... None of the exemplars of these trends ... are British. In any case to exploit the new philosophy we need a new class of visionary business leader, a financial system that comprehends their mission and will back it, and a system of company law that fosters team building organizations, rather than profit-maximizing deal makers. Not to mention a highly educated and participating workforce.

Note here that the issue of technology is not one of the problems since its capacity is taken for granted; there are problems in adopting it but these have nothing to do with the technology itself.

One of the most popular representations of the importance of this new form of manufacturing, flexible specialization, and the deterministic implications of technical change, is Womack et al., *The Machine that Changed the World* (1990), a review of the development of the motor car and a prescription for lean management. As they state very explicitly at the beginning: 'how we make things dictates not only how we work but what we buy, how we think and the way we live' (1990: 11). The radical implications of this technical determinism are partly contradicted three pages later, when lean management is described as inducing: 'changes [in] how people work but not always in the way they think' (1990: 14).

Whatever the inconsistencies here, Womack et al. assert that, just as Ford's manufacturing advances owed little to new technology, the same can be said of Ford's later rival, Toyota. The latter's pioneering efforts in just-in-time systems and lean management systems owe very little to the adoption, let alone the determining effects, of new technology (see Grint, 1992). (In fact, Toyota's refurbished Toyota City Plant, when making the RAV4 vehicle, de-automated some elements of the assembly line to rescue its falling productivity and quality figures). Traditionally, Toyota's innovations lay in the organizational developments of delegating responsibility for quality as far down the hierarchy as possible, coupled with a permanent attack upon all forms of human and non-human waste, which provides for the very high levels of productivity and quality found amongst the best Japanese – and some non-Japanese – plants. As Womack et al. summarize their argument:

> The truly lean plant has two organizational features: It transfers the maximum number of tasks and responsibilities to those workers actually adding value to the car on the line and it has in place a system for detecting defects that quickly traces every problem, once discovered, to its ultimate cause ... in the end, it is the dynamic work team that emerges as the heart of the lean factory. (1990: 99)

Paradoxically, one might be tempted here to note just how different this approach is to classical models of manufacturing organization, where technology-led developments are perceived to be the way forward. However, Taylor himself was never enamoured of such an approach and always accepted that organizational sophistication was the route to business success, for: 'there is no question that when the work to be done is at all complicated a good organization with a poor plant will give better results than the best plant with a poor organization' (1903: 62).

Lean production is also similar to Taylor's approach in its elimination of waste or slack of any kind, 'management by stress' as Slaughter (1987) has called it. Nevertheless, lean production is grounded, in theory at least, on the integration of manual and mental labour, things which Taylor sought to separate. This reintegration of skill, and the associated dispersal, and devolvement, of control and responsibility, necessarily implies a dispersal of managerial authority; and the role of management itself tends to be perceived as one concerned primarily with co-ordination rather than with control, especially in terms of the team-based design and production techniques. Yet it is worth highlighting the significance of language in the creation of distinct images for mass and lean production. For Womack et al., 'the most important distinction [is] between the mind-numbing tension of mass production work and the creative challenge of constant improvement in Lean Production' (1990: 168). Contrast this, once more, with Kamata's (1982) account of 'the creative challenge' of working for Toyota:

> Overtime for an hour. I come back with Takeda who works next to me ... Suddenly he says, 'This job's dull, don't you think?' Dull as hell all right ... I'm so worn out I feel numb all over ... This is my exciting everyday life when I'm on the first shift! It's becoming almost as mechanical as my job. Sensations move monotonously by me like parts on a conveyor. (1982: 45–6)

Exactly ten years later, at Toyota's Tsutsumi plant in Japan, monotony appears not to be in the minds of two new trainees, recently interviewed. The first 'want(s) to stay for 30 years with Toyota'; the second 'came for security and to get on. The atmosphere's so positive' (quoted in *The Guardian*, 27 May 1992). Almost simultaneously, the Confederation of Japan Automobile Workers' Unions published a report (1992) suggesting that Japanese car workers were exhausted by 'lean' regimes and a new approach to work was essential. The point here is not to argue that Womack et al.'s account is more or less accurate than Kamata's, or that Kamata's ethnography has received considerable support from the Japanese unions, nor even to register surprise that the two trainees quoted are British, seconded from the new Toyota plant in Derbyshire; the point is to note the importance of the interpretative action: for some workers lean production may well be interpreted as creatively challenging, for others it may be little different from Taylor's ideal. To try and develop an account which denies the validity of one or the other, in the quest for an 'objective' account of life as a car worker, is to miss the point. These people create and sustain different accounts of their world, they appear not to be determined by the technology. But does this interpretative freedom extend beyond the organized production systems to organized consumption systems?

## Organizations as consumers of technologies

There has certainly been a consistent recognition that technological determinism has had severe problems in accounting for the apparent effects of technical change. Reviewing their version of the 'truth' of the significance of automation for work in 1968, the British Social Science Research Council (SSRC) argued that several general effects were clear: automation would reduce the number of supervisors, the size of work groups and the amount of communication between supervisor and employee, while it would increase the amount of supervisory responsibility and the centralization of authority. Where studies did not reveal similar 'effects' the report called for a 'general theory in terms of which the deviations from the normal experience might be explained' (SSRC, 1968: 29).

The problem of explaining the diverse 'effects' of computers, especially with regard to the 'effects' they had upon workers was also an early concern of Shepard, who concluded on the basis of his comparative study of factory and office work that: 'Automation in the factory appears to have a somewhat uniform impact on the nature of work. On the other hand, computerization in the office has thus far resulted in the existence of markedly different worker relationships to technology' (1971: 125).

An alternative approach is to assume that, however significant the location or design process may be, the consumption of technology is a crucial variable missed by most scholars. Thus, just as most sociology of work has turned out to mean the sociology of the factory assembly line so, most of it has turned on the *production* of artefacts through technology rather than the *consumption* of technological artefacts. But, unless we assume that technology does indeed determine its own use, the process of consuming technologies should exhibit considerably different aspects of what we take to be the same technology. The development of interest in consumption, rather than production, is a relatively recent development in the social sciences (see Bocock, 1992; Du Gay, 1996; Featherstone, 1990), and, perhaps more than anyone else, Rob Kling has pioneered this approach in social analyses of information technology.

According to Kling (1991, 1992), it is because such systems are consumed rather than simply deployed that they are 'potentially socially transformative'. That is, they can play 'key roles in restructuring major social relationships – interpersonal, intergroup and institutional' (1991: 344). This transformative *potential* is in contrast to the *necessary* transformative effects of computer systems that Kling accords to the approaches of Strassman (1985), Shaiken (1984), Zuboff (1988) and the like, who appear to insist on the significance of 'one dominant logic': either all transforming or all non-transforming. For Kling the starting-point must be to stop analysing technology and start considering technolo*gies*; clearly, for Kling at least, some technologies are transformative and others are not.

The potential for restructuring apparently inherent to some computer technologies is derived from the way that computer systems can alter 'the kinds of information readily available, [and] reorganize patterns of access to information, organizing the cost and work of organizing information, and shifting patterns of social dependencies for key resources' (Kling, 1991: 344). This approach of Kling's implies that although technology does not *determine* change it nevertheless has an independent effect; whether that effect is transformative or not depends upon the nature of the technology itself and the way it is produced, disseminated and consumed.

Kling attempts to demonstrate this approach by running through a series of case studies undertaken over the last two decades, and concludes that 'the different technical features of computer systems and the social organization sometimes do matter'; that, for instance, the:

> difference in the architecture of database management systems matters ... Why should such a difference in the architecture of database management matter to a social analyst of technology? If one asks whether computerization leads to changes in skill level of jobs, then the extent to which the systems people use enable them to develop new or expanded skills is an important part of the answer. (1991: 356)

In short, although conventional accounts suggest that only the technology matters, Kling's approach rescues the human side, but simultaneously looks at the way technology has impacts upon social organization under certain conditions.

The clearest example, perhaps, relates to the notion of deskilling and reskilling. For Shaiken (1984), as for Braverman (1974), new technology leads to deskilling; for Strassman (1985) (and Bell, 1973), new technology necessarily leads to reskilling or enskilling; but for Kling whether the effects of new technology are enskilling or deskilling depends upon the specific nature of the technology in question; some databases reskill and some deskill. Here, then, lies the answer to the problem Kling begins with – how can we assimilate the contradictory conclusions of previous scholars, with some suggesting technology deskills and others that it reskills? Once we stop talking about 'technology' in an abstract sense and begin to discuss technology in a particular material form we can distinguish between differing effects – and from here between socially transformative and non-socially transformative computer-based technologies. But the problem is that Kling's examples suggest a rather more radical approach is appropriate; one that focuses not upon the technical capacities and capabilities of technology but on the significance of interpretative action by actors.

For example, one of his case studies concerns the Urban Management Information System (UMIS) at Riverville. Here the computer system is portrayed by the UMIS operators to the public and the Federal funding authorities as providing a more rational service, reducing paperwork, improving managerial control etc., yet Kling argues that these effects were either difficult to measure or did not occur. Hence, Kling concludes that the 'primary value (of UMIS) was in *enhancing the welfare agencies' image*' (1991: 348; original emphasis).

Another of Kling's examples compares a mortgage bank (Western Mortgage) with an order-taking group in a sales department of a pharmaceuticals firm (Coast Pharmaceutical). Both organizations revamped their computer systems in 1989 with Coast Pharmaceuticals spending considerable time and money involving employees and managers in the new system installation and Western Mortgage doing much less in the training field, with the result that Western Mortgage employees were considerably more dissatisfied. As Kling concludes: 'In these two work groups, *different management approaches* have resulted in very different changes from the computerization projects' (1991: 351; our emphasis). This, one might argue, is a clear denial of the independent role of technology. But he goes on to argue that the Coast Pharmaceuticals case 'is transformative in nature'; to be 'transformative' the computer system has to play 'a key role' in restructuring major social relationships – yet it would seem that the key role here is management. Indeed, in the Western Mortgage case, the technology: 'was relatively non-transformative – the new computer system *was seen* as a simple substitute for the manual procedures and outside computer system. Managers appear to have initially *believed* that jobs would not be significantly changed as the computer system was implemented' (1991: 351; our emphasis). Again, we would argue that the critical issue here is interpretation of the technology, not the capacity of the technology in and of itself; whether the technology has identifiable capacities and effects is something from which Kling himself appears to skate away.

The third example drawn from Kling's work which undermines the 'independent effect' approach is that of PRINTCO. This high-technology manufacturing firm adopted a computerized inventory control system called a Material Requirements Planning (MRP) system. Once again, Kling notes how the claimed advantages of the MRP users were impossible to verify, but that they were taken for granted by the users. This enabled one group (the material managers) to secure control over another (the purchasing staff); but note that the role of MRP is not one of independent technology but one grounded in rhetoric: 'The *ideology of MRP impacts* helped the material managers *mobilize support* for the organizational changes needed to make the system work locally' (1991: 353; our emphasis). Unless ideology can be reduced to the objective and consensual redescription of 'technological effects' we remain unconvinced that the MRP system played a role independent of human attribution at PRINTCO.

The final example relates to the adoption of particular technologies by Artificial Intelligence (AI) professionals and computer scientists. As Kling remarks:

> AI researchers have eschewed IBM mainframes for years, and have often generalized their dislike to PCs. Computer Scientists have generally galvanized around Macs rather than PCs, even though there are technical ways to configure them similarly, and economic incentives for buying PCs. Consequently, people's behaviour with computer-based technologies can hinge on their ascribed social characteristics as much as on their technical features. (Kling, 1991: 356–7)

Since, according to Kling, Macs and PCs can be configured similarly, we would argue that Kling's analysis itself demonstrates the poverty of the 'independent technical effects' approach. Whether Macs can be configured like PCs or not is not what appears to determine the actions of AI professionals and computer scientists; rather, their action depends upon their interpretation of the technology in question.

In conclusion, we would argue that Kling's approach is a valuable contribution to the field in two areas: first in his able destruction of the technological determinist and single logic approach; second in the mine of empirical information thrown up by his and his colleagues' research. But his quest for the reasonable middle way, between technological and social determinism, where technology is just one, albeit an important, variable, is unsupported by his own evidence. It is not that technology has a social as well as a technical face but that what counts as technical is a social construct.

This image-enhancing role of technology appears to be especially important where the technology in question is at the leading edge of innovation, and the more information technology people use, the more they appear to think they will be regarded as competent and innovative.

This technological beguilement, in which the technology is used to sell itself rather than the product of the technology, is also evident in many other 'high tech' establishments. As one company president is reported to have said to a colleague: 'I don't think a guy will be able to go to his country club if he doesn't have a CAD/CAM system in his factory. He's got to be able to talk about his CAD/CAM system as he tees off on the third tee – or he will be embarrassed (*The Economist*, 30 May 1987, cited by Badham, 1990).

This inversion of Veblen's (1899) 'conspicuous consumption', such that the technology itself becomes public in 'conspicuous production', involves not just the promotion of a 'superficial' search for status rather than a logic of production, but promotes the production technology as a symbol of the company's ethics. Hence the image of a solid and environmentally friendly Volvo is demonstrated by adverts showing the multi-skilled, team-based work methods; Fiat demonstrated their adoption of 'new' technology for the Strada car by proclaiming a model 'built by robots' (Badham, 1990).

Now it would seem clear from this that whatever the 'capacity' or 'effects' of the particular technology involved, what really matters is the way the technology buttresses an image of efficiency, since the efficiency claims associated with new technologies in particular often appear to be very difficult to support with any kind of empirical data. It is equally difficult to argue that such technology has specific and identifiable 'effects'. What 'effects' it may have appear to lie within the persuasive rhetoric of the users rather than anything else. But is the technology of contemporary organizations as harmless as 'mere words'?

## Organizations as technological panopticons or empowerers?

If the organizations promoting the consumption of technology in organizations would like to persuade us that the road to utopia is lined with ever-improving computers there are others who take a quite contrary view. Foucault, in particular, has been associated with developing a perspective on social developments that lies much closer to Bentham's panopticon than Ford's freedom city. As Foucault states: 'the panopticon became the architectural program of most prison projects. It was the most direct way of expressing "the intelligence of discipline in stone"; of making architecture transparent to the administration of power; of making it possible to substitute for force or other violent constraints the gentle efficiency of total surveillance' (1984: 217). For Foucault the detailed observation and monitoring of daily life in prisons became the method of control which (as Bentham had originally suggested) many other institutions, including schools and factories, copied (cf. Giddens, 1985; Webster and Robins, 1993). Naturally, any form of surveillance has resource implications and many traditional bureaucratic forms have been regarded as simply too costly to maintain: the detailed actions of workers can be observed and controlled but only through prohibitively expensive numbers of supervisors to monitor each worker. More recently, the totalitarian implications of widespread surveillance through massive databases to create a 'superpanopticon' have been the subject of Poster's ideas (1990). In the world of work organizations it has been argued that information technology, notably that utilized in JIT systems and in Total Quality Control (TQC) (which devolves responsibility for quality down to the operative and denotes a switch from producer- to customer-orientation) can alleviate some of these problems, both by making the production process itself more visible, by stripping all buffer stocks and by relating quality errors to individuals. For all the novelty of the technology and the organizational forms, there is a striking resemblance between the methods of flagging the responsible individual in contemporary 'high tech' manufacturers, such as the one described by Sewell and Wilkinson (1992), and Robert Owen's approach. In Sewell and Wilkinson's factory, any manufactured component failure 'would result in the normative sanction of an identifying or "black" mark being placed above the operator's station' (1992: 280). Robert Owen used similar 'silent monitors': a piece of wood mounted over a machine with one of four colours on it to denote daily performance. (Arkwright went one better and provided different dresses to denote quality of performance) (Pollard, 1968: 225). But, if nineteenth-century owners constantly battled to control recalcitrant employees through various forms of technology, Sewell and Wilkinson (1992) suggest that:

> the development and continued refinement of electronic surveillance systems using computer-based technology can provide the means by which management can achieve the benefits that derive from the delegation of responsibility to teams whilst retaining authority and disciplinary control through the ownership of the superstructure of surveillance and the information it collects, retains and disseminates. (1992: 283)

This, as they acknowledge, is close to Zuboff's (1988) 'information panopticon', though they prefer the term 'Electronic Panopticon'. Thus, for Sewell and Wilkinson it is the use of computers to trace faults back to the individuals responsible *immediately* which acts as a powerful disciplining mechanism. However, they produce little empirical evidence to support the notion that the technology does have this objective effect. So we are once again left with an assessment of the significance of the technology rooted in technicist assumptions about technical capacities. The point here is not that Sewell and Wilkinson are wrong to suggest technology can be enrolled in a disciplinary system, but that the role of the technology can only be deduced from the accounts provided by those involved – and these accounts are not objective reflections of the technology. Hence whether the technology is a significant aspect of the disciplinary system depends on who says it is, or is not, and how persuasive these various contending accounts are.

This is probably best developed through an analysis of work by Zuboff. In a similar approach to that of Sewell and Wilkinson, Zuboff argues that managers prefer to exercise power through information control, rather than through more overt and physical forms of control, because the former can 'transmit the presence of the omniscient observer and so induce compliance without the messy conflict-prone exertions of reciprocal relations' (1988: 323). That said, Zuboff's examples of managerial technology seem not to fulfil their informational potential, since various groups used the monitoring technology to their own advantage: 'There were examples of operators using the data from the Overview System to prove to managers that they were not to blame. There were other cases where managers used the data to protect their own subordinates from being blamed for an error' (1988: 342). As one manager asserted in relation to the development of one such controlling database: 'When everybody looks at the database it should be obvious – data become the focus not the people. People hear words differently, but with the right data, we have something objective, beyond what each person hears ... You don't have to debate; you can see what is true' (1988: 349). If such a statement were accurate we would presumably have seen a rapid decrease in disputes where computer data, rather than human debate, formed the basis of decision-making: it is hard to think of any such decrease.

More generally, Zuboff considers the significance of the computer at work in terms of a traditional dilemma: either computer-mediated work will lead to the loss of meaningful employment and increasingly hierarchical control, or it will provide the opportunity for revitalizing work and enhancing its participatory potential. Either way, we are faced with crucial choices; yet 'computer-based technologies are not neutral; they embody essential characteristics that are bound to alter the nature of work within our factories and offices, and among workers, professionals, and managers' (1988: 7). So, 'how can the very same technologies be interpreted in these different ways? Is this evidence that the technology is indeed neutral?' (1988: 8).

While she does not take technology to be neutral, Zuboff does take information technology to be qualitatively different from prior forms of machine technology. While machine technology can *automate* it does nothing but act upon the object. However, information technology is reflexive in the sense that it generates additional information, thus providing 'a deeper level of transparency to activities that had either been partially or completely opaque' (1988: 9). In Zuboff's terms, information technology *informates* as well as automates. This distinction is important to Zuboff, since she claims that failure to recognize the significance of the informating potential – an 'intrinsic quality' – leads users to perpetuate the automating approach – a 'contingent' choice: work is rationalized through decreasing the level of dependence on human skill. In the absence of an informating perspective, information technology is assumed to have unintended consequences. In effect, information technology poses new and radical choices about work: 'the informating capacity of the new computer-based technologies brings about radical changes as it alters the intrinsic character of work' (1988: 11). Now the problem is that this 'intrinsic' character embodies a form of essentialism – it denies the mediated characteristics of *all* relations and asserts that some processes have qualities that are beyond interpretation, beyond the analyst's gaze. The essentialist position implies, for example, that it is the very act of typing which has 'intrinsic' characteristics that make it boring or exciting to experience. Note that this act cannot be both boring and exciting since this would assume that the qualities were attributed to the human typist, not the technical process of typing. This is precisely the point; since people do appear to experience what we conventionally assume to be similar actions as very different then it is this attributing process, rather than any inherent characteristic, that can best explain the divergences of experience.

Nevertheless, Zuboff's approach does not assume a deterministic tone since we can ultimately ignore the potential of informating technologies, but to do so is then to leave us open to 'dysfunctions'- which usually turn out to be the reproduction of the status quo. Dysfunctional for whom? might be the next question, but this is not something we will pursue here.

The significance of human interpretative action is displayed in the first two pages of Zuboff's book. In describing the nature of an airlock system, which is supposed to separate the bleaching area of a mill from its control room, Zuboff notes how the system is regularly subverted by the operatives:

They step through the inner door, but they do not wait for that door to seal behind them before opening the second door. Instead they force their fingertips through the rubber seal down the middle of the outer door and, with a mighty heft of their shoulders, pry open the seam and wrench the door apart ... the door is crippled. (1988: 21–2)

For Zuboff this example resonates with human resistance to technology; the action of the workers is not determined by the automatic doors because the workers interpret the doors as being too slow but potentially compliant. Nevertheless, this interpretative approach is only pursued in so far as the interpretation leads either to the realization of the technology's potential or its non-realization. In effect, the interpretative freedom enjoyed by Zuboff's humans is not extended to the technology. The impression given is that there can be no dispute over the potential capacity of the technology, just over whether or not this (actual) potential has been realized. The paucity of examples of fully realized potential suggests to us that interpretative dispute, not executive failure, is the key.

What precisely is this technical potential and why is IT so different? For Zuboff, IT marks the point of departure from a pre-automated industrial system which required considerable physical resources and provided commensurate opportunities for the acquisition of skills to an automated one which required less of the worker and provided correspondingly less in terms of facilities for skill acquisition. However, informating technologies, while requiring little in terms of physical input, since they require mainly symbolic manipulation, imply that new knowledge may be acquired through the same process.

For instance, in discussing the computerization of traditional pulp mills Zuboff argues that 'the medium of knowledge was transformed by the computers' (1988: 62). That is to say that, before computerization, workers used their sentient skills of touch and sight to 'know' what was happening; subsequently they were required to analyse electronic symbols for this same level of knowledge. The workforce associated this loss of 'immediate knowledge' of 'tangible objects' with a loss of control and sight; they were no longer able to 'feel the machine' (1988: 64). In the words of one, 'our operators did their job by feeling a pipe – "Is it hot?" We can't tell them it's 150 degrees. They have to believe it' (1988: 63). But does the computer have this objective 'effect' on the workers or is it the result of participants' interpretative action? Just how unmediated was the previous system? Feeling a pipe is not equivalent to feeling the water in the pipe. Their equivalence is established through conventions of practice and representation. Through interpretative practice, the mediation becomes discounted so that feeling the pipe comes to stand for feeling the water. This makes it difficult to see how in principle computer use could be any more or less mediated than the 'hands on' approach. Zuboff's approach assumes that sentient knowledge is not symbolic, but it is difficult to see how 'feeling the machine' can be anything but an exercise in symbolic manipulation. Does the novice on entering the mill immediately recognize the pulp as 'ready' or does she or he require some experience in interpreting symbols before this skill is acquired? This is not, of course, to say that the operatives (and Zuboff) are mistaken about their experiences. It simply reaffirms that their knowledge, constructed through discourse, is necessarily symbolic. What is crucial is not the (actual) 'effects' of the computers but the interpretations of the computer operatives.

Zuboff goes on to distinguish between 'action-centred skills' and 'intellective skills'. The distinction is manifest in a quote from an operator: 'Before computers, we didn't have to think as much, just react. You just knew what to do because it was physically there. Now, the most important thing is to learn to think before you do something' (1988: 74). Note here the assumption that action-centred skills are intuitive and learned wholly by experience of a physical presence: almost as if one can become an expert in (mechanical) pulp-milling without any mental activity! Zuboff further argues for a difference in the meaning system associated with a symbolic medium (computer) and an (allegedly) non-symbolic medium (non-computing artefact): 'In a symbolic medium, meaning is not a given value; rather, it must be constructed. This is a problem that action centred skills are not required to address. The medium of equipment and materials conveys its meaning in its own immediate context' (1988: 76). Zuboff attempts to demonstrate this by arguing that a pot handle gains its (undisputed) meaning through its immediate 'normal' context: 'the handle means that human hands grasp objects in particular ways' (1988: 76). Where a handle is in 'abnormal contexts' (photographs, paintings etc.) 'its meaning becomes problematic and must be constructed by the observer' (ibid.). But, to take an everyday example of a 'normal' British context, publicans frequently ask pint-drinkers whether they would like a handled glass or a straight glass. Does this imply that some pint-drinkers dispute the meaning of the handled glass? Surely, not, since Zuboff implies that meaning can only be problematic in abnormal situations. We would argue, then, that meaning is always constructed by the observer: why else should debutantes spend time learning to hold china cups with their little fingers pointing outwards, if not to differentiate themselves from 'popular' ways of grasping a handle on a tea cup? Why else would some non-Japanese regard the intricacies of cup-holding in the Japanese tea ceremony as bizarre, while some Japanese regard the cavalier approach of some Westerners as contemptible?

Yet Zuboff later appears to embrace the interpretative approach: 'Significance is not a transparent feature of the data from the system; rather, significance is a construction that emerges from the application of intellective skill to the available data' (1988: 80). But this interpretative approach is restricted to computer-mediated work since the computer mediates between the world and the worker in a way that, presumably, never used to occur. In itself this 'epistemological distress' as Zuboff calls it, is dubious, even for work processes like pulp-milling: do the operatives have direct – i.e. transparent – knowledge of *all* the pulp or just the portion they can see or smell or touch? Going further back historically, to a time when one might presume epistemological distress was not generated by machine mediation, did farmers 'know' what was happening to their seeds under the soil? Or to the seed's roots when the leaves emerged? Or did they also have to interpret from the data they had? Zuboff suggests not: 'in the world of action-centred skills ... the context allowed a worker to know what kinds of detail to look for and what kind of data to expect' (1988: 95). Unless we suppose farmers gain knowledge direct and 'unmediated' from the plant, without the use of any interpretative skills, it is difficult to accept Zuboff's claim. Her argument that computers are significantly different technologies because they informate the work process implies, for her, that symbolic manipulation and theoretical knowledge will rise to pre-eminence amongst the workforce. We would not wish to speculate whether or not this will come about. But on one thing she is clear: 'Managers must have an awareness of the choices they face, a desire to exploit the informating capacity of the new technology, and a commitment to fundamental change in the landscape of authority if a comprehensive informating strategy is to succeed. Without this strategic commitment the hierarchy will use technology to reproduce itself' (1988: 392).

In sum, it is not so much that Zuboff makes exaggerated claims for the capacities and effects of computer technology but that the symbolism and the interpretative nature of this technology undermine her assumptions about its objective capacity. In our approach, *all* technologies, by virtue of being cultural artefacts (Woolgar, 1996b), necessarily require and involve interpretative action. They are all symbolic media. It is not, then, that Zuboff is radical in her claim for the qualitative difference of computers from other machines, but that she is insufficiently radical and unreflexive about 'epistemological distress'. In effect, whether information technology will lead to a 'superpanopticon' or the technological empowerment of those currently in subordinate positions within organizations, is couched as a technicist question which implies technology has effects independent of interpretative action. Our argument is not that information technology is irrelevant, but that its relevance depends upon the mediating effects of the interpreter not the transparent effects of the technology.

Zuboff's more recent (1996) foray into the field reveals, if anything, a hardening of her attitude towards the coercive effects of technology. From a concern to establish the *choices* made available to managers through technological change, Zuboff has demonstrated her frustration at their apparent refusal to accept the invitation to the liberatory ball by suggesting that market forces will eliminate all those who reject the invitation. Where the new information technology still promises to replace the adversarial relationships of old, forged in the traditional hierarchies of command and control, she predicts their demise within twenty-five years, for: 'environmental conditions will select for success firms that proactively adapt their organizational methodologies to the moral, social and psychological requirements of an information economy' (1995: 17). Admittedly, she calls for a new social contract to be promulgated and for the old 'division of love' – between the haves (managers) and have-nots (workers) – to be displaced by a new form of co-operative endeavour but, beyond the humanist foundations there is only one driving force in this game: technology (see Willmott, 1995, for a 'political' critique of Zuboff's approach).

As we mentioned at the beginning of this chapter, the appeal to 'revolutionary' technology as a way of transcending the stalemate of organized conflict and dysfunctional hierarchies of command and control is not new. Let us close, and preface the final chapter, by comparing another 'hard' case where, eighty years ago, a previous technical revolution also promised the same answer to the same problem for the oldest profession in the world.

The First World War was fought on the basis of what Travers (1993) calls 'the cult of the offensive' in which the development of military technology, in particular fire-power, was subordinated to the cultural norms of combat. Such norms, at least from the British side, involved assumptions that war was traditionally won by superior willpower over technology. Hence, when it appeared that the war would generate huge numbers of casualties, the typical response of the military command was not to use technology to win the battle but to prepare for what would win the war: nerve in the face of deadly technology. Artillery would be used to 'soften' up the enemy but one's own troops would be 'hardened' by the enemy's artillery. Once this state of affairs had been achieved then the willpower of the two sides would be tested through the application of an 'old-fashioned' – and therefore respectable – form of human-technology network: the bayonet charge. As Brigadier General Kiggell argued in 1910: 'Victory is won actually by the bayonet charge or by the fear of it' (quoted in Travers, 1993: 67). Hence, when 'alien' technologies like the tank were deployed – against considerable resistance from many within the establishment – it was not as a revolutionary technology that could determine the outcome of the war but as a device to facilitate the 'necessary' attack by the infantry. Tanks were first deployed in action during the battle of the Somme in September 1916 and then during the Nivelle offensive (April 1917) and the battle of Cambrai in November 1917. In the latter battle 324 tanks were used to break through German lines, but ten days later the German's counter-offensive restored the land balance. Indeed, it was not the tank that broke the stalemate created by rigid hierarchies of command and control but a tactical change. Using small teams of fully trained and lavishly equipped elite 'storm troopers', where authority for decision-making was devolved down to the lowest officer in the field, the move from slow, methodological and mass attack to rapid, flexible and small attacks was instantly successful. The Spring offensive by the Germans in 1918 propelled them to the brink of victory and – ultimately – defeat as their very success exposed them to unsustainable casualties (Parker, 1995: 276–90). The technically determined 'victory' of the tank had failed because, amongst other things, it had not undermined what many considered to be the dysfunctional hierarchies of command and control. In short, the perception of the tank had critical and practical consequences for its use. Is there any reason to assume that computer technology will be more successful in removing hierarchies at work?

## Conclusion

In this chapter we have subjected a series of arguments and analyses about the relationship between technology and organization to a post-essentialist critique. Again, our point is not to assert the irrelevance of technology and its displacement by human actors and social forces, but to argue that the relevance of technology lies in actors' interpretative activities rather than in any objective account of its capacities or effects.

Whether Fordism was ever predominant, as a form of manufacturing production or economic regulation is not the issue here. Rather, we have been concerned with the relevance of technology in the development of Fordism and its alleged replacement, post-Fordism or flexible specialization. We have attempted to show that, despite the claims of many authors, technology neither dictates features of the manufacturing process nor has effects independent of the human actors involved. The objective effects of technology are anything but self-evident. In each case the effect of technology necessitates some form of human interpretation; even if debate about such effects may be brought to (temporary) closure, and a consensus constructed around the alleged effects, this consensus is socially constituted, not the result of an autonomously and exogenously imposed truth.

We then considered the issue of organizations as consumers of technology through the work of Kling and suggested that his research carries with it a much richer and more interpretative potential than he allows. It does seem that the symbolic aspects of technology are critical in their 'effects' and that no 'effect' can be known except through human articulation.

Finally, we considered the argument that computer technology is radically different from any other. Ultimately we found this approach, represented by Zuboff's work, lacking. Despite some equivocation about the 'effects' of technology, Zuboff's argument remains couched in the technicist vein. Against this, we insist on the need for careful interrogation of the assumptions and claims which inform our discussions of whether or not computer technology *is* revolutionary. Whether the machine, old or new, embodies a god depends crucially on the faith of the believer; no amount of contrary evidence will shake a zealot's belief in the wonders of the new technology. For the sceptic it is the zealot, not (just) the machinery which is the wonder to behold. In the final chapter we take the post-essentialist critique to its most difficult terrain: its social, political and moral consequences.

# 6

# What's Social about Being Shot?

The tanks had rolled forward to clear away the remaining students clustered around the Monument to the People's Heroes. Then a lone figure stepped into their path. For long minutes the man with the plastic shopping bag would not let the four Chinese Army tanks past.

Amnesty International report of a student, possibly called Wang Weilin, in Tiananmen Square, Peking, 1989

## Introduction

Our aim has been to explore the implications of recent social perspectives for our understanding of technology. We have surveyed various alternatives to bald technological determinism, noting in particular how these alternatives offer varying degrees of challenge to essentialist ideas about the nature and capacity of the machine. Thus, in chapter 1 we showed that, in many pluralist perspectives, technology was displaced as the single determining variable but, since it was reaccommodated as one among several variables, these perspectives retained their essentialist core. In chapter 3, we stressed the need to understand the processes whereby the apparently essential characteristics of the machine are built in: the socially contingent ways in which the *deus* becomes inserted into the *machina*. We proposed the metaphor of technology as text as a way of relating the contingent uses and interpretation (reading) of the machine to its design and development (writing). In chapter 4, we argued that even those approaches which advocate a strident anti-essentialism, notably many feminist and constructivist perspectives on technology, have yet to interrogate their own residual dependence on facets of essentialism. Post-essentialism is a programme which tries to go beyond anti-essentialism.

The whole thrust of our argument, then, has been to demonstrate the important implications of these new perspectives on technology for our thinking about the relation between technology and work, an area which has, on the whole, followed a determinist line by concentrating on the effects upon work organization of the introduction of new technologies. As we have seen, especially in chapters 2 and 5, these new perspectives propose considerably more flexibility in the interpretation, use and implementation of technology in work situations.

Our discussion has demonstrated the considerable variety and richness of the new perspectives on technology, which we shall generically term 'sceptical' – we have referred among others to pluralism, sociotechnical alignments, actor-network theory, constructivism, feminism, social shaping approaches, and anti-essentialism. However, there is considerable room for confusion arising directly from the degree of residual essentialism associated with each approach. Thus, for example, most commentators find the claim that an understanding of technology must 'take social factors into account' entirely unobjectionable in general terms. But when this is claimed to mean, as it is in some social constructivist approaches, that 'social factors' are largely responsible for what we come to accept as the technical capacity of a new technology, many find this entails an unacceptably high dose of scepticism. Moreover, this scepticism seems to pose severe problems for our engagement in social and political affairs: if there is no definitive truth, merely contending truth claims, then how can sceptics choose sides? And if they do not choose sides does this not allow the strong to prevail over the weak? As Law (1991: 4) has pointed out, it may seem odd that 'just at the moment when women appear to be finding a powerful political and analytic voice, it turns out that (some) men have suddenly discovered the virtues of epistemological pluralism'. Although we have already touched on these issues, here we want to go one step further and consider what might be regarded as a particularly 'hard case'. If what counts as the truth is socially constructed then surely constructivists must stand exposed in debates where the effect of the technology is obvious? How can anyone deny that, to take the example of Wang Weilin, a tank is inevitably going to win out against a unarmed civilian? However much Wang Weilin denied the determinism of the tanks facing him, many of his compatriots did not. Can it really be denied that a bullet has an objective effect upon human flesh? Relatedly, if scepticism 'impedes' social or political action because of its stance on truth claims, sceptics must presumably refuse to enter important policy debates concerning environmental damage, Aids or access to guns. According to the critics, scepticism must lead its adherents to disbelieve their own eyes and, by default, allow the environment to decay, Aids to go unchecked and gangsters to rule our streets. In this final chapter we want to tackle these epistemological and moral points head on by clarifying the sceptical stance on realist questions about morality and its relationship to epistemology. In its starkest form, 'what's social about being shot?'

## 'Excessive' relativism

Proponents of (some forms of) feminism regard many of these sceptical currents as simply beyond the pale. They are viewed as an extreme form of relativism which represents a distraction from the urgent demands of political action. What we described in chapter 4 as 'a failure of nerve' would be regarded by many anti-essentialists as the necessary stopping point beyond which further scepticism might jeopardize the possibilities of effecting change. This reaction assumes that political action requires a touchstone of analytic realism upon which (recommendations for) policy and action have to be based. But to what extent is this the case, and what disadvantages accrue from a move away from essentialism? Is there more to be lost than gained in equivocating our efforts to escape essentialism? To begin to address these questions, we first consider some specific objections to 'excessive' relativism as they have been directed to social constructivism.

For feminists such as Fox-Keller (1988), and for other anti-essentialists like Kling (1992) and Winner (1985, 1993), 'excessive' relativism implies a rejection of the possibility of establishing 'the truth' about technology or science or anything else. This might be largely inconsequential in a constructivist discussion about bicycle design (Pinch and Bijker, 1989): such analyses can throw critical light on historical processes with little fear of moral or ethical contention. But when it comes to an issue like patriarchy, they say, relativism is the font of moral compromise. Kirkup and Smith Keller (1992) put the point forcefully:

> epistemological relativism ... suggests that there are as many truths as individual people and that no single truth has any claim to be better that any other ... As a position it runs counter not only to the aims of science, but to those of feminism of the 1970s and '80s. Feminism as a theory and a political movement, claims that there are 'facts' and 'realities' about the position of women, such as rape, domestic violence and unequal pay that are a key to understanding sexual oppression, and that these have been hidden or distorted ... science and feminism have similar agendas in that they are both concerned to remedy distortion and move closer towards a more accurate description of how things are. (1992: 10)

Three issues are worthy of comment here. First, given the massive literature which contests traditional versions of science, the authors' summary invocation of the 'aims' and 'agenda' of science is contentious to say the least. Second, the authors charge that the relativist denial of a single reflective and objective truth hides the 'realities' of women's position. But the constructivist concern is precisely to support alternative truth claims rather than to side with prevailing ones. Constructivists can enrich the debate with their critical analyses of patriarchal claims to truth without automatically supporting the claims of feminists to be in possession of the alternative, truly 'real', truth. Do all feminists support the same interpretation of patriarchy? If not, then, in line with this kind of essentialism, it would follow that some feminists are in possession of the truth and others not. If, as has frequently happened, constructivists are accused of siding with the powerful in such disputes, then presumably they would be guilty of siding with the powerful feminists against the weak feminists, and so would still be no nearer the truth.

The third issue hinges on the assertion that constructivism surrounds itself with contending claims to truth between which it has no means of discriminating. Even on uncharitable interpretations of constructivism, however, this charge is misinformed. The constructivist does not assert that all claims have equal status; instead she asks which claims attract the most significant support and why. Take the example of domestic violence (by men on women). Kirkup and Smith Keller's essentialist view is that feminism, like 'science', is (and should be) intent on uncovering the truth about domestic violence, a truth allegedly hidden from view by patriarchal distortion. This approach implies that research can 'discover' the truth and that this discovery will lead, eventually at least, to mechanisms which prevent it. By denying objective truth, relativism is said, first, to allow its adherents either to sit on the fence and procrastinate about truth claims while women are battered or, second and worse, actually to sanction violence by accepting the proposition that, at any given time, the truth is the most successfully deployed discourse. The latter charge is simply wrong: assessing the strength of a truth claim through an analysis of its social construction is not equivalent to supporting that claim.

The former charge is more complex. The sceptical currents of anti-essentialism do leave one bereft of the certainties that might propel a political fanatic or religious fundamentalist; for these people the truth is self-evident and the line of action follows directly from such truth. For the sceptic there may, of course, be a pragmatic legitimation of action – doubts about truth claims are fine for the university seminar but too dangerous for the real world. Does this mean there is a clear limit to the application of Kant's injunction 'sapere aude' (dare to know)? Acquiescence in the politics of the real world – to which we are enjoined by critics of relativism – implies not just a pragmatic boundary but an epistemological, and ultimately political, flaw. Certainly Kling (1992) and Winner (1993) have attacked followers of this sceptical line for being politically naïve and implicitly conservative.

## The moral and epistemological case against scepticism

As should be clear from the previous chapters, and indeed as the discussion of the Luddite case demonstrated in chapter 2, the normative coloration of technology is hardly a new topic. Traditionally this debate has tended to centre on the political effects of technological developments or, more recently, on the inscribed politics of technologies. Sceptical approaches to technology have certainly attracted a considerable amount of hostility from social scientists of one form or another who perceive themselves to be defenders of the weak, and often defenders of the truth too. Hence Winner's (1993: 29) claim that constructivists have 'retreated into a blasé, depoliticized scholasticism'. Disinterested scepticism, it is claimed, merely leaves the field open to those who are already powerful – and by definition to people with problematic morals. On the other hand, sceptical approaches do suggest that traditional accounts be subjected to vigorous critique on epistemological, rather than moral, grounds: grounds that realists and traditionalists may find harder to reject. For example, powerful industrial corporations may be charged, by radical environmental scientists (supported by realist social scientists), with polluting the atmosphere; for the realist, a sceptical approach necessarily inhibits taking sides in the debate, and as a result the corporate polluters continue to pollute. Aside from the dubious assumption that the revelation of objective truth by committed social scientists is going to sway private corporate interests, the problem for realists is that the corporation is just as likely to generate alternative accounts of 'the truth' which demonstrate (claim) that the corporation is not a polluter. Where such 'truth' prevails the realist has no option but to accept that, indeed, the corporation is innocent of the charge. But for the sceptic the issue is not which side is telling 'the truth' – and should therefore be allowed to prevail – but why one side manages to persuade the actors who are involved in decision-making processes that their version of the truth is the only one, and why such debates have a tendency to dissolve into dualisms: truth and lies; right and wrong; good and bad. The realist concern for *the* truth invokes its opposite for all other accounts: if there is just one truth then everything else must be false. But to remain sceptical of truth claims does not imply that all such claims are 'truly' false; rather that all such claims are subject to sceptical enquiry. This permanent question-mark over the truth, then, makes it possible to maintain a scepticism about the corporate position whatever the 'evidence' deployed in its favour. Hence, when a public inquiry, hearing evidence from 'experts', 'proves' that pumping nuclear waste into the ocean is actually 'safe', the sceptic is much harder to enrol into the corporation's camp than the environmental realist.

Of course, just as realists engage in the practice of constituting objects through representation, most sceptics, as we pointed out in chapter 4, do precisely the same. Recognition of the constitutive function of truth claims is usually taken to be inconsistent with scepticism. As with many forms of relativism, the problem remains that a denial of objective knowledge is itself grounded in a consistency that smacks of objectivity. Whatever the philosophical tail-catching wrapped up in this debate, the significant effect, for liberal-minded realists at least, is the inability of relativists to develop sustainable normative critiques of the status quo. This is most typically expressed in the notion that if all accounts are equally valid (or invalid) then sceptics are barred from engaging with the practical ramifications of the debate. The argument is analogous to classical pluralists' notions of the role of the state in the development of civil society: since all elements of civil society are (ultimately) equal, the role of the state is to remain neutral. For radicals and liberals the upshot of non-engagement is to allow the strong to retain perpetual control of the ring while the state wanders round, impotent to intervene.

Before focusing on this issue in detail we need to specify the ground rules. Contrary to realist assumptions, scepticism about truth claims does not mean that constructivists accept all truth claims as equally valid. Their aim is to assess why some claims are considered true and others false, or some more true than others. To emphasize the constitutive function of representations does not entail accepting them all as equally true or untrue. Indeed, since there is a tendency for 'successful' truth claims to be deployed through the resources of powerful actors, constructivist critiques tend to deconstruct the claims of the powerful rather than those of the weak. In this sense, the constructivist approach has normative relevance, even though this does not depend on the inference that because the claims of the powerful are not objective the claims of the weak are objective. Instead, the scepticism is applied to any claim to have found the 'truth' or 'the only way for all humanity to prosper'. Being sceptical of truth claims, messiahs, and all things eschatological is one thing; being willing to join the march to the promised land is quite another. This makes Winner's (1993: 5) attack upon constructivism, for being 'self-consciously imperial', bizarre in the extreme.

Radder (1992), for example, suggests that constructivism can lead to absurd results. If discourse about the hole in the ozone layer ceased, he says, then 'the hole would simply disappear at the very moment we stopped discoursing about it' (1992: 156). It is not clear how this applies to constructivism. His point might be that our knowledge of the hole constitutes the hole, and that in the absence of any knowledge about it we have no way of knowing whether it exists or not. But this is not the same as saying: 'the truth is that there is no hole'. Nor is it the equivalent of saying: 'if we all stop discoursing about it the hole will disappear'; this implies that all knowledge of the hole can be erased from human memory and from its physical inscription. If this was the case, thanks to some fiendish alien plot to destroy the earth's atmosphere, then Radder's claim would be: 'although we have absolutely no knowledge of anything going on up there [the term 'ozone hole' would have been erased too presumably] we know there is truly a hole'. How, one is tempted to ask, can we know this to be true? It is not a question of saying it is *not* true but of asking how we know that it *is* true.

Notwithstanding the problems facing 'alienated' humans, how does a sceptical approach answer some of the more pressing demands of contemporary society? To answer this we choose the most 'difficult' case we can imagine, one in which the 'effects' of the technology are apparently self-evident, and where these effects are directly seen or experienced by ourselves, rather than through the accounts of others. It would also be helpful if the moral positions were clear-cut – with all decent social scientists on one side and the wicked of the world on the other: murder, rather than the link between poverty and population growth in the Third World, would be the preferable topic of debate. Further, if the side which the social scientists ought to support was the one which had the least resources and which was most in need of academic support, the sceptics would really be up against it. Finally, if the case also had its foundation within an archetypically male culture then all the necessary ingredients for the debate would be set up.

Thanks to a previous debate, Rob Kling (1991, 1992; see also Grint and Woolgar, 1992; Woolgar and Grint, 1991) has already provided such a scenario: how can social scientists stay out of the debate on the issue of gun control in the USA? (A similar scenario could be developed for the UK.) Realists might imagine that guns provide a case of a technology in which sceptics' allegedly dubious normative position can be clearly revealed and, realists might imagine, found wanting. Are not guns quintessentially technologies with clear-cut, objective effects; the most masculine of technologies; implicated in the destruction of hundreds of weaker members of society by stronger members; and is not the moral case against the right to bear arms the hallmark of all 'right-minded' (i.e. liberal/humane/decent/normal) people? If anything is a technical event, rather than a social construction, then being shot is it! How can being shot be regarded as a social construction and how can constructivists maintain a pious indifference to the bestiality of gun-related murders on the streets of our cities?

Note here the 'Manichean trap' which realists lay for the unwary sceptic. If sceptics are unwilling to decry bestial acts, it is assumed they must be in favour of them. It is relatively easy to parody this epistemological McCarthyism: those against hanging murderers are assumed to favour releasing them from prison. But if, to take other examples, sceptics hesitate to blame social evils on particular groups (drug-users, prostitutes, homosexuals, witches, gypsies, conservatives, socialists, trade unionists etc.) there may be good reasons for doing so. Does this mean that sceptics can only be *against* extremism and *against* absolutism because of their doubts about truth claims? Can sceptics be *for* anything if everything is relative?

Before entering the fray proper it is worth considering the ethics of the topic itself. After all, since guns are popularly regarded as the most macho of all masculine technologies, does a discussion centred around guns merely confirm the criticism that constructivism's disinterested approach to truth claims merely reproduces the culture of the powerful? (See Law's (1991) response to this claim.) In short, does a discussion of guns buttress patriarchy (Elam, 1994)?

We would argue the reverse. It is precisely because guns are an icon of masculine technology, and because being shot offers such a notoriously 'hard case' to deconstruct, that this topic forms the substance of our final chapter. If analysis of the military is left to normatively right-wing analysts does this improve the chances of normatively left-wing or liberal politicians or academics acting to restrain the influence of the military? Actor-network approaches to such topics focus on similarly powerful networks of actants to explain their powerful associations and there does seem to be a tendency to consider what Radder (1992) calls winners rather than losers: the more powerful not the less powerful. But those seeking to oust the powerful might do well to consider how that power is produced and reproduced if they intend to undermine it.

Yet the realists argue that the strong remain strong as the result of scepticism. For example, Kling (1992) argues that the most powerful voices in debates about computerization are the designers, sellers and government agencies directly involved:

> They have a stake in shaping the public discourse about computerization in a way which lets them advance their interests through unfettered experimentation ... And when organizations invest tens of millions of dollars in specific computerized systems/services, their agents and academic allies can be quite merciless in stifling serious social enquiry ... the key national discourses about technology are usually framed by commercial interests, except when there have been strong counter-movements, such as in the case of nuclear energy. (1992: 351)

Constructivists, it seems, are not just disinterested but actively neutral observers, allowing the rhetoric of the powerful to hold sway over the rhetoric of social scientists. Does this mean that Kling accepts our argument about the social construction of capabilities? To argue that technologies *do have* some inherent capabilities and simultaneously to struggle against the closure of debate is itself a tension-ridden approach. We would suggest that our approach to the inherent ambiguity of technical capability is supported precisely by the importance Kling allocates to social debate. It is *because* technology is ambiguous and the product of social construction that debate should not be stifled. If we could ascertain the capabilities of a technology in some objective manner then it would not matter whether debate was allowed – we would simply listen to disinterested experts, weigh up the 'facts' and decide on that basis. To acknowledge the social construction of technologies and texts (including this one) is not to proscribe practical engagement in policy issues. It is instead to set it on a different footing.

Kling takes his case one stage further in noting that: 'In the case of computing, this (constructivist) approach suggests that technologists, managers or politicians, have the legitimacy to talk about the social roles of technologies, while social analysts can only examine their discourse' (1992: 354). But to assert that technologists miss out on social issues is fundamental to, not a contradiction of, the sceptical approach. Further, our argument is not that scepticism must remain 'needlessly mute' (ibid.) on such issues but that engagement derives from analysis by those actors directly involved. We are not making, selling, buying, deploying, using, decrying, destroying or avoiding the technology; we are conducting research upon those who do. Far from making us mute, this provides us with the empirical data to assess the nature of human–technology relationships. So the sceptic does not suffer the 'self-denying ordinance' which Kling imagines to be characteristic of 'sociologists of technology'. Rather, the difference between us and Kling lies in the way we construe technology. For Kling:

> Sociologists of technology should be able to legitimately construct compelling narratives about technology ... They must also be able to make knowledge claims about technologies and their role in a social order, not just simply be commentators about others' claims ... They would deny SST [Social Studies of Technology] any legitimate possibility of substantively addressing issues where the use of technologies can play important roles in social welfare. (1992: 355–6)

The sceptical approach does not deny anyone, let alone sociologists, the freedom to construct any kind of narrative. The point is that such narratives – whether or not they are 'compelling' – are social constructs; they do not derive their force from transparently (re)describing the technical capacity of technology but by providing a (more or less) persuasive, and socially constructed, narrative. This does not mean that sociologists cannot engage in discussions about the role of technology in social welfare. Note here the moral coercion – sociologists qua defenders of the weak is fine but sociologists as supporters of something rather less liberal and humane ... Kling's own research on Riverville (see chapter 5) is a good example of disinterested sociological research generating knowledge that may be used to defend the weak from the powerful. If welfare funding is being funnelled into technology, yet the unofficial discourse of the users suggests that the technology is being purchased to support organizational images rather than fulfil official claims of increased efficiency, then the weak have a stronger case against the powerful.

Whether or not sociologists are actively engaged in policy-related issues, they cannot simultaneously claim that the discourse of the powerful is socially constructed (and distorted?), but that the discourse of the poor or of their friendly sociologist is a 'legitimately constructed compelling narrative' (therefore undistorted?). The sceptical approach tries to avoid determinations of distortion (or of the lack of it) and instead insists that constructed narratives are accounts, not reflections, of technical capacity.

What are the political, moral or practical consequences of this sceptical line? If one assumes that there is no single objective truth, only competing truth claims – accepting that not all claims are equal – does this imply a moral naïvety on the part of the sceptic that, by default, allows the accounts of the powerful to prevail over the accounts of the weak? Kling argues that the constructivists' stance leaves them unable to comment upon such emotive public issues as the relationship between guns and murder. Hence, while constructivists sit and twiddle their thumbs people are shot dead on the streets. For Kling and other liberal realists, it is not enough to be *against* suffering – one must be *for* specific policies derived from the 'truth' about the connection between guns and murder. There is, then, an implicitly better life to be had by all, if everyone adheres to the 'true' solution to life's problems.

There are several problems with this. First, let us reiterate the point that constructivists do not *necessarily* deny the existence of a world beyond our capacity to reconstruct it; the point is that our reconstructions of whatever it is are not true reflections of it. Thus it is not a question of saying 'guns don't kill anybody' but of asking how we know that, in this case, a particular causal relationship exists between gun ownership and murder.

Second, if the policy of the liberal realists derives from a 'true' picture of the world, what happens if 'the truth' as they see it, points the other way; for example, that gun ownership leads to a *decrease* in murder? (*Congressional Quarterly Researcher*, 1994). For the constructivist the 'truth' remains constructed, not reflected, the positional scepticism remains intact and there is no direct connection between accounts of the truth and necessary policies. But for the realist the case is much simpler and coercive – now he or she must accept the truth and should vote for a wider gun distribution. Indeed, some supporters of wider gun distribution in the USA have pointed to the 20,000 readership of the publication *Women & Guns*, the increasing numbers of women carrying guns (between 12 and 20 million according to the National Rifle Association), and to the fact that the NRA's current president is a women, Marion Hammer. From the car bumper sticker which asserts that 'God didn't make men and women equal, Samuel Colt did', to Laura Ingraham's (Washington attorney and self-styled 'activist') claim that: 'Smith & Wesson and the NRA are doing more to "take back the night" than the National Organization of Women and Emily's List' (quoted in The Guardian, 21 May 1996), there are clearly counterclaims to the 'truth' in this issue.

Let us take this argument in a (yet) more precarious direction: the death penalty. For the liberal realist the 'truth' is that there is no connection between the death penalty and the murder rate, hence liberals should support the abolition of the death penalty – even if the majority in many states tend to favour it. The constructivist is then accused of sitting on the fence because of his or her scepticism about the nature of the truth. This, it is said, leads the constructivist to avoid direct involvement in the case because they cannot offer any grounds for acting one way or the other. But what happens if future research, methodologically acceptable to realists, 'proves' that the death penalty does deter murder? (Presumably this really means that it reduces the murder *rate*, since the act of execution for any individual murderer implies the deterrent did not work.) The liberal realist then has a problem: to support the death penalty or accept an increase in the murder rate. But does this mean the constructivist has any better basis for a guide to action? In this case, the sceptic could remain very dubious about any such causal claims and more than reluctant to support any executions, both on the grounds of doubts about evidence and especially about irrevocable decisions based on such evidence. Hence, while the liberal realist may be coerced into supporting the execution of an alleged murderer – because of the truth as reproduced in the evidence of individual guilt and the truth about the effectiveness of the deterrent – the constructivist remains unconvinced by any truth claim. This does not mean that constructivists would allow all alleged murderers to walk free, but it does mean they would be dubious about sanctioning an act from which there is no recovery. As has often happened after sentencing, either to execution or imprisonment, evidence of innocence can appear after the event. For those executed this is usually a little late.

Thus, to return to the original argument, scepticism over claims about the connection between guns and murder does not entail constructivist support for the gun lobby. For liberal realists it becomes almost impossible to accept that anyone looking at the evidence would deny the truth as they see it; but for the anti-liberal realist gun supporter the same applies. Under these conditions it is the constructivist who may offer an explanation of the conflict that goes beyond the impasse of the 'you-are-lying-I-am-not' format. This still does not mean that constructivists have the answer to the problem of murder – or the answer to the related question – what is the (truly) good life? Constructivists, then, are not the kind of people to lead their followers into battle in pursuit of utopia; we have seen enough of this over the last 2,000 years and most of such battles have led to untold misery. Indeed, liberal realists should not condemn constructivists for failing to develop a model of utopia but rather consider why no model has yet appeared to resolve all human problems, and whether such utopias as do exist are more likely to compound the problem they set out to resolve.

But if we leave utopias aside there is still an epistemological problem. For Kling, the kind of scepticism embodied by constructivism appears to reduce socio-technical systems to social relationships, and hence render technology irrelevant. The charge of irrelevance makes constructivists appear as crazy as those who argue that 'guns don't kill people, people do' or, in the case of arguing that being shot is a social construction, attributes to constructivism the absurd position of denying that: 'it's much harder to kill a platoon of soldiers with a dozen roses than with well placed high speed bullets' (1992: 362).

Kling argues that calls for disinterested examination of claims made about technologies make sociologists unable to participate in the debate about gun sales. Sociologists are restricted merely to discussing the nature and terms of the debate, thereby leaving participation in it to self-appointed experts whose interests may not represent the interests of the population as a whole, let alone the victims of gun-related murders. As we have already noted, however, disinterested enquiry does not entail encouragement by default. Rather, radical interpretivism provides an insight into such debates that other approaches miss or suppress. For example, in the Gulf War, the 'fact' that the 'capacity' of Scud missiles to destroy lives in the Kuwait conflict was described by the military 'experts' as minimal appears not to have persuaded the population awaiting attack or watching events on television. Popular interpretation of a Scud's capacity for destruction – and the consequences for Israeli opinion – proved to be a more powerful narrative

form than the military version. If the allied forces had adopted an interpretative, rather than a 'technical capacity', approach to the Scud
threat, they may have operated in a rather different fashion early on.
As it was, the allied air forces appear to have spent a considerable
amount of time searching out Scud launchers specifically because they
came to accept that the popular interpretation of the threat was more
potent than their own. When many American lives were lost in a single
Scud attack even the military interpretation of its capacity altered.

Does this imply that we now know what a Scud can do or what a
Patriot can do to a Scud? Can we say that as a result of watching the
Gulf War TV coverage of laser-guided weapons, we actually now know
the effects of this technology? Once again, our knowledge is the upshot
of our interpretations of other people's interpretations. How do we
know how many weapons hit their targets and how many didn't? Why
should we believe one account but not another? Although the Patriot
system appeared to have undeniable effects upon Scud missiles, these
facts have recently been challenged. For example, Postol (1992) argues
that the system was inoperative during three attacks while software
errors were being resolved (one error apparently encouraged the
Patriot to attack underground missiles). Of 158 Patriots fired during the
war there is only detailed information on three of them. The truth
about the Patriot system technology is evidently a contingent temporary
upshot of complex interpretation. Relatedly, official accounts deny that
chemical or biological weapons were used against allied troops in the
Gulf War while many of the soldiers involved claim to be suffering the
consequences of a 'syndrome' that manifests itself in ways usually
related to precisely these kinds of weapons. How do we know which
side is telling the truth here?

Kling notes that, although the power of nuclear weaponry has been
deployed through narrative rather than actual use, it was the initial
effect of the two bombs on Hiroshima and Nagasaki which spawned the
narrative of terror. The sceptical point, however, is not to deny that
technology exists – we are not solipsists. Rather, our argument, in this
example, is that what the nuclear bombs 'did', and what they can 'do', is
not derived through a transparent reflection of the technical components of the bombs but results from the interpretative, narrative and
constructive work of various agencies and organizations (scientists, military experts, historians, victims etc.). We do not know precisely what a
bomb will do just by looking at it, nor just by watching it go off but by
reading or listening to accounts given by others (including ourselves).
We only need point to the controversy over the 'nuclear winter' predic-
tions and denials in the 1980s to note that nuclear 'experts' simply do
not agree on what nuclear bombs will 'do' nor on how accurate they are
(see MacKenzie, 1991). Some accounts may be more persuasive than

others, but they are still accounts, not definitive, uncontested and undeniable truths that are transferred in some unmediated fashion from the
technology directly to the humans: how do we know what the bomb
did? If we stood and watched it go off would we know then? If we read
all the technical reports of the scientists involved in the raid would we
know then? If we read everything about it would we know? In either of
these examples we still only know anything about the 'effect' of the
bomb by reading or listening or watching other people's reconstructions. In short we do not have to deny that the nuclear bombing of
Japan was influential in its surrender to deny a categorical truth about
what the bomb did. The nuclear bomb example seems infused with
mediations about its 'actual effects'. So let us turn instead to the apparently objective effects of a technology much closer to home.

## An onion model of the sociology of technology: between Russian roulette and a 'hard case'

A common strategy in sociological explanation is to choose a case or
example where one's theoretical perspective is least likely to apply. If
one can then show that in this hard case it does apply, one has the basis
for generalization to other 'less hard' cases. Probably the best-known
example is Goldthorpe et al., *The Affluent Worker* (1968). Initial scepticism about the *embourgeoisement* thesis was 'tested' in a setting which,
if the thesis held good, should have been one of the most 'embour-
geoised' areas in Britain. On the other hand, if 'in the cases we studied,
a process of *embourgeoisement* was shown *not* to be in evidence, then it
would be regarded as extremely unlikely that such a process was occurring to any significant extent in British society as a whole' (1968: 2). In
similar vein we now focus on a case which is particularly hard for the
sceptic position. To that end we have taken up the challenge of providing a social construction of Russian roulette.[1] If technology has no
'objective' effects – and these 'effects' are actually the result of social
reconstructions – is Russian roulette – and the likely result of a bullet
entering the flesh – also a social construction?

The realist argument is that the 'social aspects' of Russian roulette
are irrelevant in explaining the effect of the bullet on human flesh: a
bullet is a bullet and no amount of wishful thinking will wish it away. As
Kling (1992: 358) puts it:

> An analyst who argues that technologies do nothing by them-
> selves is staking a position close to the folk saying that 'guns don't
> kill, people do'. In contrast, I would speculate that an increase
> by 300,000 guns per year in pistol, assault rifle and associated

·ammunition sales to teenagers in Los Angeles would almost certainly increase the number of murders by shooting.

Kling accepts that to assume that a gun has a fixed capability does not
imply that it must be used in particular ways, nor does he deny that,
with the passage of time, the guns of today may have different meanings
for those who have them in future years:

> But in 1991, contemporary pistols and assault rifles also have
> unique capabilities of tearing flesh and splintering bone with high
> speed bullets, when compared with other kinds of weapons, such
> as knives and hands. Without a gun, it's hard to tear so much flesh
> and splinter so much bone so rapidly and readily and with such
> focus while standing ten feet away from the intended victim.
> Today, they also have special capabilities in expediting murders
> which should not be lost in endlessly iterative reinterpretations . . .
> physical objects like guns and roses, have some capabilities which
> are not only arbitrarily derived from the talk about them. It's
> much harder to kill a platoon of soldiers with a dozen roses than
> with well placed high speed bullets . . . the capabilities of specific
> technologies can be real enough that differences in the equipment
> and ways of organizing it do matter in ways that can't readily be
> neutralized by 'better talk' after the fact. (1992: 362)

Let us set out precisely the case against constructivism here: first, that
technologies *do* have specific capabilities; second, to deny this is to
assume that any technology can do anything providing the narrative is
persuasive enough. In short, our argument is, allegedly, that guns (and
any other technologies) are irrelevant; in contrast, the realist position is
that, at the heart of the socio-technical system, under all the social layers, lies a technical core which remains impervious to the sociologist's
gaze: a black box.

This concern for the core technical characteristics of technology, the
effects of which do not require interpretation, suggests the operation of
what we call an onion model of technology. Critics of sceptical positions
(like constructivism) seem to concede the existence of social and cultural 'factors' but tend to construe these layers surrounding a technical
core. This hard core resists social analysis. Once it is reached sociological analysis stops and objective technological description takes over. In
this instance, the model implies the core characteristics of a bullet,
which is impervious to social analysis and which has effects independent
of human interpretation. In what follows we descend through the various skins of the onion and attempt to demonstrate the various ways in
which it can be argued that being shot is a social process. As the descent

continues progress becomes more difficult. The effort in continuing to peel away layers increases. Ultimately, we suggest, it is only the surrounding layers and the associated difficulty of removing them which sustains the illusion that there is anything at the centre.

We might begin our descent through the onion skins by continuing the metaphor in the guns and roses couplet. What makes this a 'hard case'? After all, flowers are often related to death either through a causal analysis – didn't Socrates allegedly die from hemlock poisoning? – or one which highlights the symbolic significance of the wreath at funerals. But this is obviously not going to satisfy our critics – they could say we have barely scratched the surface.

From a social shaping approach it might be argued that the design of the revolver was the result of social factors – it could and did evolve in different directions, producing, for example, automatic pistols. Using an automatic pistol to play Russian roulette tends to alter the nature of the ritual – but once the trigger is pulled the technology 'takes over' and the bullet acts independently of the human user. The effect of the bullet is obvious. Of course, the design of the gun does not necessarily determine its deployment or use. A gun may jam or misfire – but if it does go off the effect of the bullet is again self-evident and independent of the social aspect of the situation.

At another level the argument can be reconstructed through a version of the actor-network approach – Russian roulette is not simply the experience of a bullet entering flesh but a complex social ritual which involves human and non-human actors in a potentially lethal 'game' of chance. The technological object – the bullet – is the end-product of prior social constructions, technical artefacts, contemporary social rituals and norms of human behaviour. Hence Russian roulette is a social, as much as a technological, phenomenon. At its crudest, being shot in battle or being shot in the back or being shot with an 88 mm shell or using a pistol other than a revolver does not equate with the rules of Russian roulette; hence Russian roulette is a particular kind of sociotechnical activity. Thus being shot playing Russian roulette is a social process, as well as a technical one. It is not, therefore, difficult to argue that Russian roulette is an inescapably social and cultural event, and not something simply determined by the technology. Even a standard dictionary (Collins, 1979) implies as much: 'a game of chance in which each player in turn spins the cylinder of a revolver and presses the trigger with the barrel against his own head'. There are (at least) six distinct aspects to this procedure:

1 It is a 'game' in that luck plays a significant part, though it is anything but a 'game' in terms of its potential consequences.
2 The game involves rule-bound behaviour; especially turn-taking.

3 Only a revolver is permissible.
4 Live ammunition must be used, but there must only be one bullet in the revolver at any one time.
5 There must be at least two participants who must spin the cylinder 'properly' and place the end of the barrel against the side of their own heads.
6 The participant with the revolver must then press the trigger once, if the gun does not go off he or she passes it to the next participant and so on until some resolution of the game is achieved. This usually involves one participant being shot.

Despite this kind of elucidation of the (social) rules, there remains the realist claim that, stripped of all the social and cultural aspects, there is a technical core – in this case the revolver and bullet – which affects humans irrespective of all the interpretative accounting. Once the bullet enters the flesh, doesn't the technical core take over?

Not according to some forms of actor-network theory (see Callon, 1986a, 1986b; Latour, 1988; Law, 1988, 1991), and social constructivism (for example, Bijker, 1995; Pinch and Bijker, 1987). In these approaches, being shot, either in the Sahara or Los Angeles, is not simply a technical act, not merely the experience of a bullet entering flesh, but a complex action involving human and non-human actors. The technological object – the bullet – is the end-product of prior social constructions and contemporary social actions. In this sense, being shot by a drug gang is a social process, as well as a technical one. This is perhaps best illustrated by noting that although handguns are the weapons most often cited in American murder cases it is knives that are allegedly used by most Asian and Native American murderers (Kastenbaum, 1991: 198).

This approach poses a fundamental problem for what we might call Kling's 'self-acting gun' argument: his distaste for the gun lobby's claim that 'guns don't kill, people do'. The gun lobby would have us believe that the guns are innocent tools in the hands of killers – one might argue here that providing automatic rifles to nuns would not result in an escalation of violence within a convent. The gun lobby's opponents try to persuade us that it is the ease of access to weapons that facilitates such actions. But both perspectives can be undermined if we assert that only when *potential* killers unite with guns do we have such problems: gun-less killers do not shoot people any more that killer-less guns do; but the fusion of human and non-human can lead to devastating results. This does not mean that we can abandon the interpretative approach in favour of an 'objective' analysis of weapons systems and psychopathology. What counts as a weapon that should be prohibited (pistols or automatic assault rifles or knives), and which individuals are liable to use them against other humans (known criminals, particular ethnic groups or 'nice liberals minding their own business on the subway'), are not issues that 'experts' have been able to agree on. It is not a question, therefore, of saying that the gun had an independent effect, because it only exists in the network as a result of its fusion with specific human actors. To break the network into its components parts – for the sake of analytic understanding – is to misunderstand the nature of the event as a holistic process.

Furthermore, this does not mean such an approach cannot be used in public debates. To assert that the Los Angeles problem is not related wholly to the availability of guns is not to support 'guns for children' but to support policies that go beyond the availability of guns. Guns are much more widely available in armies than in some of the world's poorest residential areas – but they do not automatically lead to higher murder rates in these armies than in our streets. Again, this does not mean we are indifferent to the sale of guns. It signals our rejection of the theory of 'the self-acting gun'. In practical policy terms this approach might well lead to a decrease in gun availability. The self-acting gun theory cannot distinguish between which British police officers should and should not be licensed to carry weapons. After the shooting of Steven Waldorf, a television technician shot in error by police in 1983, the number of police officers authorized to carry weapons decreased, according to the police, from 13,044 to 7,411 in 1992. It was said that 'glory seekers', 'weapons freaks', 'loners' and 'cowboys' are regarded as unfit to carry arms (*The Guardian*, 3 January 1992).

For the socio-technical alignment argument, for example Hill (1988), the revolver would only persist as a weapon if it was aligned with the cultural forces of the period. Such weapons are easier to obtain in the USA than in the Sahara desert precisely because of the cultural factors at work. Thus the problem facing Los Angeles is not one that would be reproduced in the Sahara. However, assuming that a weapon could be found in Sahara the bullet still has an independent effect upon human flesh: being shot in Los Angeles surely has the same effect as being shot in Sahara, doesn't it? Kling's own 'reconstructive interpretivism' would presumably consider the precise nature of the interacting elements involved and note the role of social and cultural forces in generating such an attack. For example, the comparative time involved in securing hospital treatment if one was shot in the Sahara or Los Angeles would very probably make a considerable difference to one's chances of survival. Similar kinds of arguments are made about the effects of blows to the head in professional boxing. It is thus said that many boxers would avoid cerebral atrophy and death if neurological treatment was close at hand for all fights. This argument implies that what we take to be precisely the same kind of blow to the head would have markedly different effects if delivered during the first Olympics 2,500 years ago rather than in the current games.

The crucial role played by social and cultural forces in the development and deployment of technologies of sport and war are, of course, related. Similar examples can be traced at different historical periods. For example, in ancient Greece the city states: 'entered into a convention among themselves to use against each other neither secret missiles nor those discharged from a distance' (Polybius, quoted in Connor, 1988: 19). These conventions primarily protected the Hoplites, heavily armoured Greek foot soldiers, from arrows, javelins and stones. Such missiles were the responsibility of lower-class Greeks who could not afford the armour of the Hoplite class and the agreement ensured that fighting between middle-class Greeks was a gentlemanly affair. That fifth- and sixth-century Greeks recognized that such technology could be valuable in war is manifest in its use against barbarians, that is, non-Greeks.

Another notable example of the cultural constraints on the technology of war is Henry V's difficulty at Agincourt in persuading his knights to butcher the captured French knights in retaliation for the French murder of the English baggage boys. The English knights simply refused to undertake such an ignoble action and it was left to the lower-class archers to do the grisly deed (Keegan, 1976: 108–12). A century later, the Japanese had their first taste of firearms. Yet even after the Meiji restoration in the second half of the nineteenth century there were still samurai rebellions which refused to use firearms, on the grounds that these were foreign and dishonourable weapons (Turnbull, 1989). Precisely what counts as dishonourable in war, of course, is very much influenced by culture. For example, Robert Graves, wading through the human and animal corpses on the Somme, noted that he was 'shocked by the dead horses and mules; human corpses were all very well, but it seemed wrong for animals to be dragged into the war like this' (quoted in Holmes, 1986: 106).

Probably the clearest example of the significance of this socio-technical alignment approach to more recent technical developments is James Fallows' (1985) account of the development of rifles used by the Americans in Vietnam. The American Special Services had disregarded the older M16 rifle in favour of the lighter Armalite which used smaller-calibre ammunition. This ammunition also allowed the shooter to maintain greater control when firing on automatic than was possible with the heavier-calibre M16. The latter may have been more accurate over long distances – a snipers' rifle – but was less useful in the close-range fire fights that conventionally happened in war. Despite this evidence the army retained the M16. According to Fallows' account, the army regarded the Armalite as an inappropriate weapon for several reasons.

First, the calibre was too small. For the army, a .22 was a boy's toy, a weapon which boys used to shoot squirrels back home. No self-respecting man went to war with such a toy. Second, the Armalite had a plastic stock – useful for reducing the weight of the weapon, but it could not be used to club an enemy. Third, the weapon had an effective range considerably less than the 1,000 metres plus of the M16. In sum, the Armalite was not the weapon for 'real' men. The Armalite Company retorted, using the experience of the American Special Forces, that most killings occurred within a 40 metre range – which was about all you could see in the Vietnamese jungle anyway – and that the lighter ammunition facilitated a much higher rate of fire than could be achieved with the M16. Furthermore, since the .22 tended to tumble on impact more than the heavier-calibre bullet, it was likely to cause a higher level of casualties (an argument relayed to British troops during the Second World War to account for Japanese weapons strategy (G.C. Grint, 1991). Moreover, since the effectiveness of the Armalite as a killing machine was far superior to that of the M16 there would be no need for a metal stock and, since the ammunition was lighter, far more of it could be carried. The army was eventually persuaded to take the Armalite, but only after insisting on an increased rifling and higher-velocity ammunition, all of which, according to Fallows, led to a significant deterioration in the weapon's effectiveness and to the death of a large number of American servicemen. A similar account can be reconstructed of the British army's refusal to adopt a smaller-calibre rifle at the end of the Second World War. Despite its alleged technical advantages it was rejected, amongst other reasons, for its ceremonial inadequacy. Soldiers bringing the gun to the 'present arms' position could not secure a 'decent-sounding slap' from its small frame (Lambe, 1992).

Having taken all these social and cultural aspects of war into account, does this not still leave the question of the effects of the bullet entering flesh? In what ways can lead tearing flesh sensibly be construed as a social construct (other than being an extraordinarily anti-social act)?

One approach might focus upon the way the results of the bullet are mediated by cultural influences. For example, whether the effects of a bullet or shell leads to immediate attempts to care for the wounded depends partially upon the gender of the wounded. As became clear in 1948, when female Israeli soldiers were shot, 'Men who might have found the wounding of a male colleague comparatively tolerable were shocked by the injury of a woman, and the mission tended to get forgotten in a general scramble to ensure that she received medical aid' (Holmes, 1986: 104). Exactly the same kind of arguments against deploying women in battle can be found in parts of the British army where women (officers) have only undergone weapons training since

1984 (BBC2, 7 July 1992). Similarly, the effect of shelling upon witnesses can depend not upon the shell's 'objective' effects but upon the
cultural mores of the witness. Even the level of pain is not determined
by the technological intrusion of the bullet or shell: not just in the sense
that drugs can numb the body to withstand any amount of physical
damage but also in the way that the apprehension of pain can be experienced as worse than the pain itself – a visit to the dentist will suffice for
this example. Experience of pain varies with the context (Scarry, 1985),
but at least with the dentist you know who is inflicting the pain. Russian
roulette is similarly transparent. But to be shelled by an unseen enemy
is something altogether different. As William Langer notes in his auto-
biographical account of the First World War: 'shellfire seemed a bit
unfair . . . the advantage is all with the shell and you have no comeback'
(quoted in Holmes, 1986: 232). Or, in the words of Paul Dubrulle, a
Jesuit priest serving in the French army in the same conflict, 'To die
from a bullet seems to be nothing; parts of our being remain intact; but
to be dismembered, torn to pieces, reduced to pulp, this is a fear that
flesh cannot support and which is fundamentally the great suffering of
the bombardment' (quoted in Holmes, 1986: 232–3).

But even if we accept the significance of social and cultural aspects of
war and weapons, this does not stop a bullet or shell having an objective
effect once it has hit the target, does it? It is one thing to argue that culture inhibits the deployment of technology but quite another to suggest
that the *effects* of technology are socially constructed. Let us move
down to another layer of the onion.

Consider the initial damage – as opposed to the subsequent effects
upon all and sundry. The first point is that it is not necessary to deny
that bullets may tear flesh and splinter bone to argue that it is nevertheless a social construction. If the gun goes off and the victim falls over
with a hole in his or her head you would have to be insufferably stubborn to deny that the bullet has made the hole. But the point is that
how we come to know that the bullet made the hole depends upon a
series of social (re)constructions. If the victim was dead or unconscious
or unaware of the dangers then he or she would not be able to account
for the injury. So only victims still conscious, or the shooter or those just
watching would be able to verify what had happened. Only those familiar with guns would assume a relationship between bullet and human
reaction: the assumption that the bullet made the wound is a cultural
assumption – those who are unfamiliar with such weapons would not,
and indeed in the North and South American experience of invading
Europeans did not, automatically connect the two. Only those certain
that the victim was not an actor in a film set would be fairly sure that
the wound was 'real'; only those actually present could verify the connection – the hospital surgeon retrieving the bullet could not guarantee

that the wound was caused by the bullet. In short, most people would have to take it on trust – a social construct – that the wound was caused by the bullet. We need look no further than the assassination of J. F. Kennedy to consider the difficulty of providing an irrefutable, 'objective' account of the damage caused by 'the bullet' – or was it two bullets?

This still leaves a knowledgeable agent who directly witnesses the events; is not this witness justified in claiming that the bullet caused the wound as a material and objective event, untainted by social processes? The circumstances leading to the event itself may have been a social construct but once the trigger was pulled the rest was non-social.

We beg to differ. It may be clear that something has happened but how that event is interpreted depends upon social factors, not technological ones. For example, it may be that the observer is unable to ascertain anything other than that the victim has suffered some form of injury; in the absence of sufficient medical knowledge (a social product) the observer cannot tell what the injuries are. But say the observer is medically proficient – surely we have now eliminated all the social aspects and are left with an objective analysis of the injury sustained? Well, do medical 'experts' necessarily (or even normally) concur on the extent and form of injury? It is not only in TV dramas that medical 'experts' disagree profoundly about the form of injury or illness a patient may have and, therefore, on the necessary form of medication or therapy.

Those who are familiar with weapons might want to ascertain the nature of the exit hole rather than entry hole in their assessment of the result: the effect, therefore, seems to depend upon levels of experience with bullets. But what if we have two soldiers who are identically experienced – would their account of the damage be the same? Being a soldier does not necessarily require medical knowledge; the medically ignorant might assert that the individual had been shot, that the exit hole was bigger than the entry hole, and that he or she had been shot in the chest, but that would be about all that could be said – and perhaps done – for the victim. A medically knowledgeable soldier, on the other hand, might want to suggest that the bullet had damaged the left ventricle but that the victim could be saved. Here, the same bullet appears to have different effects depending on the expertise of the person providing the account. But if we had two identically qualified individuals surely we would then get a transparent description of the effects of the bullet? We may do, but we may also get a disagreement. After all, the very phrase, a 'second opinion' is synonymous with the medical profession and implies that such expertise is not based upon transparent reflections of patients' problems.

But what if the victim is dead? Have we now reached the end of the social layers and hit the technical core? Perhaps not. First, we might want to argue that what counts as death is a social and cultural construct. For some Australian aborigines death can occur when an individual is expelled from the tribe. For some religions there is no death, there is just a transmutation from one bodily form to another. But let us forget all this cultural stuff, a dead body is a dead body isn't it? That depends; certainly the fear of premature burial was significant enough for the development of 'dead houses' where those defined as dead by doctors would be laid out – just in case they were not. In Mark Twain's (1883) graphic description of one such establishment in Munich:

> Around a finger of each of these fifty still forms, both great and small, was a ring; and from the ring a wire led to the ceiling, and thence to a bell in a watch room yonder, where, day and night, a watchman sits always alert and ready to spring to the aid of any of that pallid company who, waking out of death, shall make a movement – for any, even the slightest movement will twitch the wire and ring that fearful bell. (quoted in Kastenbaum, 1991: 30)

Does death, then, mean the absence of pulse, or fixed dilated pupils, or the absence of brain activity, or something else? Even if we narrow the definition down to 'brain death' (itself a relative newcomer deriving from 1959) we are still left with three different versions of this: 'whole brain death', 'cerebral death' and 'neocortical death'; the precise nature of each is not as important as the point that there is still disagreement as to which definition is the most acceptable (Kastenbaum, 1991), and, consequently, at what point in time the individual is deemed to be dead.

Nor are such disputes confined to medical journals or irrelevant because of their 'academic' nature. For example, some research by Kemp and Sibert (1991) on child drownings suggests that we should take great care in describing a person as dead. Between 1988 and 1989 330 children 'drowned' in England and Wales. Of these thirty-three were taken from the water with fixed dilated pupils (usually taken as a sign of death), and of these ten recovered fully, thirteen 'died' and ten survived with brain damage. One of those who survived had been under water for sixty minutes and had a body temperature of 23°C. The current record for recovery without brain damage is sixty-six minutes submerged, suffered in 1986 by Michelle Funk, aged 2 from Salt Lake City (*The Guardian*, 29 December 1995). Kemp and Sibert argue that under certain conditions (i.e. hypothermia) the requirement for oxygen is much reduced and thus 'dead' children can be brought back to 'life'. Since then, an accident in Wakefield, West Yorkshire, saw a medical team of twenty spend five hours trying to resuscitate three people who had been submerged under ice for two hours (*The Guardian*, 29 December 95).

Even when we leave the macro-level of collective statistics and descend to the micro-level of individual cases it is not always clear what counts as death – as Daphne Banks discovered in January 1996 having been pronounced 'dead' by her own doctor but subsequently pronounced 'alive' by the mortuary assistant preparing to put her body in a fridge (*The Observer*, 7 January 1996). Nor does the number of disagreements seem to decline with increased medical experience. Cameron and McGoogan's research (cited in Open University, 1992) compared correlations between diagnoses of death in 1,000 hospital autopsies which had previously been diagnosed by clinicians of various kinds. The pathologists' autopsies disputed 39 per cent of the clinicians' diagnoses of cause of death; 66 per cent of patients had discrepancies between clinicians' diagnosis and pathologists' autopsies. Now one might want to argue that discrepancies can be so minor as to be irrelevant to the argument about the social construction of evidence. However, Cameron and McGoogan suggest that in half the cases the discrepancies would have affected the treatment. One might also want to argue that, by definition, only difficult cases reach the pathologist so, again, the difficulty of diagnosis pre-exists the correlation between clinician's diagnosis and pathologist's autopsy. Yet in the case of myocardial infarction (one form of heart attack) 198 patients were diagnosed with this by both clinician and pathologist: in fifty-eight cases the clinician's positive diagnosis was not confirmed by the pathologist, and in fifty-one cases the clinician's negative diagnosis was disputed by the pathologist.

Of course, we might still want to argue that the clinician is seldom in the best position to diagnose the cause of death and thus we would expect the pathologist to be closer to the 'truth' than the clinician. But, first, the discrepancies between the two are large enough to suggest that clinicians are not the kind of people one should go to if one was feeling ill. Second, this implies that pathologists agree on the evidence – but do they? If the 'truth' is automatically reflected in the tissues of the body one might wonder how there can be a dispute over the cause of Robert Maxwell's death or whether Rudolf Hess really killed himself. How can pathologists disagree unless the evidence is in a perpetually opaque state?

And if we did get agreement on the diagnosis, is this the reflected truth or a consensual account of the effects? The argument that the effects of technology are socially constructed does not fail where a consensus forms; on the contrary, it is not that anyone's account is as persuasive as anyone else's but that certain individuals and groups are able to construct privileged accounts or narratives of technology which the rest of us tend to accept uncritically. One might, for example, be forgiven for assuming that we *know* that a lifestyle of smoking, high-fat diets and minimal physical activity are sure ways to make the chances of heart attack significantly higher; after all, countless medical experts have been saying as much for years now and there is a popular consensus that we now have the truth. However, David Barker's research suggests that many health problems can be traced back to the nutritional health of the mother, rather than the lifestyle of the subsequent individual (*The Observer*, 24 May 1992). The point here is not that Barker's research *proves* the geneticists or the environmentalists wrong but that it poses a question-mark over all such claims to objective truth – including those that appear to have settled into some form of consensus (see Payer, 1988 for other 'unsettling' accounts of cultural variation in the diagnosis and treatment of 'ill health').

Even at the very centre of the onion, then, we would argue that there is no residual technical core which is in principle impervious to social analysis. In principle layers can continue to be stripped away until it is evident that there is nothing at the centre. The layers themselves are what constitute the core. The incremental costs of removing further layers might persuade us to stop at any particular point. At that point the notion of the core becomes a convenient shorthand for the fact that we have been persuaded that further deconstruction is inappropriate. The 'effect' of a bullet in the head is no more transparent than the 'effect' of technology on society – both forms of argument depend on uninterrogated essentialism. Far from destroying the case for a sceptical approach, Russian roulette and the case of the self-acting gun provide evidence that even the most self-evident case of determinism is, to capture the metaphor, shot full of holes.

## Conclusion: truth as the basis for political action

The sceptical perspective on technology (in the examples above mostly a constructivist perspective) does not argue that technology (the bullet) is irrelevant, but it does argue that the process by which we come to know about its relevance is irredeemably social. Nor is it a consequence of sceptical perspectives that they make it impossible to engage in policy debates. Sociologists generally can 'make a difference' to the world they live in. They are better equipped to do so if they resist the convention that accounts of technology derive unproblematically from some technical essence.

We have argued throughout against grand narratives, against the pursuit of utopias and against those who, whatever their liberal pretensions, seek to outlaw alternative accounts. To assume that technology is impervious to social analysis – of whatever variety – is to subordinate oneself to what may be dubious truth claims. Rather, the capacity and effects of technology are essentially contingent. Our

knowledge of the capacity and effects of technology is socially constructed, not a technically transparent description. Although the technology becomes progressively 'harder' – that is, more costly – to
deconstruct as we move through each successive layer of the onion, this
is both possible and, in some circumstances, desirable.

We have already cast doubt, in general terms, on the presumption
that recommendations for political action have a coherent basis in anti-
essentialism. Independently of our position on the policy implications
of these diverse accounts, we remain sceptical of the theoretical
premises from which policies may flow. Some examples of policy recommendations can help us expose the incoherence of the analyses used
to justify them.

Consider, for example, the assertion that almost all forms of technology are essentially masculine. As a problem for women, this implies a
requirement for a feminine technology. In direct contrast to the claims
of some other feminists that what counts as masculine and feminine are
culturally and historically variable, this commits the essentialist to specify the enduring characteristics of essential masculinity/femininity. The
arguments tend to focus on a technology which does indeed appear
unvarying in space and time; it is asserted that military technology – or
just weapons, for example – have always been masculine. Yet knives,
for instance, have been used for a whole variety of purposes other than
wounding or killing others. Also, there is considerable evidence that
women would – if 'masculine regulations', or at least a powerful masculine culture, would allow them – become involved in all forms of military endeavour from the infantry to flying combat aircraft in war
(Dixon, 1976; Moskos, 1990; Shields, 1988; Wheelwright, 1992). For the
post-essentialist, what counts as a feminine technology lies in the interpretation, not in the technology itself – since our apprehension of what
the technology is requires that very interpretative effort. This is not to
say that technology constructed by women *and* consensually defined as
feminine would be irrelevant to the undermining of patriarchy. If the
significance of technology lies in the interpretation rather than in the
technology, then a radically feminist interpretation may well have some
influence in the policy arena. For example, if a computer destined for
use in schools was defined as 'girl-friendly' it may well dissuade boys
from attempting to monopolize it, thus providing greater opportunities
for girls to acquire high levels of computer literacy. Potential changes in
use now result from a different apprehension of the computer's gender,
rather than from an intrinsically 'female' computer.

For the anti-essentialist liberal feminist, the problem lies not in the
technology but the unequal opportunities which deter girls and women
from engaging with computers. As Kreinberg and Stage (1983: 28)
recount, with regard to US examples: 'The biggest barriers to women

taking advantage of the computer revolution are the myths and stereo-
types about technology that are well established in children's minds at a
very early age ... Changes must take place in schools and outside of
schools so that women will have equal access to computer technology.'
Thus, we are more likely to see support for female pupils and students
expressed in a variety of ways: advertising campaigns, more resources,
stronger targeting of female pupil and students, 'awareness' campaigns
and, perhaps, some provision for girl- or women-only computers and IT
courses. In effect, for the liberal, technology cannot be the problem and
it is far more likely that the problem lies in women's 'failure' to realize
their own potential.[2] It may or may not be coincidental that the great
majority of such policies appear, at least so far, to have been abject failures. Such policies will, in all probability, continue to fail, precisely
because they refuse to countenance the possibility that what we take to
be the same technology is apprehended in radically different ways by
different people. If the different people see technology differently, then
no amount of lens-cleaning will help. We need to recognize that people
are using different lenses rather than assume that some people are
wearing smudged glasses.

Thus one might want to question just how non-essentialist and liberal such a perspective really is. If the essentialist model is one in which
the 'essence' of a phenomenon explains its behaviour or actions, then,
although the liberal model rejects the idea that technology is distorted
through its male origins, it nevertheless implies that all humans, regard-
less of sex, have an essence. Admittedly, in the case of women, this
essence is distorted through the gendered inequalities that persist; but
once equal opportunities are deployed then the true and equal essence
of men and women will prevail. In effect both liberal feminist and eco-
feminist positions have at their heart a similar essentialist position.

We have argued that the anti-essentialism of much feminism and
(especially the designer technology variant of) constructivism precludes
a coherent basis for recommendations for political action – recommendations which, we have already said, may well be laudable on other
grounds. We have also said that charges of excessive relativism are misguided. Nonetheless, it might still be said, a commitment to the true
facts of the matter is surely a prerequisite basis for political action.

We believe this last point of view reveals a fundamental weakness in
this style of political radicalism. Research in social studies of science
and technology has repeatedly and overwhelmingly demonstrated
how truth is the contingent upshot of social action rather than its
prerequisite. Knowledge claims are deemed to be true as a result of a
particular concatenation of social relationships; truth is the ex-post
shorthand for agreement on a state of affairs; facts become true (facts)
by virtue of actors' beliefs; beliefs are not caused by true facts. More

specifically, we contend that the form of political radicalism which depends on essentialism misunderstands the relation between its claims and its putative audiences. Typically, essentialism assumes a relation between a knowledge claim and a passive receptive audience – the identity of which is usually left unexplicated – such that 'the truth will out'. Against this, research in a wide variety of areas, from literary theory to anthropology to social studies of technology, tells of the myriad processes whereby audiences are identified, defined, recruited, configured, enrolled and performed by the textuality of knowledge claims. The rhetoric of truth may feature as part of these processes, but this rhetoric is emphatically insufficient to guarantee the 'appropriate' audience response.

The essentialist elements of much anti-essentialism render feminism and constructivism inconsistent, hamper their renewal and testify to their lack of audacity.[3] In some respects, however, the same charge could be made about our own argument: to specify the faults of anti-essentialism we have had to specify its 'essential' features. Our articulation of the limits of constructivism and feminism entailed our specification of the essential character of these endeavours; our argument about their reliance upon the realist language game has itself been couched within the terms of that game. What is the consequence of this observation? One interpretation is that it simply casts doubt on the force of our criticism. We have hardly progressed much beyond the use of conventions which support and reaffirm essentialism; ours is an argument well within the 'tu quoque' (you too?) (Ashmore, 1989).

More interesting, however, is the sense in which this observation reinforces the argument we advance (but, admittedly, do not here exemplify). Adopting a post-essentialist mode seems to entail doing away with, or at least taking issue with, the 'critical attitude'. Whereas criticism is regarded as a token of the political motivations of its perpetrators, non-criticism is all too easily identified with a lack of politics. Thus realist conventions not only confine us to parameters of essentialist argument but also commit us to *a particular form of politics*. The question is, then, whether an exploration of alternative forms of post-essentialism can define an alternative form of politically relevant enquiry. Essentialism seems to constrain critical space. Should we not be exploring the possibility of defining a critical space which moves us beyond merely political radicalism?

So where does this leave our machined deity? Is it a god or a goddess? Does it matter anyway? We have suggested, against both essentialism and anti-essentialism, that the gender of a technology does not lie encased in the fabric of the material. It is instead the temporary, contingent upshot of ongoing interpretation by designers, sellers and users. The politics and values of technology, in this perspective, lie in the gaze of the human, not in the gauze of the machine. This does not mean that the machine is neutral. Since the machine, its capacities, and its representations are social constructions, not objective reflections, the machine always appears (to steal a phrase from Lévi-Strauss) cooked and never raw. Technological practices and descriptions of technology, by which we come to know it, necessarily embody social and political values, but these do not lie within the hard creases or soft folds of the machine. When a goddess or devil appears in machine form, we construct him or her. The truth of the nuclear bomb appears to combine two diametrically opposite truths: it is inescapably a political device, even a masculine machine, destined first to terrorize and then obliterate the entire human race (that is, the god of war); or it is a neutral amalgam of chemicals and metals destined to eliminate the threat of world war (that is, the deity designed to protect the human species). What the thing actually is, even what its exact capabilities and effects are, is not something that any kind of detached, objective or realist analysis seems capable of constructing. What it is depends on who is describing it, although not every account of it is equal: self-evidently, the eco-feminist account is not powerful enough to persuade political leaders completely to abandon the technology. But this is precisely why post-essentialism can provide resources for those seeking to change the world rather than just to account for it. If Foucault is right that truth and power are intimately intertwined, those seeking to change the world might try strategies to recruit powerful allies rather than assuming that the quest for the truth will, in and of itself, lead to dramatic changes in levels and forms of social inequality. If the deity in the machine is male, if technology in a patriarchal society is essentially masculine, then no amount of reiteration of this point will alter 'reality': would men really let power slip so easily from their grasp? But if the gendered significance of a technology lies in the interpretative framework within which it is constructed, then there is a possibility of deconstructing and subsequently reconstructing the technology. As Prometheus found to his cost, even male gods with magical technologies to empower men can find themselves powerless. But whether the deity in the machine is a god or a goddess – or just an actress or actor – depends crucially on the active construction achieved by the audience rather than the assembly of wood, wire and flesh on the stage.

# Notes

## Introduction: *Deus ex Machina*

1   The dramatic device dates from the 5th century BC; a god appears in Sophocles' *Philoctetes* and in most of Euripedes' plays to solve a crisis by divine intervention (*Encyclopedia Britannica*, 4: 41).
2   Perhaps the most bizarre example of this developed in (what was) the Soviet Union under Stalin when Alexei Gastev, then head of the influential Central Institute of Labour, designed and constructed a 'social engineering machine'. This machine, never completed, comprised an array of pulleys, wires and levers which was destined to make society, and therefore the Soviet people, ever more rational. Ultimately, it should have turned out perfectly rational humans, and one social engineering machine was to be installed in every major population centre across the entire Soviet Union (*Pandora's Box*, Channel 4, 11 June 1992). Here, truly, was a deity in machine form – albeit one that failed.

## Chapter 1   Theories of Technology

1   We subsequently broaden the discussion to refer to the tendency towards essentialism, the persistent assumption that entities contain essences, in a variety of literatures other than sociology of technology. Technicism can be understood as a particular example of essentialism, manifest in treatments and discussions of technology.
2   As we shall see, for example in ch. 5, proponents of constructivism themselves differ considerably as to which kinds of factors are responsible for constraining interpretations of technology.
3   See Grint (1991) for a review of technological determinism in industrial sociology.
4   See also n. 1.

5   This brief account does scant justice to the range of approaches which can be subsumed under the general 'constructivist' label. For an appreciation of some significant emerging differences see, for example, Pickering (1992), Lynch (1993) and Jasanoff et al. (1995).

6   It is a central feature of many arguments which deploy this ironicizing move – the 'same' technology but different interpretations/meanings – that they assert the essential unchanging character of the object which is being interpreted. See also Woolgar (1983, 1991a).

7   This contrasts with the sense of 'technology as a text' developed below in ch. 3.

8   Actor networks are also influential in the construction of received 'truth'. This is demonstrated in ethnographic analyses of laboratory life (Knorr-Cetina, 1981; Latour and Woolgar, 1986; Lynch, 1985) in which the messiness of science becomes progressively cleansed and tidied up into 'truth' through various 'inscription devices', devices which 'provide a visual display of any sort in a scientific text (Latour 1987: 68) and which, where successful, carry the 'truth' constructed by scientists far beyond their laboratory (see Latour, 1987; Pickering, 1992). Actor networks, then, feature human and non-human actors in a contingent and seamless web of relationships, which, through certain strategies – especially the transformation or institutionalization of human resources into non-human resources, either material (for example, in technologies) or symbolic (for example, in law) – may reduce the degree of inherent contingency (Grint, 1992).

9   See also ch. 2.

10  The link between technicism and aspirations to causal type explanation has important implications for questions of policy, to which we return in later chapters.

## Chapter 2   The Luddites: *Diablo ex Machina*

1   We cannot pretend to provide anything like a full history of the Luddites nor of the woollen industry in the late eighteenth and early nineteenth centuries (see Berg, 1987; Dinwiddy, 1979; Peel, 1968; Randall, 1982, 1986, 1988, 1991; Reid, 1986; Thomis, 1970; Thompson, 1968). Since our purpose is to illustrate and assess the utility of different analytic approaches to the relation between technology and society, we concentrate on the events in West Riding around 1812 – the area and time of the greatest physical resistance to the 'new' technology.

2   Although Smith was in favour of *laissez-faire* and the 'invisible hand', he was very antagonistic towards factory owners and their ilk; see Brown (1992).

3   Noble (1983: 13) takes this to mean that 1,000 *mills* were destroyed.

4   In line with our general argument about the contingency of interpretation of technical attributes, there is some ambiguity about which precise aspects of gig mill usage were prohibited by these earlier legal statutes. Randall (1991: 120) discusses how the Luddite clothiers pressed their own retrospective interpretations.

5   One implication of this is that different agents may have interpreted the 'problem' very differently. Thus, the West Country Luddites did not imbue

the technology with evil intent, but for the West Riding Luddites the problem *was* the technology.
6    See the quote from the York trial transcript on p. xx.

## Chapter 3    Configuring the User: Inventing New Technologies

1    Bromley (1994) lists further examples. Critical studies in education: do schools act systematically to reproduce the status quo or do participants in educational institutions regularly find ways to thwart the reproductive process? Women's history: are women victims or active agents? Policy sociology: are public policies to be imposed by the state or should they result from a 'policy cycle' of negotiation between all involved parties?

2    For a discussion of the different senses in which technology can be understood as a text, in an analysis of attempts to 'apply' constructivism in the sociology of technology, see Cooper and Woolgar (1993, 1994), Woolgar (1991a, 1996b).

3    Of course, the idea of 'playing against' a metaphor is itself to be understood metaphorically.

4    Unfortunately, this prevents us from making any detailed comments on the way the company name featured in talk between company members. In addition to the common shorthand reference to the company by the initials of its name (see also n. 6), some engineers played with the company name by rearranging a set of magnetic letters on one of the notice-boards, to form various cryptic, sometimes lewd, anagrams.

5    One reaction to the description below of the usability trials is that the company appears 'rather unscientific' in its testing. It is therefore worth stressing that despite (or perhaps because of) this, the company has been very successful.

6    Nobody I talked to in the company had any difficulty in using the acronym 'DNS' in a sensible way. Many were aware of the (intended) technical specifications, the broad purposes, the target market for this new computer. But even at an early stage in my time at the company, I met a surprising number of people who had difficulty telling me what DNS stood for. A standing joke which enjoyed popularity around the time of the first shipment went as follows:

'What's DNS stand for?'

'Don't No, Sorry!' (or 'Don't kNow, Squire!')

Several months after first shipment, a number of people were using a corruption of the acronym to refer to the machine as 'Dennis'.

When I once remarked upon the prevalence of these coded terms throughout the company (and the computer industry more generally), my colleague in hardware design initially looked blank. When I gave a few examples – DNS, RAM, ROM, IBM, MCA, etc. – he said, 'Oh, you mean all the TLAs'. TLA, he explained, means Three-Letter Acronym. (S.W.)

7    Somewhat less idealistic forms of scepticism suggest that the possibilities of different readings are only limited by imagination. Imagination, that is, of the different circumstances prevailing at the point of the reading being carried out.

8    In Smith (1978) and other textual analysts influenced by ethnomethodology, the deterministic status of the text is present although muted. The usual formulation is that the organization of the text provides for a particular reading. It thus delimits the interpretative options, rather than determining them.

9    The notion that the technical support section is the fount of the various 'atrocity stories' circulating in the company is developed in an analysis of hotline calls to the company (Woolgar, 1993a):

Why are personal computers so hard to configure? Dave Methvin relates a few horror stories.
DEAR MARGE, MY PC WILL NOT BOOT UP, WHAT SHOULD I DO?
Anyone who's worked with PCs for a while has a personal set of horror stories on configuration ... (*PC Week*, 20 March 1990, p. 6)

10   One of the engineers who read this passage proposed a counter-example: the isolated user who, by virtue of his isolation and lack of contact with the company, was forced frequently to reconfigure the machine on his own and had, as a result, built up a detailed knowledge of the inner workings of the machine while knowing nothing about the inner workings of the company. The example may be re-subsumed under the explanatory scheme proposed here by noting his isolation from other users, or at least from 'users' as projected by the company. In a sense, his isolation had had the effect of forcing him to become part of the company.

11   Newcomers with experience of microcomputer assembly in other companies would have little interest in the manufacturing induction.

12   For a further example of the symbolic value of the machine boundary, played against the metaphor of transgressing organizational boundaries, see the analysis of computer virus stories in Woolgar and Russell (1990).

13   Cf. the front cover of Woolgar (1991b). Pelaez (1990) similarly makes the analogy between protection of texts and of software by including a warning on the front cover of her paper: 'Anyone who opens this paper will be deemed to have agreed not to quote, copy, reproduce, communicate or otherwise divulge any of the ideas contained herein without being granted express licence in writing by the author.'

14   Other occasions include, notably, telephone calls to the company hotline. See n. 9.

15   We use 'settled' in an attempt to avoid the connotations of 'closure'. In the sociology of technology, 'closure' refers to the delimitation of different technological choices. For example, when bicycles (usually?) came to have two similar-sized wheels – rather than, say, the penny farthing configuration – technological closure is said to have occurred. 'Closure' in this usage refers specifically to a choice between design options. In the current case study, the focus is more generally on interpretation of capacity; 'settling' thus denotes a (temporarily) sufficient interpretation.

16   It could be argued that the identity of the user became more settled when the project code-name 'DNS' was superseded by the name chosen by marketing: 'Stratus'.

17   Once again, we should note the reflexive ties involved in these kinds of determination of 'fault'. It is not that faults occurring in machines under

development straightforwardly or unproblematically give rise to the machine being blamed when the user is an expert. Rather, fault assignation involves finding the error to be just-that-kind-of-error-associated-with-a-machine-under-development. Similarly, the assignation is not straightforwardly independent of the status of expert. Rather, this works in virtue of the expert's recognition of a fault revealing and displaying the sense in which she is being an expert.

18 The messages from the machine are, of course, designed to have a rough equivalent in self-diagnostics such as 'How did I get that?' and 'Where did I go wrong?' But this is only a rough equivalent. For a start the latter are questions addressed to self rather than to the machine, whereas the former are designed as informative diagnostic statements for consumption by the user.

19 This may be partly because, until recently, it had dealt with a homogeneous and fairly close-knit set of customers. Giving privileged access to a small number of these would have jeopardized their relationship with the wider body of customers.

20 The user products section had the idea of video-taping the trials. The idea of using the audio-tape recorder was mine. (S.W.)

21 However, I later discovered that it had been the practice to rewind the video-tape over sections where things had gone wrong, or where it had turned out to be embarrassing, or where it was thought boring. The (complete) audio record provides an interesting contrast, revealing which episodes were deemed (videographically) irrelevant as far the testers were concerned. (S.W.)

## Chapter 4   Some Failures of Nerve in Constructivist and Feminist Analyses of Technology

1 An earlier review of this field, by Wajcman (1991), is a good example of this kind of theoretical approach. Wajcman adopts an overtly anti-essentialist model and stresses the socially and culturally constructed nature of gender, with the implication that what counts as a patriarchal technology is a social not an objective, phenomenon.

2 We return, in ch. 6, to a critical evaluation of the assumption, often implicit in 'political' critiques of technology, that some form of essentialist (objectivist) account is a necessary basis for political (and policy) action (Elam, 1994; cf. Woolgar, 1992). In brief, the problem with this assumption is that it entails unexplicated preconceptions of the nature and identity of the relevant audiences, and of their motivations and user practices.

3 This view accepts there may be disagreements and ambiguities as to what precisely that technical capacity is, but holds *de facto* to the view that some objective view of technical capacity is in principle available.

4 For example, Winner (1993) makes much of the particular differences in antecedent circumstances selected by his approach and by members of what he calls 'social constructivism'.

5 The same problem occurs in some symbolic interactionist accounts of language which, bizarrely, speak of items having meaning 'attached to them'. (Oh, excuse me, my meaning has just fallen off.)

6     Similar equivocation over the realist basis of purportedly anti-essentialist arguments has been identified in the 'labelling theory' (Pollner, 1978) and 'social problems' (Woolgar and Pawluch, 1985) literatures.

7     Of course, it follows from our observation that practical argument conventionally entails realist auspices, that it is difficult for ontological agnosticism – when couched within these conventions – to make itself heard. For similar reasons, constructivist arguments are often decried for their (allegedly) absurd (ontological) implications, usually through appeal to the brute facts of material objects and/or death. See Edwards et al. (1992) and Ashmore et al. (1994).

8     We discuss below some implications of this point for own attempt to move away from essentialism.

9     Which means, of course, that no historian has (yet) done the constructivist work to (re)constitute these intentions. See Stanley (1992) for some artefacts designed by women that have been 'rediscovered'.

10    That strength is an attribute which can be enhanced through practices which are themselves gendered is not something we wish to go into here.

11    In considering objections to our analysis, it is evident that a whole series of auxiliary hypotheses can be mobilized to protect the central essentialist argument. It could be said, for example, that few scythes were in fact available to the sickle-wielding gangs of 1921, or that, by employing women part-time, Post Office managers were alerted to the inherently tiring prospects of making them carry loads full-time. It seems our charges of inconsistency can thus always be countered by the invocation of other antecedent circumstances which keep the basic essentialist characterization of the technology intact. This is a reflection of the conventional view that there is always more room for debate about antecedent circumstances than about the inherent properties of a technology.

12    See Margaret Atwood's *The Handmaid's Tale* for a fictional account of this scenario.

13    See n. 11.

14    This process has a very long history which we will not cover here (see Donnison, 1977; Ehrenreich and English, 1976; McNeil, Varcoe and Yearley, 1990; Oakley, 1976; Wajcman, 1991; Witz, 1986, 1990).

15    Rothschild (1983) coins the phrase dea ex machina to suggest not just that language is gendered but that women's role in the construction, development and deployment of technology is all but invisible and this has led to a particular relationship between people and technology. On both counts we would agree, though she does not go on to question whether the technology itself is gendered through the language or the language merely reflects the gender allegedly inherent to the technology.

16    As feminists have long since charged, language is not neutral in this scene nor, as (some) other anti-essentialists argue, is it a mere carrier of meaning: language may be gendered but is also the means by which meanings are constructed rather than reflected.

17    Or should that read: putting scare quotes around 'everything'?

18    Some moves in this direction can be found in explorations in reflexivity (Ashmore, 1989; Woolgar, 1988b); the creation of hopeful monsters (Law, 1991); cyborgs (Haraway, 1991) and quasi-objects (Latour, 1993).

## Chapter 6   What's Social about Being Shot?

1   The example was not of our own choosing but the result of an exchange of e-mail messages with Rob Kling.
2   See Cockburn (1991) and Kvande and Rasmussen (1986) on women's 'failure' in organizations.
3   Thanks to comments from Marianne de Laet for inspiring this section.

# References

Adorno, T. 1974: *Minima Moralia*. London: New Left Books.

Aguren, S., Bredbacka, C., Hansson, R., Ihregren, K. and Karlsson, K.G. 1984: *Volvo Kalmar Revisited: Ten Years of Experience*. Stockholm: Efficiency and Participation Development Council.

Albin, P. and Appelbaum, E. 1988: 'The Computer Rationalization of Work' in Jenson, J., Hagen, E. and Reddy, C. (eds.): *Feminization of the Labour Force: Paradoxes and Promises*. Cambridge: Polity Press.

Allen, J. 1992: 'Fordism and Modern Industry' in Allen, J., Braham, P. and Lewis, P. (eds.): *Political and Economic Forms of Modernity*. Cambridge: Polity Press.

Althusser, L. 1969: *For Marx*. Harmondsworth: Penguin.

Althusser, L. and Balibar, E. 1970: *Reading 'Capital'*. London: New Left Books.

Anderson, B.S. and Zinsser, J.P. 1990: *A History of their Own: Women in Europe from Prehistory to the Present*. Harmondsworth: Penguin.

Apple, M. 1992: 'New Technology: Part of the Solution or Part of the Problem?' in Beynon, H. and MacKay, H. (eds.): *Technological Literacy and the Curriculum*. London: Falmer Press.

Armstrong, P., Glynn, A. and Harrison, J. 1991: *Capitalism since 1945*. Oxford: Blackwell.

Ashmore, M. 1989: *The Reflexive Thesis: Wrighting the Sociology of Scientific Knowledge*. Chicago: Chicago University Press.

Ashmore, M., Edwards, D. and Potter, J. 1994: 'The Bottom Line: The Rhetoric of Reality Demonstrations'. *Configurations*. 2, 1–14.

Atkinson, J. 1985: 'Flexibility: Planning for an Uncertain Future'. *Manpower Policy and Practice*, 1 (Summer), 26–9.

Badham, R. 1990: 'Machine Metaphors and Conspicuous Production'. Paper presented to the CRICT seminar series, Brunel University, October.

Baines, S. 1992: *Living with Information Technology: Women, Men and the Adoption of Home Computing in Distance Education*. Newcastle: University of Newcastle Programme on Information and Communication Technologies, Working Paper No. 5.

Bansler, J. 1989: 'Trade Unions and Alternative Technology in Scandinavia'. *New Technology, Work and Employment*, 4, 2, 92–9.

Barker, J. and Downing, H. 1985: 'Word Processing and the Transformation of Patriarchal Relations of Control in the Office' in Mackenzie, D. and Wajcman, J. (eds.): *The Social Shaping of Technology*. Milton Keynes: Open University Press.

Barley, S. 1986: 'Technology as an Occasion for Structuring: Evidence from Observation of CT Scanners and the Social Order of Radiology Departments'. *Administrative Science Quarterly*, Vol. 31, pp. 78–108.

Barley, S, 1990: 'The Alignment of Technology and Structure through Roles and Networks'. *Administrative Science Quarterly*, 35, 61–103.

Bates, T., Kaye, T., Kirkup, G., Laurillard, D. and Stannett, C. 1988: *Applying IT to Education and Training*. Milton Keynes: Open University Press.

BBC2. 1992: *Women at Arms*. 7 July.

Beaumont, G. 1812: *The Beggar's Complaint*. (repr. 1972). New York: Arno Press.

Beirne, M. and Ramsay, H. 1988: 'Computer Redesign and Labour Process Theory' in Knights, D. and Willmott, H. (eds.): *New Technology and the Labour Process*. London: Macmillan.

Bell, D. 1960: *The End of Ideology*. Glencoe, Ill.: The Free Press.

Bell, D. 1973: *The Coming of Post-industrial Society*. New York: Basic Books.

Berg, A.J. 1991: *He, She and I.T. – Designing the Technological House of the Future*. Trondheim: Institute for Social Research in Industry, IFIM Paper No. 12/91.

Berg, A.J. 1992: 'The Technological House of the Future'. Paper presented to the CRICT seminar series, Brunel University, May.

Berg, M. 1980: *The Machinery Question and the Making of Political Economy 1815–1845*. Cambridge: Cambridge University Press.

Berg, M. 1987: 'Workers and Machinery in Rule, J. (ed.): Eighteenth Century England' in Rule, J. (ed.). *British Trade Unionism 1750–1850: The Formative Years*. London: Longman.

Berger, P. and Luckman, T. 1966: *The Social Construction of Knowledge*. Garden City, NY: Doubleday.

Berggren, C. 1989: 'New Production Concepts in Final Assembly – the Swedish Experience' in Wood, S. (ed.): *The Transformation of Work?* London: Unwin Hyman.

Berggren, C. 1990: *Det Nya Bilarbet*. Lund: University of Lund Archiv Dissertation Series, No. 32.

Berggren, C. 1992: *The Volvo Experience: Alternatives to Lean Production*. London: Macmillan.

Bijker, W.E., Hughes, T.P. and Pinch, T. (eds.) 1987: *The Social Construction of Technological Systems*. Cambridge, Mass.: MIT Press.

Bijker, W.E. and Law, J. (eds.) 1992: *Shaping Technology/Building Society*. Cambridge, Mass.: MIT Press.

Bimber, B. 1990: 'Karl Marx and the Three Faces of Technological Determinism'. *Social Studies of Science*, 20, 331–51.

Bishop, A. and Simpson, D. 1991: 'Toys for the Boys'. *The Higher*, 22 November.

Bland, A.E., Brown, P.A. and Tawney, R.H. (eds.) 1963: *English Economic History: Select Documents*. London: Bell and Sons.

Blauner, R. 1964: *Alienation and Freedom*. Chicago: Chicago University Press.
Bloor, D. 1976: *Knowledge and Social Imagery*. London: Routledge and Kegan Paul.
Bobbio, N. 1987: *The Future of Democracy*. Cambridge: Polity Press.
Bocock, R. 1992: 'Consumption and Lifestyles' in Bocock, R. and Thompson, K. (eds.): *Social and Cultural Forms of Modernity*. Cambridge: Polity Press.
Braverman, H. 1974: *Labor and Monopoly Capital*. New York: Monthly Review Press.
Briggs, M. and Jordan, P. 1958: *Economic History of England*. London: University Tutorial Press.
Bromley, H. 1994: 'The Social Chicken and the Technological Egg'. Paper read to the American Educational Research Association Annual Meeting, April.
Brown, G. 1977: *Sabotage*. Nottingham: Spokesman Books.
Brown, V. 1992: 'The Emergence of the Economy' in Hall, S. and Gieben, B. (eds.) *Formations of Modernity*. Oxford: Polity Press.
Brontë, C. 1974: *Shirley*. Harmondsworth: Penguin.
Bruland, T. 1985: 'Industrial Conflict as a Source of Technical Innovation: The Development of the Automatic Spinning Mule' in MacKenzie, D. and Wajcman, J. (eds.): *The Social Shaping of Technology*. Milton Keynes: Open University Press.
Burnes, B., Knights, D. and Willmott, H. (eds.) 1988: *New Technology and the Labour Process*. London: Macmillan.
Burns, P. and Doyle, M. 1981: *Democracy at Work*. London: Pan.
Button, G. (ed.) 1993: *Technology in Working Order: Studies of Work, Interaction and Technology*. London: Routledge.
Callon, M. 1986a: 'The Sociology of an Actor Network' in Callon, M., Law, J. and Rip, A. (eds.): *Mapping the Dynamics of Science and Technology*. London: Macmillan.
Callon, M. 1986b: 'Some Elements of a Sociology of Translation: Domestication of the Scallops and the Fisherman of St Brieuc Bay' in Law, J. (ed.): *Power, Action and Belief: A New Sociology of Knowledge?* London: RKP.
Callon, M. 1991: 'Techno-economic Networks and Irreversibility' in Law, J. (ed.): *A Sociology of Monsters: Essays on Power, Technology and Domination*. London: Routledge.
Callon, M. and Latour, B. 1992: 'Don't throw the baby out with the Bath school! A Reply to Collins and Yearley' in Pickering, A. (ed.): *Science as Practice and Culture*. Chicago: Chicago University Press.
Cavendish, R. 1982: *Women on the Line*. London: Routledge and Kegan Paul.
Chabaud-Rychter, D. 1995: 'The Configuration of Domestic Practices in the Designing of Household Appliances' in Grint, K., and Gill, R. (eds.): *The Gender–Technology Relation*. London: Taylor and Francis.
Clark, J., McLoughlin, I., Rose, H. and King, R. 1988: *The Process of Technological Change in the Workplace*. Cambridge: Cambridge University Press.
Cockburn, C. 1983: *Brothers: Male Dominance and Technological Change*. London: Pluto Press.
Cockburn, C. 1985: *Machinery of Dominance: Women, Men and Technical Know-How*. London: Pluto Press.
Cockburn, C. 1991: *In the Way of Women*. London: Macmillan.
Cohen, G.A. 1978: *Karl Marx's Theory of History: A Defence*. Princeton, NJ:

Princeton University Press.

Cole, G.D.H. and Wilson, A.W. 1965: *British Working Class Movements: Select Documents 1789–1875*. London: Macmillan.

Collins, H.M. 1985: *Changing Order: Replication and Induction in Scientific Practice*. London: Sage.

Collins, H.M. 1986: 'The Core Set and the Public Experiment'. Unpublished manuscript, cited in Mackenzie, D., Rudig, W. and Spinardi, G. 1988: 'Social Research on Technology and the Policy Agenda: An Example from the Strategic Arms Race' in Elliott, B. (ed.): *Technology and Social Process*. Edinburgh: Edinburgh University Press.

Collins, H.M. and Yearley, S. 1992: 'Epistemological Chicken' in Pickering, A. (ed.): *Science as Practice and Culture*. Chicago: Chicago University Press.

Confederation of Japan Automobile Workers' Unions (CJAWU) 1992: *Japanese Automobile Industry in the Future: Towards Coexistence with the World, Consumers and Employees*. Tokyo: CJAWU.

*Congressional Quarterly Researcher*, 1994: 4, 22, 507–22. Washington, DC: Quarterly Inc.

Connor, W.R. 1988: 'Early Greek Land Warfare as Symbolic Expression'. *Past and Present*, 119, 3–29.

Conti, R. 1992: 'Work Practice Barriers to Flexible Manufacturing in the US and the UK'. *New Technology, Work and Employment*, 7, 1, 3–14.

Cooley, M. 1968: *Architect or Bee?* Slough: Langley Technical Services.

Cooley, M. and Crampton, S. 1986: 'Criteria for Human Centred Systems'. Paper presented to the Working Conference on Production Systems, CIM Europe, Bremen, May.

Coombs, R., Knights, D. and Willmott, H. 1990: 'Culture, Control and Competition: Towards a Conceptual Framework for the Study of Information Technology in Organizations'. Paper presented to the CRICT seminar series, Brunel University, May.

Cooper, G. 1990: 'Context and its Representation'. Paper presented to the Discourse Analysis Workshop, University of Lancaster, 25–6 September.

Cooper, G. and Woolgar, S. 1993: *Software is Society made Malleable: The Importance of Conceptions of Audience in Software and Research Practice*. Brunel University: CRICT Research Policy Paper, No. 25.

Cooper, G. and Woolgar, S. 1994: 'Software Quality as Community Performance' in R. Mansell (ed.): *Information, Control and Technical Change*. London: Aslib.

Corea, G. et al. 1985: *Man-Made Women: How New Reproductive Technologies Affect Women*. London: Hutchinson.

Coulter, J. 1989: *Mind in Action*. Cambridge: Polity Press.

Cowan, R.S. 1983: *More Work for Mother: The Ironies of Household Technology from the Open Hearth to the Microwave*. New York: Basic Books.

Crossman, E.R.F.W. 1966: 'Taxonomy of Automation'. Paper presented at the Conference on the manpower aspects of automation and technical change. Paris: OECD.

Culley, L. 1986: *Gender Differences and Computing in Secondary Schools*. Loughborough: University of Loughborough, Department of Education.

Culley, L. 1988: 'Girls, Boys and Computers'. *Educational Studies*, 14, 1, 17–31.

Dain, J. 1991: 'Women and Computing'. *Women's Studies International Forum*, 14, 3, 217–55.

Dankbaar, B. 1988: 'New Production Concepts, Management Strategies and the Quality of Work'. *Work, Employment and Society*, 2, 1, 25–50.

Dankbaar, B. and Hertog, F. den. 1990: 'Labour Process Analysis and Socio-technical Design: Living Apart Together?' *New Technology, Work and Employment*, 5, 2, 122–34.

Darvall, F.O. 1969: *Popular Disturbances and Public Order in Regency England*. Oxford: Oxford University Press.

DES (Department of Education and Science). 1986: *Education Statistics for the United Kingdom*. London: HMSO.

Dierkes, M. and Hoffman, U. (eds.) 1992: *Research on the Social Shaping of Technology in France, Germany, Norway, Sweden, the United Kingdom and the United States*. Berlin: Wissenschaftszentrum Berlin für Sozialforschung and Hoffmann.

Dinwiddy, J. 1979: 'Luddism and Politics in the Northern Counties'. *Social History*, 4, 1, 33–63.

Dixon, N.F. 1976: *On the Psychology of Military Incompetence*. London: Futura.

Dobbins, J. 1990: 'Good For Business, Death for the Joy of Work: An Ethnography of Quality in a Microcomputer Company'. Unpublished B.Sc. dissertation, Brunel University.

Donnison, J. 1977: *Midwives and Medical Men: A History of Inter-Professional Rivalries and Women's Rights*. London: Heinemann.

Doray, B. 1988: *From Taylorism to Fordism*. London: Free Association Books.

Du Gay, P. 1996: *Consumption and Identity at Work*. London: Sage.

Dumont, L. 1977: *From Mandeville to Marx: The Genesis and Triumph of Economic Ideology*. Chicago: Chicago University Press.

Dundelach, P. and Mortensen, N. 1979: 'Denmark, Norway and Sweden' in International Labour Office: *New Forms of Work Organization*. Geneva: ILO.

Dunlop, C. and Kling, R. (eds.) 1991: *Computerization and Controversy*. San Diego, Ca.: Academic Press.

Dutton, W.H. 1988: 'The Automation of Bias' in Open University: *An Introduction to Information Technology: Social and Technological Issues* (DT200). Milton Keynes: Open University Press.

Easlea, B. 1983: *Fathering the Unthinkable: Masculinity, Scientists and the Nuclear Arms Race*. London: Pluto Press.

Edge, D. 1973: 'Technological Metaphor' in Edge, D. and Wolfe, J. (eds.): *Science in Context*. London: Tavistock.

Edge, D. 1988: *The Social Shaping of Technology* Edinburgh: University of Edinburgh PICT Working Paper, No. 1.

Edwards, D., Ashmore, M. and Potter, J. 1992: *Death and Furniture: The Rhetoric, Politics and Theology of Bottom Line Arguments against Relativism*. Loughborough: University of Loughborough, Department of Social Sciences.

Edwards, P.N. 1990: 'The Army and the Microworld: Computers and the Politics of Gender Identity'. *Signs: Journal of Women in Culture and Society*, 16, 1, 43–59.

Ehrenreich, B. and English, D. 1976: *Witches, Midwives and Nurses: A History of Women Healers*. London: Writers and Readers.

Elam, M. 1994: 'Anti Anticonstructivism, or Laying the Fears of a Langdon Winner to Rest'. *Science Technology and Human Values*, 19, 1, 101–6.

Elliott, D. 1980: 'The Organization as a System' in Salaman, G. and Thompson,

K. (eds.): *Control and Ideology in Organizations*. Milton Keynes: Open University Press.

Equal Opportunities Commission. 1983: *Information Technology in Schools*. Manchester: EOC.

ERGO. 1984: *Workshop on Production Technology and Quality of Working Life*. Gothenburg: Volvo Publications.

Fallows, J. 1985: 'The American Army and the M-16 Rifle' in MacKenzie, D. and Wajcman, J. (eds.): *The Social Shaping of Technology*. Milton Keynes: Open University Press.

Farrant, W. 1985: 'Who's for Amniocentesis? The Politics of Prenatal Screening' in Homans, H. (ed.): *The Sexual Politics of Reproduction*. Aldershot: Gower.

Faulkner, W. 1985: 'Medical Technology and the Right to Heal' in Faulkner, W. and Arnold, E. (eds.): *Smothered by Invention: Technology in Women's Lives*. London: Pluto Press.

Featherstone, M. 1990: 'Perspectives on Consumer Culture': *Sociology*, 24, 1, 5–22.

Finnegan, R. and Heap, N. 1988: *Information Technology and its Implications*. Milton Keynes: Open University Press.

Firestone, S. 1970: *The Dialectic of Sex*. New York: William Morrow.

Fish, S. 1980: *Is There a Text in This Class? The Authority of Interpretative Communities*. Baltimore: Johns Hopkins University Press.

Foucault, M. 1980: *Power/Knowledge*. Brighton: Harvester.

Foucault, M. 1984: *Discipline and Punish*, excerpts in Rabinow, P. (ed.): *The Foucault Reader*, Harmondsworth: Penguin.

Fox-Keller, E. 1988. 'Feminist Perspectives on Science Studies'. *Science, Technology and Human Values*, 13, 2, 235–49.

Francis, A. 1986: *New Technology at Work*. Oxford: Oxford University Press.

Freeman, C. 1987: 'The Case for Technological Determinism' in Finnegan, R. et al. (eds.): *Information Technology: Social Issues*. Milton Keynes: Open University Press.

Friedman, A.L. (with D.S. Cornford). 1989: *Computer Systems Development: History, Organization and Implementation*. Chichester: John Wiley.

Gallie, D. 1978: *In Search of the New Working Class*. Cambridge: Cambridge University Press.

Garfinkel, H. 1967: *Studies in Ethnomethodology*. Englewood Cliffs, NJ: Prentice-Hall.

Gartman, D. 1979: 'Origins of the Assembly Line and Capitalist Control of Work at Ford' in Zimbalist, A. (ed.): *Case Studies on the Labor Process*. New York: Monthly Review.

Gatrell, V.A.C. 1994: *The Hanging Tree*. Oxford: Oxford University Press.

Gay, P. 1973: *The Enlightenment: An Interpretation. Vol. 2: The Science of Freedom*. London: Wildwood House.

Gergen, K.J. 1992: 'Organization Theory in the Postmodern Era' in Reed, M. and Hughes, M. (eds.): *Rethinking Organization: New Directions in Organization Theory and Analysis*. London: Sage.

Gerver, E. 1985: *Humanizing Technology*. London: Plenum Press.

Giddens, A. 1979: *Central Problems in Social Theory*. London: Macmillan.

Giddens, A. 1984: *The Constitution of Society*. Cambridge: Polity Press.

Giddens, A. 1985: *The Nation State and Violence*. Cambridge: Polity Press.

Gill, C. 1985: *Work, Unemployment and the New Technology*. Cambridge: Polity Press.

Godelier, M. 1980: 'Work: The Words used to Represent Work and Workers'. *History Workshop*, 10, 164–74.

Golby, J.M. (ed.) 1986: *Culture and Society in Britain, 1850–1890*. Oxford: Oxford University Press.

Goldthorpe, J.H., Lockwood, D., Bechofer, F. and Platt, J. 1968: *The Affluent Worker: Industrial Attitudes and Behaviour*. Cambridge: Cambridge University Press.

Gordon, R.B. 1988: 'Who Turned the Mechanical Ideal into Mechanical Reality?' *Technology and Culture*, 30, 4, 744–78.

Gray, A. 1987: 'Behind Closed Doors: Women and Video' in Baehr, H. and Dyer, G. (eds.): *Boxed In: Women on and in TV*. London: Routledge.

Gray, R. 1987: 'The Languages of Factory Reform in Britain, 1830–1860' in Joyce, P. (ed.): *The Historical Meanings of Work*. Cambridge: Cambridge University Press.

Grint, G.C. 1991: Personal communication.

Grint, K. 1991: *The Sociology of Work: An Introduction*. Cambridge: Polity Press.

Grint, K. 1992: 'Sniffers, Lurkers, Actor-Networkers: Computer-Mediated Communications as a Technical Fix' in Beynon, J. and Mackay, H. (eds.): *Technological Literacy and Education*. London: FalmerPress.

Grint, K. 1993: 'Japanisation? Some Early Lessons from the British Post Office'. *Industrial Relations Journal*, 24, 1, 14–27.

Grint, K. 1995: *Management: A Sociological Introduction*, Cambridge: Polity Press.

Grint, K. and Gill, R. (eds.) 1995: *The Gender–Technology Relation*. London: Taylor and Francis.

Grint, K. and Willcocks, L. 1995: 'Business Process Reengineering in Theory and Practice: Business Paradise Regained?' *New Technology, Work and Employment*, 10, 2, 99–109.

Grint, K. and Woolgar, S. 1992: 'Computers, Guns and Roses: What's Social about Being Shot? *Science, Technology and Human Values*, 17, 3, 366–80.

Gunzburg, D. 1978: *Industrial Democracy Approaches in Sweden*. Melbourne: Productivity Promotion Council of Australia.

Habermas, J. 1971a: *Towards a Rational Society*. London: Heinemann.

Habermas, J. 1971b: *Knowledge and Human Interests*. London: Heinemann.

Hacker, S. 1989: *Pleasure, Power and Technology*. London: Unwin Hyman.

Haddon, L. 1988: 'The Home Computer: The Making of a Consumer Electronic'. *Science as Culture*, 2, 7–51.

Hamilton, P. 1992: 'The Enlightenment and the Birth of Social Science' in Hall, S. and Gieben, B. (eds.): *Formations of Modernity*. Cambridge: Polity Press.

Hammerström, O. and Lansbury, R.D. 1991: 'The Art of Building a Car: The Swedish Experience Re-examined'. *New Technology, Work and Employment*, 6, 2, 85–90.

Hammond, J.L., and Hammond, B. 1948: *The Village Labourer*, vol. 2. London: Guild Books.

Hammond, J.L., and Hammond, B. 1949: *The Town Labourer (1760–1832)*, vol. 1. London: Guild Books.

Handy, C. 1978: *Gods of Management*. London: Pan.

Håpnes, T. and Rasmussen, B. 1992: 'The Production of Male Power in Computer Science'. Paper presented to the CRICT seminar series, Brunel University, May.

Håpnes, T., and Sørenson, K. 1995: 'Competition and Collaboration in Male Shaping of Computing: A Study of a Norwegian Hacker Culture' in Grint, K., and Gill, R. (eds.): *The Gender–Technology Relation.* London: Taylor and Francis.

Haraway, D. 1991: *Simians, Cyborgs and Women: The Reinvention of Nature.* New York: Routledge.

Harding, J. (ed.) 1986: *Perspectives on Gender and Science.* London: Falmer Press.

Heilbroner, R. 1972: 'Do Machines Make History?' in Kranzberg, M. and Davenport, W.H. (eds.): *Technology and Culture: An Anthology.* New York: Meridian.

Held, D. 1980: *Introduction to Critical Theory: Horkheimer to Habermas.* London: Hutchinson.

Heller, F. 1987: 'The Technological Imperative and the Quality of Employment'. *New Technology, Work and Employment,* 2, 1, 19–26.

Hill, C.P. 1961: *British Economic and Social History 1700–1939.* London: Arnold.

Hill, S. 1981: *Competition and Control at Work.* London: Heinemann.

Hill, S. 1988: *The Tragedy of Technology: Human Liberation Versus Domination in the Late Twentieth Century.* London: Pluto Press.

Hirsch, E. 1995: 'New Reproductive Technologies and the "Modern Condition" in Southern England' in Grint, K., and Gill, R., (eds.): *The Gender–Technology Relation.* London: Taylor and Francis.

Hirschauer, S. and Mol, A. 1995: 'Shifting Sexes, Moving Stories: Feminist/Constructivist Dialogues' in Woolgar, S. (ed.): *Feminist and Constructivist Perspectives on New Technology.* Special issue of *Science, Technology and Human Values* 20, 3.

Hirschhorn, L. 1984: *Beyond Mechanization.* Cambridge, Mass.: MIT Press.

Hobsbawm, E. 1964: 'The Machine Breakers' in Hobsbawm, E. *Labouring Men.* London: Weidenfeld & Nicolson.

Hobsbawm, E. and Rude, G. 1969: *Captain Swing.* London: Lawrence and Wishart.

Holmes, R. 1986: *Firing Line.* Harmondsworth: Penguin.

Horkheimer, M. and Adorno, T. 1972: *Dialectic of Enlightenment.* New York: Herder and Herder.

Hounsell, D. 1984: *From the American System to Mass Production 1800–1932: The Development of Manufacturing Technology in the United States.* Baltimore: Johns Hopkins University Press.

Hoyles, C. (ed.) 1988: *Girls and Computers.* London: Institute of Education, Bedford Way Papers, No. 34.

Hughes, M., Brackenridge, A., Biby, A. and Greenhough, P. 1988: 'Girls, Boys and Turtles: Gender Effects in Young Children Learning with Logo' in Hoyles, C. (ed.): *Girls and Computers.* London: Institute of Education, Bedford Way Papers, No. 34.

Hughes, T.P. 1979: 'The Electrification of America: the Systems Builders'. *Technology and Culture,* 20, 1, 124–62.

Hughes, T.P. 1987: 'Evolution of Large Systems' in Bijker, W.E., Hughes, T.P.

and Pinch, T. (eds.): *The Social Construction of Technological Systems.* Cambridge, Mass.: MIT Press.

Hutton, W. 1991: *The Guardian*, 16 September.

Inglis, B. 1971: *Poverty and the Industrial Revolution.* London: Panther.

Jasanoff, S., Markle, G.E., Petersen, J.C. and Pinch, T. (eds.) 1995: *Handbook of Science and Technology Studies.* London: Sage.

Jayaweera, N.D. 1987: 'Communication Satellites: A Third World Perspective' in Finnegan, R., Salaman, G. and Thompson, K. (eds.): *Information Technology: Social Issues.* Sevenoaks: Hodder and Stoughton/Open University Press.

Jenkins, D. 1978: *The West German Humanization of Work Programme: A Preliminary Assessment.* Aston University Work Research Unit Occasional Paper No. 8.

Jennings, H. 1995: *Pandemonium: The Coming of the Machine As Seen by Contemporary Observers.* London: Macmillan.

Jessop, B. 1989: 'Conservative Regimes and the Transition to Post-Fordism: The Cases of Great Britain and West Germany' in Gottdiener, M. and Komninos, N. (eds.): *Capitalist Development and Crisis Theory: Accumulation, Regulation and Spatial Restructuring.* London: Macmillan.

Jones, B. 1987: 'Flexible Automation in Britain: Societal Conditions and Social Consequences'. Paper presented to the conference on the social problems of the introduction of flexible automation, Turin.

Jones, B. 1988: 'Work and Flexible Automation in Britain: A Review of Developments and Possibilities'. *Work, Employment and Society*, 2, 4, 431–80.

Jones, B. 1990: 'New Production Technology and Work Roles: A Paradox of Flexible versus Strategic Control' in Loveridge, R. and Pitt, M. (eds.): *The Strategic Management of Technological Innovation.* Chichester: John Wiley.

Jones, S.R. 1994: 'The Origins of the Factory System in Great Britain: Technology, Transaction Cost or Exploitation?' in Kirby, M.W. and Rose, M.B. (eds.): *Enterprise in Modern Britain.* London: Routledge.

Joyce, P. 1992: *Visions of the People: Industrial England and the Question of Class.* Cambridge: Cambridge University Press.

Kamata, S. 1982: *Japan in the Passing Line.* New York: Pantheon.

Kaplinsky, R. 1984: *Automation: The Technology and Society.* Harlow: Longman.

Kastenbaum. R.J. 1991: *Death, Society and Human Experience.* New York: Macmillan.

Keegan, J. 1976: *The Face of Battle.* Harmondsworth: Penguin.

Kelly, J. 1982: *Scientific Management, Job Redesign and Work Performance.* London: Academic Press.

Kemp, A. and Sibert, J. 1991: 'Cold water deaths can be reversed'. *The Guardian*, 19 April.

Kerr, C., Dunlop, J.T., Harbison, F.H. and Myers, C.A. 1964: *Industrialism and Industrial Man.* London: Oxford University Press.

Kidder, T. 1982: *The Soul of a New Machine.* Harmondsworth: Penguin.

Kimble, C. and McLoughlin, K. 1992: 'The Impact of Integrated Computer-based Information Systems on the Roles and Skills of Managers: Some Evidence from Case Studies'. Paper presented to the PICT national conference, Newport, March.

Kirkup, G. 1992: 'The Social Construction of Computers: Hammers or Harpsichords?' in Kirkup, G. and Smith Keller, L. (eds.): *Inventing Women: Science, Technology and Gender*. Cambridge: Polity Press.

Kirkup, G. and Smith Keller, L. 1992: 'The Nature of Science and Technology' in Kirkup, G. and Smith Keller, L. (eds.): *Inventing Women: Science, Technology and Gender*. Cambridge: Polity Press.

Klawe, M. and Leveson, N. 1995: 'Women in Computing: Where are we Now?' *Communications of the ACM*, 38, 1, 29–35.

Klein, R. 1985: 'What's "New" about the "New" Reproductive Technologies?' in Corea, G. et al.: *Man-Made Women: How New Reproductive Technologies Affect Women*. London: Hutchinson.

Kling, R. 1991: 'Computerization and Social Transformation'. *Science, Technology and Human Values*, 16, 3, 342–67.

Kling, R. 1992: 'Audiences, Narratives and Human Values in Social Studies of Technology'. *Science, Technology and Human Values,* 17, 3, 349–65.

Knorr-Cetina, K.D. 1981: *The Manufacture of Knowledge*. Oxford: Pergamon Press.

Knorr-Cetina, K.D. 1982: 'The Constructivist Programme in the Sociology of Science'. *Social Studies of Science*, 12, 32–4.

Kramarae, C. 1988: *Technology and Women's Voices*. London: Routledge.

Kreinberg, N. and Stage, E.K. 1983: 'Equals in Computer Technology' in Zimmerman, J. (ed.): *The Technological Woman: Interfacing with Tomorrow*. New York: Praeger Publishers.

Kumar, K. 1978: *Prophecy and Progress: The Sociology of Industrial and Post-Industrial Society*. London: Penguin.

Kuper, A. 1994: *The Chosen Primate: Human Nature and Cultural Diversity*. Cambridge, Mass.: Harvard University Press.

Kvande, E. and Rasmussen, B. 1986: *Who Lacks Courage – the Organizations or the Women?* Trondheim: Institute for Social Research in Industry. NOTAT Paper No. 5.

Laet, M. de 1993: Discussants' remarks in the workshop on European Theoretical Perspectives on New Technology: Feminism, Constructivism and Utility. CRICT, Brunel University, 16–17 September.

Lambe, K. 1992: Personal communication.

Lass, A.H., Kiremidjian, D. and Goldstein, R.M. 1994: *Dictionary of Classical and Literary Allusion*. Ware, Herts.: Wordsworth.

Latour, B. 1987: *Science in Action*. Milton Keynes: Open University Press.

Latour, B. 1988: 'The Prince for Machines as Well as for Machinations' in Elliott, B. (ed.): *Technology and Social Process*. Edinburgh: Edinburgh University Press.

Latour, B. 1991: 'Technology is Society made Durable' in Law, J. (ed.): *A Sociology of Monsters: Essays on Power, Technology and Domination*. London: Routledge.

Latour, B. 1993. *We Have Never Been Modern*. Hemel Hempstead: Harvester Wheatsheaf.

Latour, B. and Woolgar, S. 1986: *Laboratory Life: The Construction of Scientific Facts*. Princeton, NJ: Princeton University Life.

Law, J. 1986: 'On the Methods of Long Distance Control: Vessels, Navigation and the Portuguese Route to India' in Law, J. (ed.): *Power, Action and Belief: A New Sociology of Knowledge?* London: RKP.

Law, J. 1987: 'Technology and Heterogeneous Engineering: The Case of Portuguese Expansion' in Bijker, W., Hughes, T.P. and Pinch, T. (eds.) *The Social Construction of Technological Systems*. Cambridge, Mass.: MIT Press.

Law, J. 1988: 'The Anatomy of a Socio-technical Struggle' in Elliott, B. (ed.): *Technology and Social Process*. Edinburgh: Edinburgh University Press.

Law, J. 1991: 'Introduction' in Law, J. (ed.): *A Sociology of Monsters: Essays on Power, Technology and Domination*. London: Routledge.

Lazonick, W. 1985: 'The Self-acting Mule and Social Relations in the Workplace' in MacKenzie, D. and Wajcman, J. (eds.): *The Social Shaping of Technology*, Milton Keynes: Open University Press.

Leavitt, H.J. and Whisler, T.L. 1958: 'Management in the 1980s'. *Harvard Business Review*, 36, 41–8.

Lee, C.H. 1986: *The British Economy since 1700: A Macroeconomic Perspective*. Cambridge: Cambridge University Press.

Leeson, R.A. 1979: *Travelling Brothers*. London: Granada.

Littler, C.R. (ed.) 1985: *The Experience of Work*. Aldershot: Gower.

Lowe Benston, M. 1983: 'For Women the Chips are Down' in Zimmerman, J. (ed.): *The Technological Woman: Interfacing with Tomorrow*. New York: Praeger Publishers.

Lynch, M. 1985: *Art and Artifact in Laboratory Science: A Study of Shop Work and Shop Talk in a Research Laboratory*. London: Routledge and Kegan Paul.

Lynch, M. 1993: *Scientific Practice and Ordinary Action: Ethnomethodology and Social Studies of Science*. Cambridge: Cambridge University Press.

MacKenzie, D. 1984: 'Marx and the Machine'. *Technology and Culture*, 25, 473–502.

MacKenzie, D. 1991: *Inventing Accuracy: A Historical Sociology of Missile Guidance*. Cambridge, Mass.: MIT Press.

MacKenzie, D., Rudig, W. and Spinardi, G. 1988: 'Social Research on Technology and the Policy Agenda: An Example from the Strategic Arms Race' in B. Elliott (ed.): *Technology and Social Process*. Edinburgh: Edinburgh University Press.

MacKenzie, D. and Wajcman, J. (eds.) 1985: *The Social Shaping of Technology*. Milton Keynes: Open University Press.

McLoughlin, I. 1991: 'Human-Centred by Design? The Adoption of CAD in the UK'. *AI and Society*, 5, 296–307.

McLoughlin, I. and Clark, J. 1988: *Technological Change at Work*. Milton Keynes: Open University Press.

McNeil, M. (ed.) 1987: *Gender and Expertise*. London: Free Association Books.

McNeil, M., Varcoe, I. and Yearley, S. (eds.) 1990: *The New Reproductive Technologies*. London: Macmillan.

Marcuse, H. 1964: *One Dimensional Man*. Boston: Beacon Press.

Markus, M.L. and Robey, D. 1988: 'Information Technology and Organizational Change: Causal Structure in Theory and Research'. *Management Science*, 34, 5, 583–98.

Marx, K. 1954: *Capital*, vol. 1. London: Lawrence and Wishart.

Marx, L. 1964: *The Machine in the Garden: Technology and the Pastoral Idea in America*. Oxford: Oxford University Press.

Marx, L. 1988: *The Pilot and the Passenger: Essays on Literature, Technology and Culture in the United States*. Oxford: Oxford University Press.

Mathews, J. 1989: *Tools of Change: New Technology and the Democratization of Work*. London: Pluto Press.

Mathias, P. 1969: *The First Industrial Nation*. London: Methuen.

Mendels, P. 1995: 'Who's Managing Now?' *Working Woman*, October, 44–5.

Milkman, R. and Pullman, C. 1991: 'Technological Change in an Auto Assembly Plant: The Impact on Workers' Tasks and Skills'. *Work and Occupations*, 18, 2, 123–47.

Mintel. 1988: *Women 2000*. London: Mintel.

Morley, D. and Silverstone, R. 1990: 'Domestic Communication, Technologies and Meanings'. *Media, Culture and Society*, 12, 31–56.

Morris, J. 1989: 'Women in Computing'. London: *Computing Weekly*.

Morris, W. 1987: 'Useful Work Versus Useless Toil' in Richards, V. (ed.): *Why Work?* London: Freedom Press.

Moskos, C. 1990: 'Army Women'. *Atlantic Monthly*, August.

Mumford, E. 1981: *Values, Technology and Work*. Kluwer, Netherlands: Martinus Nijhoff.

Mumford, E. 1983: 'Successful Systems Design' in Otway, H. and Peltu, M. (eds.): *New Office Technology: Human and Organizational Aspects*. London: Pinter.

Mumford, L. 1966: *The Myth of the Machine: Technics and Human Development*. New York: Harcourt Brace Jovanovich.

Mumford, L. 1972: 'Authoritarian and Democratic Technics' in Kranzberg, M. and Davenport, W.H. (eds.): *Technology and Culture: An Anthology*. New York: Meridian.

NASUWT (National Association of Schoolmasters and Union of Women Teachers) and Engineering Council. 1991: *Gender, Primary Schools and the National Curriculum*. London: NASUWT.

Noble, D. 1979: 'Social Choice in Machine Design: The Case of Automatically Controlled Machine Tools' in Zimbalist, A. (ed.): *Case Studies on the Labour Process*. New York: Monthly Review Press.

Noble, D. 1983: 'Present Tense Technology'. *Democracy* (Spring) 8–27.

Oakley, A. 1976: 'Wisewoman and Medicine Man: Changes in the Management of Childbirth' in Mitchell, J. and Oakley, A. (eds.): *The Rights and Wrongs of Women*. Harmondsworth: Penguin.

Oliver, N. and Wilkinson, B. 1988: *The Japanization of British Industry*, Oxford: Blackwell.

Open University, 1992: *Professional Judgement and Decision Making* (D300), BBC2, 20 February.

Orlikowski, W.J. 1992: 'The Duality of Technology: Rethinking the Concept of Technology in Organizations'. *Organization Science*, 3, 3, 398–427.

Palfreman, J. and Swade, D. 1991: *The Dream Machine: Exploring the Computer Age*. London: BBC.

Parker, G. 1995: *Cambridge Illustrated History of Warfare*. Cambridge: Cambridge University Press.

Payer, L. 1988: *Medicine and Culture*. New York: Henry Holt.

Peel, F. 1968: *The Rising of the Luddites: Chartists and Plug Drawers*. London: Cass.

Pelaez, E. 1990: 'Soft Ware: A Peculiar Commodity'. Paper presented at PICT Workshop on Social Perspectives on Software, Oxford, 13–14 January.

Penn, R. 1982: 'Skilled Manual Workers in the Labour Process' in Wood, S.

(ed.): *The Degradation of Work? Skill, Deskilling and the Labour Process*. London: Hutchinson.

Perrole, J.A. 1988: 'The Social Impact of Computing: Ideological Themes and Research Issues'. *Social Science Computer Review*, 6, 4, 469–81.

Pfeffer, J. 1982: *Organizations and Organization Theory*. Marshfield, Mass.: Pitman.

Phillimore, A.J. 1989: 'Flexible Specialization, Work Organization and Skills: Approaching the "Second Industrial Divide" '. *New Technology, Work and Employment*, 4, 2, 79–91.

Pickering, A. (ed.) 1992: *Science as Practice and Culture*. Chicago: Chicago University Press.

Pinch, T. and Bijker, W.E. 1989: 'The Social Construction of Facts and Artefacts: or How the Sociology of Science and the Sociology of Technology Might Benefit Each Other', in Bijker, W.E., Hughes, T.P. and Pinch, T. (eds.): *The Social Construction of Technological Systems*, Cambridge, Mass.: MIT Press.

Piore, M.J. and Sable, C.F. 1984: *The Second Industrial Divide*. New York: Basic Books.

Pollard, S. 1968: *The Genesis of Modern Management*. Harmondsworth: Penguin.

Pollner, M. 1978: Constitutive and Mundane Versions of Labeling Theory. *Human Sciences*, 31, 285–304.

Pool, I. de S. 1983: *Technologies of Freedom*. Cambridge, Mass.: Belknap Press.

*Post Office Records,* 1930: 6033, *Women Clerks Equality of Opportunity in the Post Office*. London: GPO.

Poster, M. 1990: *The Mode of Information*. Cambridge: Polity Press.

Postol, T. 1992: 'Gulf War Patriot Missile Hits a Myth'. *The Higher*, 14 February.

Poulsen, C. 1984: *The English Rebels*. London: The Journeyman Press.

*Proceedings at York Special Commission*. 1813: repr. 1972: *The Luddites: Three Pamphlets 1812–1839*. New York: Arno Press.

Rachel, J. and Woolgar, S. 1995: 'The Discursive Structure of the Social–Technical Divide: The Example of Information Systems Development'. *Sociological Review*, 43, 2, 251–273.

Radder, H. 1992: 'Normative Reflexions on Constructivist Approaches to Science and Technology'. *Social Studies of Science and Technology*, 22, 141–73.

Randall, A.J. 1982: 'The Shearmen and the Wiltshire Outrages of 1802: Trade Unionism and Industrial Violence'. *Social History*, 7, 3, 283–304.

Randall, A.J. 1986: 'The Philosophy of Luddism: The Case of the West of England Woollen Workers, ca 1790–1809'. *Technology and Culture*, 27, 1, 1–17.

Randall, A.J. 1988: 'The Industrial Moral Economy of the Gloucestershire Weavers in the Eighteenth Century' in Rule, J. (ed.): *British Trade Unionism 1750–1850*. London: Longman.

Randall, A.J. 1990: 'New Languages or Old? Labour, Capital and Discourse in the Industrial Revolution'. *Social History*, 15, 2, 195–216.

Randall, A.J. 1991: *Before the Luddites: Custom, Community and Machinery in the English Woollen Industry 1776–1809*. Cambridge: Cambridge University Press.

Rasmussen, B. and Håpnes, T. 1991: 'Excluding Women from the Technologies of the Future'. Paper presented at the 16th Nordic Congress of Sociology, Trondheim, Norway, 23–5 August.

Reich, R.B. 1983: *The Next American Frontier*. New York: Times Books.

Reid, R. 1986: *Land of Lost Content: The Luddite Revolt 1812*. London: Cardinal.

Reinerstein, D. and Smith, P. 1991: *Developing Products in Half the Time*. London: Chapman and Hall.

Rice, A.K. 1958: *Productivity and Social Organization*. London: Tavistock.

Roberts, M. 1979: 'Sickles and Scythes'. *History Workshop Journal*, 7, 3–28.

Robey, D. 1977: 'Computers and Management Structures: Some Empirical Findings Re-examined'. *Human Relations*, 30, 963–76.

Roderick, G. and Stevens, M. (eds.) 1981: *Where did we go Wrong? Industry, Education and Economy of Victorian Britain*. Lewes: Falmer Press.

Rolfe, H. 1990: 'In the Name of Progress? Skill and Attitude Towards Technological Change'. *New Technology, Work and Employment*, 5, 2, 107–21.

Rorty, R. 1989: *Contingency, Irony and Solidarity*. Cambridge: Cambridge University Press.

Rose, H., McLoughlin, I., King, R. and Clark, J. 1986: 'Opening the Black Box: The Relation Between Technology and Work'. *New Technology, Work and Employment*, 1, 1, 18–26.

Rose, N. 1989: *The Productive Subject*. London: Routledge.

Rosenbrock, H.H. 1987: 'The Combined Social and Technical Design of Production Systems'. Paper presented to the international seminar on advanced information technology, Milan, October.

Rosenbrock, H.H. (ed.) 1989a: *Designing Human-Centred Technology*. London: Springer Verlag.

Rosenbrock, H.H. 1989b: 'Human Centred Technology' Paper presented to the CRICT seminar series, Brunel University, 6 December.

Rosenbrock, H. 1990: *Machines with a Purpose*. Oxford: Oxford University Press.

Rothschild, J. (ed.) 1983: *Machina Ex Dea: Feminist Perspectives on Technology*. New York: Pergamon Press.

Rowland, R. 1992: *Living Laboratories: Women and Reproductive Technologies*. London: Lime Tree.

Rubinstein, W.D. 1988: *Elites and Wealthy in Modern British History*. Brighton: Harvester.

Rule, J. 1986: *The Labouring Classes in Early Industrial England 1750–1850*. London: Longman.

Sable, C.F. 1982: *Work and Politics*. Cambridge: Cambridge University Press.

Salaman, G. 1992: 'Work Design and Corporate Strategies' in Allen, J., Braham, P. and Lewis, P. (eds.): *Political and Economic Forms of Modernity*. Cambridge: Polity Press.

Sandberg, A. 1976: *The Limits to Democratic Planning*. Stockholm: LiberForlag.

Sanderson, G. and Stapenhurst, F. (eds.) 1979: *Industrial Democracy Today*. New York: McGraw-Hill.

Sayer, A. 1989: 'Post-Fordism in Question'. *The International Journal of Urban and Regional Research*, 13, 4, 666–95.

Scarry, E. 1985: *The Body in Pain: The Making and Unmaking of the World*. New York: Oxford University Press.

Sewell, G. and Wilkinson, B. 1992: 'Surveillance, Discipline and Just-In-Time Process'. *Sociology*, 26, 2, 271–89.

Shaiken, H. 1984: *Work Transformed: Automation and Labor in the Computer Age*. New York: Holt, Rinehart and Winston.

Shaw, B. 1946: *Man and Superman*. Harmondsworth: Penguin.

Shepard, J.M. 1971: *Automation and Alienation: A Study of Office and Factory Workers*. Cambridge, Mass.: MIT Press.

Shields, P.M. 1988: 'Sex Roles in the Military' in Moskos, C. and Wood, F.R. (eds.): *The Military: More Than Just a Job?* Oxford: Pergamon-Brassey.

Silverstone, R., Morley, D., Dahlberg, A. and Livingstone, S. 1990: *Families, Technologies and Consumption: The Household and Information and Communication Technologies*. Brunel University: CRICT Discussion Paper.

Singleton, V.1995: 'Networking Constructions of Gender and Constructing Gender Networks: Considering Definitions of Women in the British Cervical Screening Programme' in Grint, K., and Gill, R. (eds.): *The Gender–Technology Relation*. London: Taylor and Francis.

Slaughter, J. 1987: 'The Team Concept in the US Auto Industry'. Paper given at the ERU conference on the Japanization of British industry, UWIST, Cardiff, September.

Smail, J. 1987: 'New Languages for Labour and Capital: The Transformation of Discourse in the Early Years of the Industrial Revolution'. *Social History*, 12, 1, 49–71.

Smail, J. 1991: 'New Languages? Yes indeed: A Reply to Adrian Randall'. *Social History*, 16, 2, 217–22.

Smith, A. 1974: *The Wealth of Nations*. Harmondsworth: Penguin.

Smith, C. 1989: 'Flexible Specialization, Automation and Mass Production'. *Work, Employment and Society*, 3, 2, 203–20.

Smith, D. 1978: 'K is Mentally Ill: The Anatomy of a Factual Account'. *Sociology*, 12, 23–53.

SSRC (Social Science Research Council). 1968: *Social Research on Automation*. London: Heinemann.

Sørensen, K.H. 1985: 'Technology and Industrial Democracy. An Enquiry into Some Theoretical Issues and their Social Basis'. *Organization Studies*, 6, 2, 139–60.

Sørensen, K.H. 1992: 'Towards a Feminized Technology? Gendered Values in the Construction of Technology'. *Social Studies of Science*, 22, 5–31.

Sorge, A. 1984: *Technological Change, Employment, Qualifications and Training*. Berlin: CEDEFOP.

Spenner, K.I. 1985: 'The Upgrading and Downgrading of Occupations: Issues, Evidence and Implications for Education'. *Review of Educational Research*, 55, 122–54.

Stanley, A. 1983: 'Women Hold Up Two Thirds of the Sky: Notes for a Revised History of Technology' in Rothschild, J. (ed.): *Machina Ex Dea: Feminist Perspectives on Technology*. New York: Pergamon Press.

Stanley, A. 1992: *Mothers of Invention*. Newark, NJ: Scarecrow Press.

Stanworth, M. (ed.) 1987: *Reproductive Technologies: Gender, Motherhood and Medicine*. Cambridge: Polity Press.

Stein, M. 1992: 'The Development, Integration and Use of Open Socio-

Technical and Psycho-analytic Group Relations Approaches in Consultancy Work with Organizations'. Ph.D. thesis, Brunel University.

Strassman, P. 1985: *Information Payoff: The Transformation of Work in the Electronic Age*. New York: Basic Books.

Streek, W. 1987: 'The Uncertainties of Management in the Management of Uncertainty' *Work, Employment and Society*, 1, 3, 281–308.

Taylor, F.W. 1903: 'Shop Management'. Repr. in Taylor, F.W. 1964: *Scientific Management*, New York: Harper and Row.

Taylor, F.W. 1911: *The Principles of Scientific Management*. New York: Harper and Row.

Taylor, R. 1812: *The Blackfaces of 1812*. Repr. 1972: New York: Arno Press.

Thomas, R. and Presland, S.M. 1992: 'DT200 Gender Analysis'. Personal communication.

Thomis, I.T. 1970: *The Luddites*. Newton Abbot: David and Charles.

Thompson, E.P. 1968: *The Making of the English Working Class*. Harmondsworth: Penguin.

Thompson, E.P. 1977: *Whigs and Hunters*. Harmondsworth: Penguin.

Tierney, M. 1992: *Negotiating a Software Career: Informality and 'the Lads' in an Irish Software Installation*. University of Edinburgh: Edinburgh PICT Working Paper No. 33.

Toffler, A. 1980: *The Third Wave*. London: Collins.

Travers, T. 1993: *The Killing Ground*. London: Routledge.

Trist, E.L. and Bamforth, K.W. 1951: 'Some Social and Psychological Consequences of the Longwall Method of Coal Getting'. *Human Relations*, 4, 1, 3–38.

Tucker, A. and Allen, J. 1992: 'Global Firms, Shrinking Worlds'. Open University TV Programme for D213, *Understanding Modern Societies*. Milton Keynes: Open University.

Turkle, S. 1984: *The Second Self: Computers and the Human Spirit*. London: Granada.

Turkle, S. 1988: 'Computational Reticence: Why Women Fear the Intimate Machine' in Kramarae, C. (ed.): *Technology and Women's Voices*. London: Routledge.

Turkle, S. and Papert, S. 1990: 'Epistemological Pluralism: Styles and Voices within the Computer Culture'. *Signs: Journal of Women in Culture and Society*, 16, 1, 41–61.

Turnbull, J.F. 1989: *Samurai Warlords: The Book of the Daimyo*. London: Blandford Press.

Twain, M. 1972: *Life on the Mississippi*. Norwalk, Conn.: The Heritage Press.

UCCA (Universities' Central Council on Admissions). 1991: *Annual Report*. London: UCCA.

Van Beinum, H. 1988: 'New Technology and Organizational Choice'. *QWLFOCUS* 6, 1, 3–10.

Van Eijnatten, F. M. 1991: *From Autonomous Work Groups to Democratic Dialogue and Integral Organizational Renewal: 40 Years of Development and Expansion of the Socio-technical Systems Design Paradigm*. Eindhoven: Eindhoven University of Technology and Maastricht Economic Research Institute on Innovation and Technology.

Van Zoonen, L. 1992: 'Feminist Theory and Information Technology'. *Media, Culture and Society*, 14, 1, 9–30.

Veblen, T. 1899: *The Theory of the Leisure Class*, New York: Macmillan.
Veblen, T. 1904: *The Theory of Business Enterprise*, New York: Charles Scribner's Sons.
Viner, K. 1992: 'In the Finals Analysis' *The Guardian*, 8 July.
Wainwright, H. and Elliot, D. 1982: *The Lucas Plan: A New Trade Unionism in the Making?* London: Allison and Busby.
Wajcman, J. 1991: *Feminism Confronts Technology*. Cambridge: Polity Press.
Webster, F. and Robins, K. 1986: *Information Technology: A Luddite Analysis*. Norwood, NJ: Ablex.
Webster, F. and Robins, K. 1993: 'I'll be watching you'. *Sociology*, 27, 2, 243–52.
Webster, J. 1988: *New Technology, Old Jobs: Secretarial Labour in Automated Offices*. Edinburgh: University of Edinburgh PICT Working Paper No. 8.
Webster, J. 1989: *Office Automation: The Labour Process and Women's Work in Britain*. Hemel Hempstead: Harvester Wheatsheaf.
Webster, J. 1991: *Automation in the Social Office: Women's Skills and New Technology*. Edinburgh: University of Edinburgh PICT Working Paper No. 21.
Wheelwright, J. 1992: ' "A Brother in Arms, a Sister in Peace": Contemporary Issues of Gender and Military Technology' in Kirkup, G. and Smith Keller, L. (eds.): *Inventing Women: Science, Technology and Gender*. Cambridge: Polity Press.
Wiener, M.J. 1981: *English Culture and the Decline of the* Industrial Spirit. Cambridge: Cambridge University Press.
Wilkinson, B. 1983: *The Shopfloor Politics of New Technology*. London: Heinemann.
Williams, R. and Edge, D. 1991: 'The Social Shaping of Technology: A Review of UK Research Concepts, Findings, Programmes and Centres' in Dierkes, M. and Hoffman, U. (eds.): *Research on the Social Shaping of Technology in France, Germany, Norway, Sweden, the United Kingdom and the United States*. Berlin: Wissenschaftszentrum Berlin fur Sozialforschung.
Willmott, H. 1995: 'A Reply to Zuboff'. Paper delivered at the IFIP WG8.2 conference on *Information Technology and Changes in Organizational Work*, Cambridge.
Winch, P. 1958: *The Idea of a Social Science and its Relation to Philosophy*. London: Routledge & Kegan Paul.
Winner, L. 1977: *Autonomous Technology*. Cambridge, Mass: MIT Press.
Winner, L. 1985: 'Do Artifacts have Politics?' in Mackenzie, D. and Wajcman, J. (eds.) *The Social Shaping of Technology*. Milton Keynes: Open University Press.
Winner, L. 1993: 'Upon Opening the Black Box and Finding it Empty: Social Constructivism and the Philosophy of Technology'. *Science, Technology and Human Values*, 18, 3, 362–78.
WIT (Women into Information Technology Foundation). 1991: *Progress Report*, June.
Witte, J.F. 1980: *Democracy, Authority and Alienation in Work*. Chicago: Chicago University Press.
Witz, A. 1986: 'Patriarchy and the Labour Market: Occupational Control Strategies and the Medical Division of Labour' in Knights, D. and Willmott, H. (eds.): *Gender and the Labour Process*. Aldershot: Gower.

Witz, A. 1990: 'Patriarchy and Professions: The General Politics of Occupational Closure'. *Sociology*, 24, 4, 675–90.

Womack, J.P., Jones, D.T. and Roos, D. 1990: *The Machine that Changed the World*. New York: Rawson Associates.

Woodward, J. 1958: *Management and Technology*. London: HMSO.

Woodward, J. 1965: *Industrial Organization*. Oxford: Oxford University Press.

Woolgar, S. 1981: 'Interests and Explanation in the Social Study of Science'. *Social Studies of Science*, 11, 365–94.

Woolgar, S. 1983: 'Irony in the Social Study of Science' in Knorr-Cetina, K. and Mulkay, M.J. (eds.): *Science Observed: Perspectives on the Social Study of Science*. London: Sage.

Woolgar, S. 1985: 'Why Not a Sociology of Machines? The Case of Sociology and Artificial Intelligence'. *Sociology*, 19, 4, 557–72.

Woolgar, S. 1987: 'Reconstructing Man and Machine: Sociological Critiques of Cognitivism' in Bijker, W., Pinch, T. and Hughes, T. (eds.): *The Social Construction of Technological Systems: New Directions in the Social Study of Technology*. Cambridge, Mass. MIT Press.

Woolgar, S. 1988a: *Science: The Very Idea*. London: Routledge.

Woolgar, S. (ed.) 1988b: *Knowledge and Reflexivity: New Frontiers in the Sociology of Knowledge*. London: Sage.

Woolgar, S. 1989: 'Stabilization Rituals: Steps in the Socialization of a New Machine'. Paper presented at the PICT conference, Brunel University, May.

Woolgar, S. 1991a: 'The Turn to Technology in Social Studies of Science'. *Science, Technology and Human Values*, 16, 1, 20–50.

Woolgar, S. 1991b: 'Configuring the User: The Case of Usability Trials' in Law, J. (ed.): *A Sociology of Monsters: Essays on Power, Technology and Domination*. London: Routledge.

Woolgar, S. 1992: 'Who/What is This For? Utility and Value as Textual Accomplishments'. Paper presented to 4S/EASST conference, Gothenberg, 12–15 August.

Woolgar, S. 1993a: *The User Talks Back*. Brunel University: CRICT Discussion Paper 40.

Woolgar, S. 1993b: 'What's at Stake in the Sociology of Technology?' *Science, Technology and Human Values*, 18, 4, 523–9.

Woolgar, S. 1994: 'Re-thinking Agency: New Moves in Science and Technology Studies'. *Mexican Journal of Behavior Analysis*, 20, 213–40.

Woolgar, S. 1996a: 'Science and Technology Studies and the Renewal of Social Theory' in Turner, S. (ed.): *The Classics and Beyond: Social Theory at the End of the Century*. Oxford: Blackwell.

Woolgar, S. 1996b: 'Technologies as Cultural Artefacts' in W. Dutton (ed.): *Information and Communication Technologies – Visions and Realities*. Oxford: Oxford University Press.

Woolgar, S. and Grint, K. 1991: 'Computers and the Transformation of Social Analysis'. *Science, Technology and Human Values*, 16, 3, 368–78.

Woolgar, S. and Pawluch, D. 1985: 'Ontological Gerrymandering: the Anatomy of Social Problems Explanations'. *Social Problems*, 32, 214–227.

Woolgar, S. and Russell, G. 1990: *The Social Basis of Computer Viruses*. Brunel University: CRICT Discussion Paper No. 17.

Zuboff, S. 1988: *In the Age of the Smart Machine: The Future of Work and Power.* Oxford: Heinemann.

Zuboff, S. 1996: 'The Emperor's New Information Economy' in Orlikowski, W., Walsham, G., Jones, M.R. and DeGross, J.I. (eds.): *Information Technology and Changes in Organisational Work.* London: Chapman & Hall.

Zwerdling, D. 1978: *Democracy at Work.* Washington, DC: Association for Self-Management.

# Index